DEFENDERS OF THE FAITH

Also by Derek Taylor

British Chief Rabbis 1664–2006

Don Pacifico – The Acceptable Face of Gunboat Diplomacy

Solomon Schonfeld – A Purpose in Life

Jewish Parliamentarians (with Greville Janner)

The Sunderland Beth Hamedresh 1889–1999 (with Harold Davis)

Thank You For Your Business: The Jewish Contribution to the British Economy

Hillel House – A Lesson in Tolerance

Chief Rabbi Hertz, The Wars of the Lord

Also:

Hotel and Catering Sales Promotion

The Golden Age of British Hotels

Fortune, Fame and Folly – The Caterer 1878–1978

How to Sell Banquets

Profitable Hotel Reception

Sales Management for Hotels

Hotel and Catering Sales – A Complete Guide

Hotel and Restaurant Advertising

Effective Hotel Sales and Marketing

Ritzy – British Hotels 1837–1987

British Hospitality Association 1907–2007

Revolutionary Hotel Marketing

Defenders of the Faith

The History of Jews' College and the
London School of Jewish Studies

DEREK TAYLOR

Foreword by
Rabbi Dr Raymond Apple

VALLENTINE MITCHELL
LONDON • PORTLAND, OR

First published in 2016 by Vallentine Mitchell

Catalyst House,
720 Centennial Court,
Centennial Park, Elstree, WD6 3SY, UK

920 NE 58th Avenue, Suite 300
Portland, Oregon,
97213-3786 USA

www.vmbooks.com
Copyright © Derek Taylor 2016

British Library Cataloguing in Publication Data:
An entry can be found on request

ISBN 978-1-910383-12-4 (cloth)
ISBN 978-1-910383-14-8 (ebook)
ISBN 978-1-910383-13-1 (paper)

Library of Congress Cataloging in Publication Data
An entry can be found on request

All rights reserved. No part of this publication may be reproduced in any form or by any means, electronic, mechanical, photocopying, reading or otherwise, without the prior permission of Vallentine Mitchell & Co. Ltd.

Printed by CMP (UK) Ltd, Poole, Dorset

Dedicated to the memory of

Philip and Rosie Taylor
and
Joe and Connie Milman

Contents

List of Photographs	ix
Preface	xi
Foreword by Rabbi Dr Raymond Apple	xiii
1. The Story So Far	1
2. Setting Down Roots	25
3. The Michael Friedländer Years	53
4. The Adolph Büchler Years	83
5. The Great War	107
6. Defending the Fort	129
7. Woburn House and the Second World War	151
8. The Golden Age of Kopul Kahana	173
9. The Isidore Epstein and Hirsch Zimmels Years	195
10. The Nahum Rabinovitch Years	215
11. Jonathan Sacks, Irving Jacobs and Daniel Sinclair	235
12. LSJS	261
13. And Then There's the Library	271
Appendix A. Jews' College Officers	291
Appendix B. Jews' College Rabbis	293

*Appendix C. Jewish Chaplains to the Forces in
the Second World War* 299

Appendix D. The Rabbinical Diploma 303

Appendix E. Jews' College Publications 307

Bibliography 309

Index 311

List of Photographs

1. Nathan Marcus Adler, the founder and inspiration.
2. Sir Moses Montefiore, undisputed leader of the Victorian community.
3. Louis Loewe, Headmaster 1855–58.
4. Finsbury Square, the first home of the college.
5. A.L. Green, Honorary Secretary 1852–83.
6. Henry Solomons, Treasurer 1855–91.
7. Michael Friedländer, Principal 1865–1907.
8. John Chapman, Honorary Secretary and distinguished teacher.
9. Hermann Adler, President and Chief Rabbi.
10. Sir Barrow Ellis, Chair of Council 1872–87.
11. The Victorian Student Journal.
12. Tavistock House, the second home of the college.
13. Queens Square, the third home of the college.
14. Charles Samuel, a friend in need.
15. Sir Adolph Tuck, financial supporter after Charles Samuel.
16. Simeon Singer, of the Singer Prayer Book
17. Adolph Büchler, Principal 1907–39.
18. Isidore Epstein, Principal during the Golden Age.

19. Nahum Rabinovitch, Principal and towering Talmudist.
20. Irving Jacobs, Principal and one of the finest academics.
21. Lord Kalms, another great benefactor.
22. Lord Sacks, student, Principal and President.

Preface

Many current and former members of the College have helped in the writing of this book and I'd particularly like to thank Rabbi, Lord Sacks, Rabbi Raymond Apple, Rabbi Geoffrey Cohen, Rabbi Abraham Levy and Rabbi Elkan Levy for their input. I am also grateful to Dayan Ivan Binstock, Simon Caplan, Lucien Gubbay, Rabbi Irving Jacobs, Esra Kahn, Professor David Latchman, Rabbi Reuben Livingstone, Lord Kalms, Jason Marantz, Clive Marks, Michael Roodyn, Professor Steve Miller, Rabbi Daniel Sinclair, Howard Stanton, Dr Tamra Wright, Rabbi Dr Raphael Zarum and Erla Zimmels for all their assistance.

In a history ranging over 160 years, there are bound to be names which have been missed or not given sufficient prominence. I apologise to their advocates for such omissions, and any errors are down to me too.

What seems to me to be important is to recognize the achievements of Jews' College over the years, and to record the sacrifices made by so many of the faculty and its supporters, to achieve the objective of keeping the religion alive and well. With Orthodox Judaism, that is a 2,000-year-old effort. It has been a privilege to document the impressive contribution of Jews' College to the education of the Jewish people.

Derek Taylor
London, 2016

Foreword
Rabbi Dr Raymond Apple

Derek Taylor is a fine historian and an engaging writer. Utilising both talents he has produced a magnificent history of Jews' College, and I am proud to represent the College graduates in writing this foreword and commendation.

There were always jokes about JC in Anglo-Jewry. Apart from Jesus Christ, the initials were used for Jews' College, for the *Jewish Chronicle*, the newspaper that called itself 'the organ of Anglo-Jewry' ... and Janus Cohen, a lawyer who once studied at Jews' College, was also referred to as JC.

In the late 1950s I enrolled in the College. I lived in its dorm, took the teacher's, minister's and rabbinical diplomas, was president of the students' union, a Council member and casual lecturer in education and youth work, and married another College student. When we left London and came to Sydney, I put FJC (Fellow of Jews' College) after my name, until people asked if it meant the Australasian Jam Company ... yet another JC!

Over the years I picked up snippets of College folklore, like the student who asked Dr Hermann Adler what blessing to make if he smelled a rat, a students' strike when Dr Büchler threw open the door of the common room and shouted 'Bolsheviks!', and a Purim when Mrs Epstein wanted the students to mimic her husband, the College Principal ...

Formal histories of the College were written by Isidore Harris and Albert M. Hyamson, but the most readable of all is this one, which vividly describes the face and place of the College over 150 years.

Rabbinic education underwent two metamorphoses in the nineteenth century. It developed the great *yeshivot*; it created the modern seminaries. There had been great ancient *yeshivot*, but they were replaced by small groups of youths who studied under the local rabbi in a largely personal and unstructured fashion. The curriculum was Talmud and codes; the aim was study for its own sake, not vocational training. Rabbis basically happened: nobody set out to mould them.

Modern *yeshivot* began in Lithuania in 1802, when Rabbi Hayim Volozhiner, a wealthy manufacturer, a follower of the Vilna Ga'on, created a large-scale *yeshivah* which drew outstanding students from far afield. It taught Talmud according to the Ga'on's system, and resisted adding Russian to the curriculum. Lithuania also saw the rise of *mussar yeshivot* based on the ethical system of Rabbi Yisra'el Salanter. All the *yeshivot* produced Talmudists (and some ignoramuses and unbelievers), not rabbis as such, though men from the *yeshivot* did often find rabbinic posts. It was largely a legend that the whole of eastern Europe was Orthodox.

Jews in lands of emancipation faced their new cultural and legal situation with a range of responses. Some rejected the ways of the past and were even ashamed of them. Some others felt that the traditional content of Judaism was sound enough but its style needed streamlining. Still others were alarmed at the thought of any compromise or concession, and wanted to go on as before without accommodating to new circumstances of any kind.

The modernists weighed their rabbis in a notional balance and found them wanting. The rabbis did not behave with urbanity, compete with gentile leaders of opinion, or couch their message in the local idiom. Hence the need for seminaries to mould modern rabbis. Between 1827 and 1886, an array of seminaries came into being. Each combined Jewish with broader culture. The emphasis was not so much on Talmud as the Jewish Humanities and ministerial skills. The teachers were renowned in Jewish *Wissenschaft*. Each had a firm commitment to Judaism as he saw it. The Continental seminaries had a more intellectual atmosphere than Jews' College, though this is no denigration of the College faculty. The London ethos was quintessentially British – pragmatic; traditional but not too much so;

not expecting the clergy to be too strict or too smart, not too different or 'foreign'.

The seminaries changed the nature of the rabbi. Hitherto, rabbis were not priests; Judaism was a religion of laymen. The rabbi was no closer to God than was any pious person. The seminaries, however, equated the rabbi with the Western clergyman and trained rabbis for a profession. The Jews of England were not entirely sure what they wanted from their College. Though medieval Anglo-Jewry had a record of rabbinic learning, by the nineteenth century the level of learning was low despite a handful of scholars from the Continent. Synagogue services were generally dreary and unembellished by 'lectures'. It was not the rise of Reform in the early 1840s that necessitated a ministerial system and college: that was already being planned.

On 11 November, 1855, the College opened in Finsbury Square. The Chief Rabbi called it 'a house to work in, teaching power to work with, and minds to work upon ... In the course of time, our schools and our pulpits will be filled with well-trained, well-furnished teachers'. The words 'our schools and our pulpits' now defined the role of the College for the whole of its 150 years as a seminary. The plan was pragmatic: schools and synagogues would be manned by professionals. Students would gain skills rather than scholarship. The clergy would conduct services and life-cycle events, give urbane (hopefully short) sermons, tend to people's pastoral needs, and enshrine the ideal of the English gentleman.

Some alumni engaged in scholarship and became intellectuals and academics; a few were Talmudists and *halakhists*; most were pastors, preachers and precentors, 'Reverends' with really only one rabbi, the Chief: 'a Chief without Indians'. All very English: a micro-version of the established Church. Newcomers from eastern Europe asked how there could be a community without real rabbis.

The College faculty had a fine name in Jewish academia. Semitic and Judaic Studies were on the curriculum, enabling students, in association with University College, to gain degrees. By the end of the century there was agitation for them to be able to gain a full rabbinical title. But there was no advanced teaching in rabbinics until the 1940s, when Dr Isidore Epstein became head of the College. He established a rabbinical diploma class conducted by a great Talmudist, Rabbi Kopel Kahana, who introduced analogies from other legal systems. In the 1950s, Dr Epstein spearheaded a Cantors' Department; an Institute for the Training of Teachers; and university extension courses. The Students' Union arranged lunchtime meetings.

As time went on, criticism grew of the old ministerial model; many wanted fully qualified rabbis at all synagogues. In the end the 'Reverend' system wound down and the old *Minhag Anglia* lost favour. Pastoral skills are still required, but so are *shi'urim* and scholarship. The *hazzanic* profession has almost evaporated, because few congregations can afford two full-time clergy and some have memories of intra-ministerial rivalry.

The College recently changed its name to the London School of Jewish Studies, an example of the adage, 'Change of name brings a change of fortune'. To the dismay of many people including myself, the ministerial department closed down, though other adult education programs remained. Thanks to the Montefiore Endowment, the Sephardim set up a rabbinic college which is now the only 'establishment' seminary in Britain. The *yeshivot* are flourishing, and many British students go to Israeli institutes of study, though few become pulpit rabbis. On the other hand, increasing numbers of British Jews now have the background to appreciate rabbinic learning and leadership, and that's what they want from their rabbis.

A factor in the changing nature of the British rabbi is the decline of the large cathedral-like synagogues with their stately architecture, pomp and ceremony, in favour of smaller, less structured places of worship which do not need a presiding prelate as much as a sage in residence. The story is fascinating. All credit to Derek Taylor for researching and writing it. I commend his book to a wide reading public.

Rabbi Dr Raymond Apple,
AO RFD, Emeritus Rabbi of
the Great Synagogue, Sydney

CHAPTER ONE

The Story so Far

Religious education was always vitally important for the maintenance of Judaism. The school, as an institution, is a joint bulwark of a Jewish congregation. It certainly wasn't the case that the hard-core of the Jewish community in Britain was ever satisfied to neglect the education of their children.

Indeed, they addressed the problem soon after Charles II rejected an appeal from merchants in the City of London to expel them in 1661. Their right to live in England was not universally approved but they had supported the King financially during his exile in Amsterdam and he didn't know if he might need them again if the remaining Cromwellians succeeded in overthrowing him; so he approved them staying, as did his brother James II when he came to the throne. It worked out perfectly well in retrospect, but the community was nervous about the future for many years; as Rabbi, Lord Sacks' book asked at the latter end of the twentieth century, would there be Jewish grandchildren?[1] It's always a deep-seated concern among Jews.

So, as early as 1664, the immigrant Dutch Sephardim had started Shaare Tikvah (Gates of Hope) School attached to their new London synagogue. They had originally come from Spain after the Jews were expelled in 1492 (Sepharad is the Hebrew word for Spain). In an age when only the rich were educated, the Sephardi children were taught not just Hebrew, but arithmetic, English and reading and writing. Haham Jacob Sasportas, the spiritual leader of the community, taught the advanced studies and his son took care of everything else. The lessons were just for children, though, and formal education for adults didn't come about for well over another hundred years.

Any synagogue was likely to have Hebrew classes and some in future would establish a Beth Hamedresh, an informal house of study, where adults could learn the Talmud, the body of law which underpinned the continuance of the religion. The main concern for the members of the immigrant community, however, was to earn a living and, for the vast majority of them, there was little time left over for study. Furthermore, to feed the family, the children often needed to find some form of employment, even if they were still under 10 years of age, and the education of both children and adults suffered from the overriding need to simply get enough to eat.

There might have been a full-scale Sephardi Yeshiva (college) in London in 1743 when Elias de Pass died and left £1,200 (at least £1 million in today's money) to build and maintain a proper Yeshiva. Unfortunately the legality of the bequest was tested in the courts and the Lord Chancellor ruled that it was illegal. He held:

> This is a bequest for the propagation of the Jewish religion: and though it is said that this is part of our religion, yet the intent of that bequest must be taken to be in contradiction of the Christian religion, which is a part of the law of the land.[2]

The spiritual leaders of the community did their best to improve the opportunities for education but sometimes they gave up in despair. Hart Lyon, the Chief Rabbi from 1756–63, had tried to promote a Talmud Torah, which was a parochial primary school, but he only managed to recruit fifteen pupils. It had actually been started in 1732, in the time of his predecessor, Rabbi Aaron Hart, so there hadn't been much progress in thirty years.

Hart Lyon eventually gave up his ministry in London to become the minister of a much smaller community in Halberstadt in Germany. The attraction was not the salary, because it was half what he was being paid. Neither was it the security of the community, because the English government was tolerant, but the Halberstadt community had been expelled from the town by its rulers in 1493 and 1594. Their synagogue had been burnt down twice in 1621 and 1669. What Halberstadt promised Hart Lyon, however, was help to establish a Yeshiva and a promise to fund the cost of maintaining twelve scholars. That was enough incentive for Lyon and it emphasized the overwhelming importance rabbis gave to traditional education in Talmud and Halachah (Jewish law).

Jewish Biblical study in eighteenth-century England remained at a low level. In some ways, though, it was still superior to that of the Church of England. When Bishop Kennicott wanted to produce the perfect English translation of the Bible, he turned to Haham Moses Cohen Dazavedo for help with those parts of the Bible and the Talmud written in Aramaic. The Bishop's problem was that only Jewish rabbis spoke the language.

What eventually spurred on some of the leaders of the community to improve the facilities for teaching the children was a redoubled effort by Christian societies in the early nineteenth century to convert Jews. They started associations like The London Society for Promoting Christianity among the Jews. Its activities were aimed at poverty stricken families; it started free schools, and offered potential Jewish pupils a meal every day and a suit of clothes.

Chief Rabbi Solomon Herschell, who was the son of Hart Lyon, was appalled. In the Great Synagogue in 1807 he preached:

> I had occasion ... to forewarn every one ... not to send any of their children to the newly established Free School until we had ... determined if it be completely free from any possible harm to the welfare of our religion ... Now having since been fully convinced ... that the whole purpose of this seemingly kind exertion is ... a decoying experiment to undermine the props of our religion; and the sole intent of this institution is ... only to entice innocent Jewish children, during their early years ... from the religion of their fathers and forefathers.[3]

As a consequence, Herschell told the community to have nothing to do with the new schools. In the event, the schools would not achieve their objective, but to combat their influence, Joshua van Oven, the

Honorary Physician to the Great Synagogue, and governor of its Talmud Torah, managed to raise £20,000 (£1.3 million today) for the creation of a Jewish school. By 1817 it had 220 pupils. By the end of the century it would be the largest school in the country with over 4,000 pupils. Its secular curriculum, however, was always much more comprehensive than its Jewish one.

Although it was called the Jews' Free School (JFS), it was not created with the prime objective of increasing the pupils' knowledge of their religion. It was started to prevent them falling into the hands of the Christian schools, and also to teach them how to earn a living when they grew up. The vast majority of the nineteenth-century Jewish community in Britain remained poverty stricken, and climbing out of the gutter was their main concern. In that objective the school had the full support of Solomon Herschell.

JFS control would always remain in the hands of the governors, and its financial stability was always guaranteed, in an emergency, by the Rothschilds. The school colours remain today the house colours of the Rothschilds. The greatest banking company in the country was a firm believer in Jewish education and supported it generously.

There was only a small percentage of well-to-do Jews but as the community's lay leaders grew in affluence, the minor restrictions on the community as a whole became more irksome to them. In 1817 Jews couldn't go to university, serve on public bodies or sit in Parliament. The emancipation of the Catholics and the Dissenters, through the 1828 Sacramental Test Act and the 1829 Roman Catholic Relief Act, gave the non-Church of England Christian sects full emancipation, but the Jews were still excluded from the benefits of the legislation.

In particular, oaths of office still had to be 'upon the true faith of a Christian' which Orthodox Jews could never assert. A few Jews had taken the oath in the prescribed form over the years, but this was very unusual.

The lay leaders, therefore, increased their efforts to gain emancipation, while those more concerned with the Talmudic study of the religion declined in importance. Of course, the chance of full emancipation was tempting even to the Orthodox. In 1841, the

Trustees of the old Beth Hamedresh of the Ashkenazi community, which had been started 100 years before, proposed to remodel the institution. It had been the centre for the study of Hebrew scriptures, Talmud and rabbinical writings. They now recommended:

> that whilst it should fulfil its original intention of promoting theological studies, it should also, in a manner suitable to the spirit of the age, serve to train up youth for the various offices connected with the ministration of our religion.[4]

It would be a recurring theme and the Trustees raised over £1,500 for their objective. Chief Rabbi Solomon Herschell was a very old man, however, and nothing much happened before he died in 1842. However the lack of suitable ministerial expertise in the community continued to be a source of aggravation for the lay leaders. The performance of such spiritual leaders as they had did not compare well with the army of ministers of the church in England. In principle they wanted a corps of congregationally able, English-speaking ministers with some Talmudic knowledge.

To acquire all the abilities was going to be very demanding though and there would be two distinct camps competing for which skill should receive the first priority. That was in the future, however; the current problem was the community's embarrassment that when the candidates for the now vacant position of Chief Rabbi were short-listed, there were fourteen possibilities and none of them came from England.

Furthermore, the Great Britain community was falling well behind the Continent. As long ago as 1704 Abraham Schwab had started a yeshiva in Metz, which became the Ecole Rabbinique de France and transferred to Paris in 1839. In 1831 the Istituto Rabbinico Lombardo-Veneto was established in Padua, under Samuel David Luzzatto.

Padua was the only Italian university which would accept Jews and it was where rabbis had given *semicha* (rabbinical ordination) to David Nietto, who had become the Haham in London in 1701. Padua had been an unimportant town in the state ruled by the Medici family, and they had decided to offer religious toleration in order to attract non-Catholic merchants to live there. The bargain worked out well for both sides.

There were other Continental yeshivot as well. In 1834 the Saadath Bachurim, which had been formed in Amsterdam in 1708 by Arye Jehuda Kalisch, was reorganized as the Nederlandisch Israelietisch Seminarium. In Lithuania in 1802 Rabbi Hayyim Volozhiner, who was a wealthy manufacturer, started a large-scale yeshivah. In 1814 Rabbi Abraham Bing moved to Würzburg and started another Yeshiva which became very famous. The curriculum was invariably Talmud and halachic codes. The aim was the study of the Talmud and the *Shulchan Aruch*[5] for their own sakes, not for vocational training.

By contrast, in England it was difficult to find many ministers who could even deliver a sermon, and even fewer who could deliver one in English. The first was delivered by Tobias Goodman in 1806 at the Seal Street Synagogue in Liverpool. Before that, such sermons as were given had been in Spanish for the Sephardim or in Yiddish for the Ashkenazim. Even the Chief Rabbis at the Great Synagogue in London were only committed to giving sermons on the Sabbaths before Passover and the New Year. Goodman did, however, move to London and then spoke at a number of synagogues, but particularly at the Western.

Afterwards, David Myer Isaacs would preach in Manchester and Liverpool, David Aaron de Sola at Bevis Marks, Morris Jacob Raphall in Birmingham, Moss Levy in Brighton, Aaron Levy Green in Bristol and Henry Abraham Henry in London. That was about all that could be mustered, and when Herman Hölzel was appointed as the *hazan* (cantor) of London's Hambro Synagogue, one of the stipulations was that he must occasionally give sermons. Most of those ministers who could preach had been to the Jews' Free School and at least were born in England; the exceptions were de Sola from Holland and Raphall from Denmark.

There had been a number of attempts by the Sephardim to create a yeshiva in the eighteenth century, with only limited success. Within the community as a whole there was still felt to be a need for such an institution and so, in 1841, the Trustees of the Ashkenazi Beth Hamedresh in London reported that:

> It cannot be denied that the Jewish community are becoming painfully alive to the want of competent religious instructors, that many of the rising generation are but slightly taught the principles of our faith, that they are athirst for true religious knowledge, and are anxiously desirous that the means of access to the sources of information and instruction shall be facilitated; it is the object of the Committee to do this, and to do it in a manner suited to the persons for whom the instruction is intended, and the age and place in which our lot has been cast. With this view, they have decided that all religious instruction, whether Scriptural or Rabbinical, shall be conveyed to the pupils in the English language.[6]

There followed the approved platitudes, but few would recognize that pious declarations would not solve the problem. It would also prove questionable whether there was, among the rising generation, that very large thirst for true religious knowledge which had been trumpeted. The evidence did not bear out the contention. What was needed – and had been needed for a long time – was a leader who could make such dreams come true.

Happily, the successful candidate to replace Solomon Herschell was Rabbi Dr Nathan Marcus Adler who was fully committed to improving Jewish education. He studied at the universities of Göttingen, Erlangen, Würzberg and Heidleberg and received testimonials in the Bible, logic, theoretical philosophy, political economy, oratory, mathematics and philology. He also studied Grecian Mythology, Practical Philosophy and Universal History, as well as the Chaldean and Syrian languages.

Adler was also a graduate of Bing's Yeshiva, from whom he had received *semicha*, and he was the first rabbi in Germany to earn a doctorate. In Hanover he had been the Land-Rabbiner for the community – a quasi-government appointment. He ministered to the community from 1830–44 and worked very hard to revitalise Jewish education during this time. He had been so successful that, towards the end of his tenure, the government even gave him a Christian primary school to supervise.

This man, who leaders of the British community would comprehensively choose, was little known to the majority of the congregations who acknowledged the spiritual authority of the Chief Rabbi in England. The press tried to sum him up: 'He is not above the middle stature but his bearing is self-possessed and well calculated to produce respect. His garb is that of a German ecclesiastic, and his head covering a species of cap made of black velvet, having somewhat the shape of a Scottish bonnet.'[7]

Nathan Marcus Adler was a realist. This was no study-bound, Talmudic scholar devoting all his time to studying the Torah, no matter how important that was and would always be to him. This was a very street-wise, determined character.

As Land-Rabbiner Adler was the Jewish representative to the government in a German state that was ruled by the King of England until 1837. There was, however, little democracy in Hanover and Jews suffered from discrimination. Adler, however, had three main supporters in England when it came to the election of a new Chief Rabbi.

The first was the Duke of Cambridge, who had been the Hanover Viceroy. When his wife was said to be dying in 1834, Adler had taken the initiative to organize services in the synagogue to pray for her recovery. When she did recover, the Duke sent him 100 gold coins, which Adler returned with the wish that the money be given to the poor. Cambridge was his admiring supporter from then until he died.

The election in London would be run by the Great Synagogue vestry and Adler's second supporter was their warden, Lionel de Rothschild, whose grandfather, Amschel Rothschild, the founder of the firm, had been a great friend of Adler's father. On one occasion, on his way through Hanover, Amschel had stopped at the Rabbi's house in the middle of the night to ask his blessing.

Finally there was the acknowledged head of the Jewish community, Sir Moses Montefiore, who was Italian born and had made his fortune as one of the twelve Jew Brokers in the City of London. His Imperial Continental Gas Association had also been very successful in providing gas to light the streets of towns on the Continent. Its first contract was for Hanover and Montefiore might well have met with the Adler family for the first time then.

Montefiore was also the first President of the Alliance Building Society and a Director of the Provincial Bank of Ireland. He was very highly regarded in the City, but he chose to retire from business in 1824 when he was 40 years old and devoted the rest of his extremely long life to good works. With his strictly Orthodox beliefs, his City reputation, his knighthood and his two-metre stature, he was very imposing and by far the best qualified Jew to lead the community for the next half century.

Montefiore was a Sephardi, and the Sephardim did not wish to be part of the Ashkenazi election process because they had their own Haham. Montefiore was still able to influence Rothschild, though, because he was his uncle and had worked with the bank. Montefiore regarded Adler highly because the rabbi had raised a substantial sum in Hanover some years before for one of Montefiore's charitable appeals, and the lay leader also admired his sermons.

The election was lauded as the first really democratic process for choosing a chief rabbi. All the British communities who acknowledged him were allowed a vote. The only problem was that to get a vote you had to give £5 a year towards the cost of maintaining the chief rabbi's office. Even a large provincial community, like Liverpool, was only prepared to offer £20 and, therefore, they got four votes.

There were 144 votes in all in the election for chief rabbi. The Great, Hambro and New Synagogues in London promised over £700 and agreed to only take ninety-five votes out of the total 144. With fifty of them in the hands of the Great Synagogue and another forty-five with the other two London *shuls*, the result was a foregone conclusion.

None of the other candidates received much support anyway. Samson Raphael Hirsch, whose important principle of *Torah im Derech Eretz* would guide Orthodox communities into benefiting from new scientific knowledge in the future, only received two votes.

Adler would use his influential friends sparingly, particularly in alliance with Sir Moses. For the most part he would plough his own furrow, well trained in Hanover to avoid giving offence and accustomed to achieve his objectives by patient argument. Time and again in the future, when serious problems arose, Adler could always be counted on to appeal for peace, 'for my sake'. He was easy to revere and deliberately difficult to catalogue. If it wasn't a situation where the *din* (law) needed protecting, he tried not to take sides. He was a very able political manipulator.

Soon after he was elected, Adler started to work towards the creation of a college to train ministers. The situation he inherited was dire. There was no tradition of yeshiva study in the country, no *semicha* courses, no British rabbinic families, and very little Talmudic knowledge. He was effectively starting from scratch and when you start from scratch it can take a very long time to reach your goals.

He also knew that the need for rabbis had to be seen in terms of the individual communities' ability to afford them, and the place they took on such communities' list of priorities. A congregation first had to have access to a *shochet*, [a ritual slaughterer], a *mohel*, [for circumcisions], an office manager and a sexton. The need for a rabbi studying the Talmud came well down the list. Adler recognized that what the communities needed first was good ministers, so when Jews' College was set up it did not have a curriculum to produce rabbis with *semicha*. Yeshivas produced rabbis; theological colleges were primarily there to produce ministers.

When the communities were more firmly established, the heads of the College could revert to concentrating on the Talmud, and they would do so with relief that they were back on the curriculum track they favoured. It would, however, take years to reach that point.

There was another consideration. While it is perfectly acceptable to be paid for acting as a *shochet* or *mohel*, a sexton or synagogue office manager, it was not considered proper in very Orthodox circles to receive any financial reward for Talmudic study. It was the responsibility of the individual to continue to learn Talmud all his life and this was the *din* (Jewish law), not part of a job specification for a synagogue post.

Indeed it was as incumbent on a layman as on a minister. Paid rabbis were a comparatively recent innovation. Up to and including the Middle Ages, rabbis had jobs or were in business for themselves. So, to some extent, Talmudic study was separate from the training of men for religious occupations within the community. This ruling, though, would necessarily be overlooked by the synagogues.

The education of the young remained vital. One of Adler's first exercises in data collection took the form of an audit of the communities who recognized his authority. One of the major questions he asked them was about their schools. He was determined to start a proper religious seminary, but the cost of maintaining such a college was always likely to be a problem. The reason for this was, primarily, the indifference on the part of most of the well-to-do families when it came to the value of religious education.

They would certainly pay lip service to the idea, but the fathers were, pragmatically, businessmen, or men who had pulled themselves up by their bootstraps. Some might support the College financially, but it was always likely to be hard going to arouse sufficient enthusiasm among enough of them.

The other constraint on providing money for the College was the alternative use for the available funds, which was to succour the poor. This was a top priority because there was no social security, no old-age pension and often no jobs for Yiddish-speaking paupers. The community were determined, as had been all Jewish communities over the centuries, to help the poor; the demands of *tsedaka*, charity, were rightly taken very seriously.

There was also the crucial factor of the relationship between the minister and the honorary officers of the synagogue. The founders had to be able to support their communities financially and were likely to be mature men. The graduates of Jews' College would usually be relatively poor youngsters and would be expected to be content to be junior to the lay leaders.

Rev. Simeon Singer would sum up the problem the youngsters faced when he addressed the Jews' College Union Society in 1906 as its

Honorary President. His words were subsequently recorded in the College's Jubilee Volume of that year:

> In no other profession is the temptation to vanity so great. A young man, generally at an age when he would be very unlikely to have any mundane business of importance entrusted to him, is suddenly raised to a position that places him on a spiritual elevation above the greater number of his brethren. He is conscious that all eyes are focussed upon him. In office he is arrayed in a distinctive uniform. Out of office he wears a garb usually closely copied from the prevailing fashion of the dominant church. He has assigned to him a distinctive title of honour and reverence. He leads the devotions of his people. He addresses with a certain note of authority, without contradiction or interruption, assemblies of men and women, many of whom are old enough to be his parents or grandparents, and not a few who are at least his equals in intellectual power and attainments ... in short he blossoms out all at once into a personage whose very office is regarded as a token that its incumbent is a man of more than ordinary wisdom and virtue ... For myself, whenever I think of it, I marvel at my own temerity ... Had I not been so young when I entered upon this sacred calling, I doubt if later I should have had the courage to do so.

If there were disputes, it would be a courageous minister who took on the founders. If the party line was not in accordance with the *din* there would be conflict. In such cases the chief rabbi would, on many occasions, be asked to arbitrate, but the relationship between the lay leaders and the minister would often be soured.

Whether or not there was harmony in the congregation depended on the personalities of individuals, and the lay leaders very seldom intended to cede authority to young college graduates, except in maintaining long-accepted traditions. It would be different on the Continent where the communities were often longer established, the ministers had *semicha* and were expected to lay down the law in all its complexity.

In the future many Orthodox teachers from the Continent at Jews' College would find the British attitude towards ministers unsatisfactory. It was often only over time that the ministers they trained would win the respect, authority and affection which the simple possession of their office provided abroad.

There was yet another source of potential conflict. The Talmudically trained minister would know the minutiae of the laws Jews were instructed to follow. The vast majority of the congregation would have found it difficult to observe them all. So, if the minister didn't emphasize them and then go on to criticize the non-observers, fewer would suffer a guilt feeling about backsliding. Orthodox Jews have guilt complexes. Therefore, in many Orthodox congregations, Talmudic knowledge was often considered a less desirable virtue in the minister than the ability to keep the community together socially.

It was for these reasons that Jews' College would be an organization to which the well-to-do usually gave their public approval but, in whose support, even Montefiore, the acknowledged leader of the community and President of the Board of Deputies, was half-hearted.

The College would have to start as a school because there were no candidates for a college with the necessary basic Talmudic knowledge or background. It needed to be fee-paying to balance the books, but to attract the children of the middle classes was also going to be a struggle; the upwardly mobile families usually did not feel that education in a Jewish environment was going to help their offspring gain acceptance into society, which was a major priority for so many of them. Such an education was also unlikely to lead to a well-paid career. A place in a public school was considered a superior option, even if the child's religious upbringing would inevitably suffer from the subsequent lack of Jewish input.

It was from that starting point that the chief rabbi knew that Jews' College would have to be built up. Over the years it would not produce a vast quantity of graduates, but it is very important to realise that even if the number of graduates was small, each man could make a major contribution to the community he went on to serve.

Without their input, those communities would have been in danger of withering. It was the minister's level of observance and dedication to the faith that played such a large part in sustaining it. They also performed their pastoral duties diligently, visiting the sick, comforting the mourners and supervising the teaching of the children.

Adler had not needed the influence of a synagogue minister. He had been taught the Talmud from an early age by his father, Rabbi Mordecai Adler, who had, himself, been a resident at a Jewish Talmudic foundation for much of his life. A Hanover Jewish banker had financed the foundation, where three students would be maintained to study Talmud, and Mordecai Adler was one of those chosen. The Adlers also came from a family of German rabbis going back at least 500 years. Two of Adler's brothers were also rabbis.

Adler was inducted in July 1845 and, as early as 1846, he arranged a meeting to discuss a proposal for the formation of a college. It was to be chaired by a very senior and wealthy layman, Isaac Cohen, but unfortunately he died on the day of the meeting and the project was delayed until its supporters could reorganize.

The problem of successfully financing the college was a sine qua non, but much of the thinking among the community was overoptimistic, if not positively illusory. The *Jewish Chronicle* discussed the prospects in 1849 and airily proclaimed:

> Our answer is simply, that every congregation will gladly contribute to the establishment of an office which will and must ultimately lead, not only to the moral improvement of the congregation, but likewise to the increase in the Synagogue funds, there being no doubt that the Synagogue would be better attended, and its frequenters be more liberal in their offerings, if a soul-stirring lecture appealed to their hearts and their purses.[8]

No, they wouldn't. They would like the better preacher, but the great majority of congregations were definitely not all ready to contribute to the cost of educating one. It would be a major and justified criticism of the British communities over the years that they felt the cost of educating ministers should fall on other shoulders than theirs.

Generous individuals would have to come to the rescue of the College finances time and again, but the future support of organisations like the United Synagogue and the Federation of Synagogues was usually miserably inadequate. Their rationale would be the financial pressures they themselves had to contend with, but with a number of congregations, this was often only an excuse; much more could have been done over the years.

At the time the best preacher, apart from the Chief Rabbi, was probably David Woolf Marks, the first minister at the breakaway Secessionist Synagogue, which would become Reform in the years to come. He had been a pupil of Solomon Herschell, who was very disappointed when Marks decided that a number of existing Orthodox practices were, in his opinion, in need of change.

Where the *Voice of Jacob* was right was when it said:

> We candidly confess that it is, to our view, rather degrading than elevating the sacred office, that the people are, under the present circumstances, compelled to seek abroad for those who can serve them. We are anxious to obtain full emancipation; and would it not be a disgrace if we were told by our Christian opponents that the Jews of England are so ignorant that they cannot find a lecturer in their community?[9]

For years, many communities couldn't. Even so, the effort to create the College lasted a very long time. Sounding out potential donors and deciding on the curriculum for the project took another six years, until 1852, when a meeting was held under the chairmanship of Sir Moses Montefiore. The Chief Rabbi had set the scene with a circular from his office on 8 December 1851:[10]

> The necessity of establishing a College for the training of Jewish Ministers and Teachers is so obvious and so generally recognized that it will suffice merely to call attention to the fact that among the numerous clerical offices of the united congregations in this Empire, some are vacant, and only a few are held by Englishmen.

That although our community on the whole is advancing in culture and intelligence, the dearest interests of ourselves and our children, our pulpits and our schools, the most precious things on earth, our character, intellect and souls, are still not seldom entrusted to men of ill-furnished minds, untutored, or at least unprepared for the performance of their sacred functions. It is no less generally acknowledged that a public Day School for the sons of our middle ranks is urgently required, especially in London, where there are good educational institutions for our poorer brethren, but none for the classes above them. Attendance in the public schools of the general community subjects our sons to this disadvantage, that they are not only deprived of one school-day in the week, but are necessarily left unprovided with sound religious instruction. That whilst their minds are necessarily engrossed by the acquisition of secular knowledge, they, for the most part, receive at home but slender and inadequate tuition in the elements of Hebrew and of our sacred doctrines.

The school for the poor brethren was, of course, the Jews' Free School, from which, in the future, many of the students for Jews' College would be enrolled.

Adler was not afraid to call a spade a spade, and he then went on to outline his plan for a school which would, 'be established in London for the purpose of affording a liberal and useful Hebrew and English education to the sons of respectable parents, and training of Ministers, Readers and Teachers'.[11]

It would be for boys between the ages of 9 and 15, who could write and read English and read Hebrew and they would be day-boys. In the Hebrew department they would be taught the translation of the prayer book, together with Bible, grammar, biblical and post-biblical history, as well as religion. They would also dip into the Pentateuch and the *Shulchan Aruch*.

In the secular department they would be taught English grammar, composition and literature, ancient and modern history, physical and political geography, arithmetic and bookkeeping. They would also learn the elements of mathematics, natural philosophy, Latin, French and German. All this for five hours every day except for Shabbat and Festivals. It was a major secular curriculum.

The school would be governed by a Council who would choose six pupils as Clerical Students. They would be taught more advanced theology and classical literature, logic and elocution at University College, London. They would have to have good characters, be in good health, and either have been born in the country or have parents who had lived in England for ten years.

The training of the Clerical Students would include taking services in the Beth Hamedresh synagogue and teaching on occasions in the day school. It was hoped, if necessary, to provide them with board and lodging and clothing. At the end of their time at the College there would be an examination for their diplomas.

The staff needed to run the school would consist of a headmaster, a second master, assistant masters and a librarian. As far as the governance of the College was concerned, the Council would consist of the president, vice president, five members, the Chief Rabbi and appropriate trustees. When it came to financing, it was expected that there would need to be an annual budget of £1,000 which would come from charitable support, the revenues of the Beth Hamedresh and school fees of £10 a year. If, however, anybody gave the College £250 they could have one pupil place free. For £1,000 they would have a free scholarship and a free Clerical Student, including the fees at University College, London. If they gave £30 a year, there would be the same advantages.

The non-Clerical Student pupils would also be able to go from the school to University College, London, which had been founded comparatively recently, to get a degree. It was an initiative to rectify the fact that Oxford and Cambridge were strongly Church of England and those belonging to other faiths could not receive degrees from them. So a number of influential non-Church of England dignitaries decided to start a purely secular college.

It opened in 1826 as London University, but against great opposition from the established church. Dr Arnold of Rugby School called it the Godless Institute in Gower Street, and Klemens von Metternich, the Austrian Chancellor, instructed his ambassador to tell the King that its establishment would bring about the ruin of England. It was later renamed University College, London and it was the obvious partner for Jews' College, if the Jewish college could be formed. It remained so for many years.

Among the most important initial financial backers of University College was Isaac Lyon Goldsmid, a prominent Jewish financier and philanthropist, but it was not until 1836 that a Royal Charter was obtained for UCL, allowing degrees to be awarded. UCL was happy to accept Jewish students and was so determinedly secular that no minister of religion was allowed to sit on its Council.

Montefiore's meeting in January 1852 was well attended and promises of support were received from those present and from many luminaries who could not attend. It was decided:

> That in the opinion of this meeting there exists among the congregations of those countries in which the English language is the vernacular tongue, a desire for the establishment of a College. That with the view to meet such desire a Jews' College be established in London. That this meeting approves of the principles embodied in the plan of the Chief Rabbi which combines three important purposes: the formation of a well regulated day school, and the objects of the Beth Hamedresh.

Here then is the first mention of the new name for the foundation: Jews' College. A Council was nominated, 'to obtain donations and subscriptions as may seem necessary for the constitution and consolidation of the Institution'.[12]

There was no problem recruiting the community's present and future leaders to sit on a committee chaired by Sir Moses Montefiore. On the list were Joshua Alexander, who would become the secretary and solicitor for the Jewish Board of Deputies; Lawrence Levy, a Vice President of the Jews Free School; Jacob Franklin, the father of Anglo-Jewish journalism; Sampson Lucas, a future Elder of the United

Synagogue; and George Jessel who, as Solicitor General, would be the first Jewish government minister. Aaron Levy Green, already a minister, was appointed Honorary Secretary.

Critics of the College in the future would attack members of the Council as has-beens, but this was certainly very unfair to the vast majority of those who gave their time and expertise to support the Institution. The Sephardim also asked to be involved and Joshua Benoliel, Nathaneel Lindo and Joseph d'Aguilar Samuda came to the meeting in April. They too were significant figures and practical men; Samuda ran the largest ship building yard in the country on the Isle of Dogs.

The Sephardi Elders had voted to give £500 to the College and were warmly welcomed. What they wanted in return for the largesse was, primarily, three representatives on the Council, at least one Hebrew master who could teach the Sephardi pronunciation, and at least one Clerical Student. In the end the Council consisted of ten Ashkenazim and two Sephardim.

There was one absolutely crucial error in the structure of the Council which would not be corrected for 75 years: 'it had previously been tacitly agreed among the Governors that residence in London was an essential qualification for membership of the Council'.[13] This was pure snobbery and not written into any constitution. It ensured that the Council would only include those considered the 'right kind of people'. It was disastrous because it meant that the College was seen in the provinces as run by the London Jewish Establishment which, of course, it was. The Council was full of eminent and dedicated men, but if the objective from the start was to get national support from the community, it should have followed that provincial councillors would be recruited in order to at least feel they had a say in the way the College was run. Yet the provincial communities were excluded from the seat of power.

Those communities were very conscious of their status. There was even considerable support for local chief rabbis, rather than just one based in London, and the irritation grew. Eventually, as far in the future as the Great War, the Chairman of the Board of Deputies would lose a vote of confidence on the Balfour Declaration because the provincial deputies had not been consulted about his proposed attitude towards it. The leaders in the provinces were every bit as proud of their positions in their communities as their London opposite numbers, but the Council took it for granted that they would support the College financially without any say in its operation.

From a fund-raising point of view, this was exactly the wrong approach, and the support the College received from provincial communities in the years to come would be very limited. After all they were far more remote from London than in modern times, when telephones, FaceTime and emails make communications easy. They had their own financial priorities and plenty of demand for the available financial resources. If London would train ministers without charging local communities, then that could be the price for excluding the provincial communities from serious involvement.

The problem with getting the support of the Empire communities was not so much their exclusion from the Council; they wouldn't have expected to come to London to attend meetings. There was, however, no real effort made to get their support for the College, even though many were very happy to accept graduates in future years.

It took nearly three more years for sufficient funds to be collected and for a suitable building to be equipped in Finsbury Square, near the Chief Rabbi's home. It involved a lot of hard work and, for Adler, 1853 was a particularly difficult year in both his personal life and as Chief Rabbi.

In June of that year his beloved wife, Henrietta, died. She had suffered from ulcers in a world where medical science could do little to cure the condition. She was in great pain for many months and an ulcer must have burst without warning because it was her servant, Mary Doyle, who was there when she died, and reported her passing. The *Rebbetzin* was only 53 years old and the devoted couple were shortly to celebrate their silver wedding. It was a devastating blow.

Henrietta had been a fine wife to Adler since they were married in 1829. She had given him three daughters and two sons, the youngest of whom was only 13 when she died. In the obituary in the *Jewish*

Chronicle we get a rare glimpse of the lady herself and the impermanence of Victorian life: 'Not a nature to shine and dazzle. She shrank from display... within a fortnight of her death, her position became alarming and every hope – humanly speaking – for recovery vanished'. Her public image was appropriate for the time: 'With increasing simplicity and singleness of heart, she discharged her domestic duties of a wife and mother.'[14]

Henrietta was the last person to be buried at the Alderney Road Cemetery in the East End of London, which had been opened as long ago as 1696. The funeral cortege consisted of fifteen coaches, with the Chief Rabbi and Sir Moses Montefiore leading the procession when it arrived at the cemetery. The coaches of the Honorary Officers of the five main London synagogues followed behind. There was, after ten years in office, a very high regard for Adler.

If his loss was not sufficient reason to distract him from the search for good teachers and the other elements involved in starting a school, Adler also, simultaneously faced a serious attack on his authority from sections of the Manchester community. To make matters worse, a number of their senior members were threatening to set up a Reform synagogue in the city, and Adler had to try to prevent that as well. In this he was not successful but the split in the community meant that the Orthodox, who remained by far the largest section of Jews in the city, reconfirmed his overall spiritual authority in Britain.

One root problem was still that of convincing the emancipationists to support the school and college project. This was well illustrated by a letter sent by Sir David Salomons, a prominent lay leader, to Adler in 1852. He wrote:

> Although I feel confirmed in the opinion first expressed to you that your proposed educational scheme as a whole was open to grave objections, I fulfil my promise of sending you a contribution. I must, however, make special conditions in respect of it. I wish to promote the education in this country of such of our Jewish fellow subjects as are destined for the Ministry of Her Majesty's Dominions and I offer my donation with that sole object in view.

> I wholly disapprove of the proposed day school as unadvisable and unnecessary. I also desire that my contribution be left distinct from the funds of the Beth Hamedresh.[15]

There was in fact no existing method of preparing school children to be sufficiently knowledgeable to enter a College to prepare them for the Ministry. So where they were supposed to come from, if there was not a school, was left in the air.

Sir Moses Montefiore was also unavailable for part of the period, as he fell very ill in February 1854. He was then 70 years old and although his stamina was remarkable, there was not much in the way of effective treatment to halt a great many diseases. Jews' College personnel would suffer from these medical shortcomings on a number of occasions in the years to come.

Eventually it was possible to hold the inaugural ceremony at 10 Finsbury Square, in the fashionable heart of the City, near the Chief Rabbi's home, on Sunday 11 November 1855. There were thirty-three registered pupils, all in the school department. After Mincha had been *davened* by Rev. Aaron Levy Green, Adler addressed the assembly. It had been a long struggle to reach this point and his speech expressed his displeasure with many who had let him down over the years. He obviously resented the lip-service. He also forecast the future with considerable foresight.

> Gentlemen, – It is my pleasing duty, a duty which fills my heart, and I am sure your hearts, with gladness, to open, this day, the Jews' College; an institution which is so important that it forms a new period in the history of our community. Allow me to address a few words to you on this occasion. After a long, very long interval between the stating of the idea and its accomplishment, we have, at last, by the assistance of the public, by the perseverance of the Council, and especially, by the aid of Almighty G-d, succeeded in opening this college to the use of the Jewish public. This is not the place to speak of the numerous difficulties which surrounded the realisation of the scheme; how some

regarded it as unnecessary, nay, injurious to the progress of the community; how others were in favour of one leading principle, but against another; how those whose support was expected left the project to its fate; how often, not without sighs and tears, I myself despaired of its attainment. It suffices to say that the doubts were dispelled, the impediments removed, and the difficulties surmounted; we are able to open it. And if it be true that the beginning is half the accomplishment, we may justly rejoice in the fact.

There may be some who have anticipated something more important, something grander and more striking, but we have, thank G-d, a house to work in, teaching power to work with, and minds to work upon. We have, in the school, the very number of pupils on which we originally founded our plan, and, in the college, we require only a very small number of students; so that the supply may not be greater than the demand. Besides, it is a known fact that every good and sound idea begins in a small degree, and grows and prospers with years ... without exaggeration or metaphor, we may truly hope that young men will obtain, in this College, a sound scientific and theological instruction, so that in the course of time our schools and our pulpits will be filled with well-trained, well-furnished teachers. We may sincerely hope that this school will afford to the youth of our middle classes a sound religious and secular education, which will go hand in hand without – as is frequently the case – injuring, curtailing and thwarting each other; we may reasonably hope and expect that the school will enlighten the intellect, warm the heart, and render them good men, faithful citizens and pious Israelites ... The permanent success of this institution will depend on some conditions and suppositions. It will depend on the support of the public at large, both in the Kingdom and the Colonies ... again the institution requires patience and perseverance. If the public expects a distinguished ministry in a very short time, or if parents hope to see immediately both blossoms and fruits sprouting, as from the rod of Aaron, or if parents will not assist the masters in their difficult task, they will be dreadfully disappointed; they will reap no fruit but that of delusion.[16]

Adler was still laying it on the line. He went on to encourage the pupils in his audience to try their hardest and to encourage the staff in similar terms. The work could now begin.

NOTES

1. Jonathan Sacks, *Will We Have Jewish Grandchildren?: Jewish Continuity and How to Achieve it* (London and Portland, OR: Vallentine Mitchell, 1994).
2. Derek Taylor, *British Chief Rabbis* (London and Portland, OR: Vallentine Mitchell, 2007), p.111.
3. Gerry Black, *JFS: The History of the Jews' Free School, London, Since 1732* (London: Tymsder Publishing, 1998).
4. Rev. Isidore Harris, *History of Jews College* (London: Luzac & Co., 1906), p iii.
5. The *Shulchan Aruch*, literally 'Prepared Table' is the most widely consulted Orthodox codification of Jewish law. It was compiled by Rabbi Joseph Caro in 1563 and published in Venice in 1565.
6. Harris, *History of Jews College*, p iv.
7. *Voice of Jacob*. 18 July 1845, p.194.
8. *Jewish Chronicle*, 12 January 1849.
9. Ibid.
10. Harris, *History of Jews College*, p.vii.
11. Ibid., p.viii.
12. Harris, *History of Jews College*.
13. Albert Hyamson, *Jews' College London, 1855–1955* (London: Jews College, 1955), p.103.
14. Ibid., p.21.
15. Harris, *History of Jews College*.
16. Harris, *History of Jews College*.

CHAPTER TWO

Setting Down Roots

English was not Nathan Marcus Adler's first language and his correspondence is, as would be expected, very formal. The family wrote to each other in a local German dialect, which is very difficult to decipher today, and his sermons were, again, carefully crafted to reflect his office rather than his inner thoughts.

At this distance in time it is helpful to have a record in English of him talking more informally. One occasion which survives was when he took the chair at the first General Meeting of the Governors of the College on 8 February 1857. He was talking to a smaller gathering than would have listened to him in the pulpit. What he had to say is, therefore, more intimate than can usually be found:

> you will allow me to make a few remarks in fuller explanation of some of the statement and details [given by the Secretary before]. And I more strongly desire your permission to do so, because I took the liberty of addressing you at the preliminary meeting at some length, [a year before] and I am perhaps now able to demonstrate and make manifest in *practice* what at that time I could only prove in *theory* ...
>
> Let me confess that there were times when I almost despaired of its [the College's] realization, and I am not afraid to say that I should have given up the project had I not kept steadily in view the greatness of the object at stake, had I not been encouraged by the conscious purity of those motives which I had so warmly cherished from the first moment of my arrival in this country – the hope to provide my community with efficient ministers and teachers for the improvement and benefit of generations yet unborn ... that while the expenditure of the year amounts to £900,

> the income is £700, and that this deficiency will be easily met by the usual benevolence and public spirit of our body ... and will reflect on the already proved groundlessness of those objections which are still urged against it.[1]

In this confident expectation of benevolence and public spirit, the Chief Rabbi and his successors were often to be disappointed. Throughout the years the financial situation of the College would be parlous and reliant on the generosity of a very small fraction of the community. Without in any way hoping that the rich would fail to reach 120 years of age, the death of supporters of the College and their subsequent bequests would rescue the General Meeting on a number of occasions from being faced with further annual losses. Over £3,400 had been raised to get the College and School started, but over the years the capital sum after the initial expenses, was slowly drawn down. Adler had other problems as well.

> Allow me to state openly some of the gravest objections referred to, which are brought forward against the College or School, and to meet those objections by facts.
> Against the training of ministers it is contended that instead of bringing boys up to an advantageous career in life, we shall render them unhappy, because they will either find no situations at all, or only poor and dependent ones ... even if we look no further than this kingdom, the demand already far exceeds the supply ... We think that were our teachers well educated and well furnished with religious and secular knowledge, they would have means and ways through public and private tuition to find an excellent living.

Again, it was a pious hope, and the benefit packages of ministers would become the subject of concern for Chief Rabbis to the present day. For too many parents considering the ministry for their sons, the old joke of 'what kind of job is that for a Jewish boy!' often had more than a grain of truth in it. Happily:

Besides, can it be denied that we have some young men, whose feelings and tastes lead them to the ministerial profession, in whom nature's hand has implanted an unconquerable love for it, and imprinted a higher bias than that for common toil. That there are some who feel a burning desire to fulfil the mission of Israel, to teach the Word of God, and to make souls happy – who would prefer this avocation to any other of worldly lucre and ambition, did not the cold voice of relatives chill such feelings and tastes.

It would indeed be fortunate for the community that there would always be men with a vocation for the ministry. That, in fact, would be Jews' College's ongoing gift to the Jewish communities both in Britain and abroad; the training of men who had the vocation but needed the right education. And also, in time, to train women to be teachers. If they were not all Talmudic giants, they still brought a great deal of carefully acquired knowledge to their future pulpits and classrooms.

On many occasions the men would arrive at the start of a congregation's life and by sheer hard work build it up into a meaningful body. As Jewish communities declined and vanished when the commercial rationale for living in the town disappeared, new congregations had to be formed, and Jews' College graduates would be crucial to that development. They lived by the motto of the College – 'The fear of the Lord is the beginning of knowledge'.

In the future the College would not only train good men who became chief rabbis and dayanim, but also ministers like Myer Berman who would serve at Wembley Synagogue for forty years, Chaim Cooper who would be at Hull for forty years, Yaacov Grunewald at Pinner for thirty-four years, and Abraham Chaitovitz at Stanmore for thirty-one years.

They would occupy overseas pulpits where, without them, an English-speaking minister would have been almost impossible to find. In the 1920s all four of the ministers in Melbourne, Australia would be Jews' College graduates. They would be found in Nairobi, Shanghai, Bulawayo in Zimbabwe, the Philippines and Denmark. In all these locations they were vital to the communities they served and often won great affection and regard.

The value of their contribution would never diminish. After the Second World War, they would revive communities in Strasbourg, Munich and Frankfurt. Their influence on innumerable individuals would be immense and it was only possible because they were given the right training at Jews' College.

The Chief Rabbi went on: 'Whether right or wrong, it is a fact, that the community prefers natives to foreigners; now I ask you, is it not paradoxical to want and desire them anxiously, and yet to do nothing for their qualification? Is it reasonable to wait until they might fall from the sky like manna?' They certainly wouldn't fall like manna. Their recruitment would always be a problem and there would be numerous struggles to encourage and sustain them through to their eventual qualifications.

> Was the Jews' Free School, set up for poor children, a possible alternative? I answer, No ... In the short time that our College has existed, it has already proved that it has its own field of culture, without interfering in the least with the work of others ... What would become of our holy religion amidst the present and future attacks from within and without, were its teachers restricted to a petty allowance of one or two hours a day.

Which was the case at the JFS. Adler was recognizing that the Jews' Free School educated its pupils to earn a living, not to become ministers. There were far more poor children than prospective clergy. The College pupils would, it was hoped, come from the ranks of the better-off Jewish families.

> Why clog it with a school? ... Gentlemen, I said at the first general meeting and I repeat it this day, supported by experience, that the School is indispensable for the support of the College both *intellectually* and *financially* ... the School teaches the man, the College the individual. The School is *general*, the College is *special*.

Chief Rabbi Nathan Marcus Adler, the founder and inspiration. Reproduced with permission from Harris, *History of Jews College*.

Sir Moses Montefiore, undisputed leader of the Victorian community. Reproduced with permission from Harris, *History of Jews College*.

The problem for the College at the outset was that there were practically no candidates sufficiently knowledgeable to attend it. In the future they would only be recruited in very small numbers, but they would need the same number and quality of teachers as if there was a far greater roll of students. They would need a building, furniture, books, and all the other elements of an academic institution. Without the school fees, the College could also never hope to be viable in the early years. Furthermore, the School was expected to be the feeder body for the College, like the public schools who had connections with primary schools for the same reason.

> The present attendance of forty pupils raised an income of £400 in school fees. This income might be regarded in many respects as an important aid and support to the College ... there is no other Jewish day school for the higher and middle classes ... We know [however] that there are gentlemen who tremble at the idea of an *exclusive* Jewish school, and think it injurious to our present or future social position.

The snobbery and class system of Victorian Britain was a core fact in everyday life. In the Jewish world, too, status mattered a great deal. There is, however, no point in trying to judge Victorian culture by twenty-first-century standards; it was simply a different world. The Jewish emancipationists were also looking for a different kind of minister from the tradition on the Continent. There:

> The modernists weighed their rabbis in a notional balance and found them wanting. The rabbis did not conduct themselves with enough urbanity, compete with the leaders of opinion and culture in the newly open European society, or couch their message in the local idiom or vernacular.[2]

They were still theologically learned. Adler pointed out the dangers of children growing up in non-Jewish schools, without any real knowledge of the religion. Those who have no real knowledge of their religion are more likely to give it up on reaching adulthood. Convincing upwardly mobile Jewish families of this though was never going to be easy.

> If they would consider all this, they would be not merely reconciled but even delighted with the existence of the School ... provide the necessary aids for the support of the College by *annual subscriptions*; the more so, as hitherto besides the munificent annual gift of £100 from the house of Rothschild, the amount from such resources is limited to £48.³

The shortfall in the accounts in the next fifteen years would seldom exceed £100, but the simple solution chosen by most charities was not adopted by the College; there would be no annual fund raising dinner until the Jubilee year in 1906. Concern about a perceived lack of dignity involved in holding such charitable occasions would seem to be the hidden agenda. Life Governorships, donations and bequests were more respectable and did not involve dedicated fund raisers. As a consequence, the £1,200 in the 1857 deposit account steadily dwindled.

Solid support continued to come from the Rothschilds, who gave their £100 a year, and the old Beth Hamedresh had funds which provided another £50. It was also possible to become a Life Governor with a donation of £10 and in 1857 there were over seventy of them. When the Liverpool banker, Israel Barned died, his demise was sincerely regretted, but he did leave the College £1,000. Such a large benefaction was, unfortunately, a rare occurrence.

When the school opened in 1855, the *Jewish Chronicle* waxed lyrical:

> The future ministers of the Anglo-Jewish congregations will be men of thorough English feelings and views, as conversant with the classics of their own language as with those of the sacred tongue, as acquainted with modern science as versed in ancient lore; men in whom the flow of the burning thought will not be impeded by heaviness of tongue, and whose ardour of enthusiasm

will break forth and rouse and kindle with Shakespearian vigour and Miltonian sweetness.[4]

There were, however, only 24 hours in the day and time spent on secular subjects reduced the hours available for Talmudic study. The writer totally underestimated the time it took to achieve even a rudimentary understanding of the *Shulchan Aruch*. Judaism is a very detailed religion. The School was always considered a necessity rather than a choice.

Rev. Aaron Green had been appointed as one of the Secretaries and would serve until 1883. He reported at the first meeting: 'Whether a time will come when the School may be dispensed with, and the connection between the two branches may be safely severed, the future alone can answer.'

The School was well located for the well-to-do families who lived in the City, but a large proportion of the pupils would not make the ministry their careers. The students of the College, by contrast, would invariably come from poor families who couldn't afford the fees, putting more strain again on the annual budget.

At least the search for a suitable headmaster had been solved by appointing Dr Louis Loewe in 1856, for three years. His contract was for an annual salary of £300. Loewe was closely associated with Montefiore, who he had met in the Middle East, and he was a brilliant linguist. In 1869 he would go on to be the head of Montefiore's new school in Ramsgate, which developed into a yeshiva.

Finsbury Square soon had a family atmosphere as James Loewe, the Headmaster's son, later recalled. He remembered, as a 6 year old, Lady Montefiore arriving with sweets for him and playing in nearby Artillery Park, while Sam da Sola was being taught Gemara in the Great Hall by his father, and Sir Moses Montefiore was in deep discussion with the Chief Rabbi.

There were five masters besides Loewe and their total cost was £730. In the early years the income from School fees never reached that figure. Two masters taught English and there was a Hebrew, French and a Drawing Master. There was rent to pay, stationary and other costs. It was, not surprising that the outgoings in the first year were

£200 more than the income.

The School actually started with thirty-three pupils and the College soon had three students. There were two school classes, evenly split in numbers. In the 1858 report the AGM heard that discipline was well maintained, and the subject of discipline would be mentioned in future years as well, usually to say it was much improved. Yet in the General Instructions for the School, detailed in the 1857 report, it had been clearly stated that: 'The discipline of the school is maintained without corporal punishment. The extreme punishment for misconduct is the removal of the Pupil from the School.'[5]

This approach might well have been unique in schools recruiting from the middle and upper classes in those days. Corporal punishment was standard practice in public schools for breaches of discipline. Its absence, however, doesn't fit in with the recollections of boys who were at the school in the 1860s.

In 1857 the oral exam to test the pupils had been delayed:

> in consequence of the absence from this country of the Reverend the Chief Rabbi. It was considered that the dignity which the presence of the Rabbi would confer, his great experience in educational matters, and the respect due to him as the Head of the College, were circumstances which rendered this step proper and expedient.[6]

Nothing was said about why the Chief Rabbi was out of the country. In fact, after he had been widowed in 1853, in August 1857, he got married again in Germany to his second wife, Celestine Lehfeld. This was right and proper because a rabbi was traditionally encouraged to remarry if he became a widower. On the other hand, to lose a wife through illness was somehow considered inappropriate in Victorian society. It was as if there had been a serious error in health management! It just wasn't talked about. The annual report had been written to follow the Victorian line.

It was reported in 1858 that the three College students could now read Hebrew without the diacritical points,[7] even if they weren't sufficiently advanced in their studies to go to UCL. This was certainly progress. The cost of attending the School was now set at £10 a year, though many prospective pupils still came from families who couldn't afford that sort of money.

Before the 1870 Education Act only between a third and a half of children went to school. So there always needed to be an effort to create scholarships which would take the financial burden off good candidates. Certainly more graduates were needed. When the Great Synagogue needed a second *hazan* in 1858 there was no British applicant.

In 1858 the Council was able to report the offer of a scholarship from the committee of the Lord Mayor's Commemoration Scholarship Association, worth £30 a year. This was to commemorate the election of the first Jew as Lord Mayor of London, the same Sir David Salomons who didn't like the idea of the School in the first place.

By 1860 the Annual Reports were becoming somewhat repetitive. The School and College were always performing very well, the staff were excellent, the books never balanced, the community would never let the College fail and the discipline was improving. Financially, the Governors continued to live in hopes that suitable candidates would emerge from all over the country and the Empire. There was one false dawn in 1860 when a Jew in Jamaica sent his son to the School to be trained as a *hazan*, but it was an isolated incident.

One notable new pupil was Samuel de Sola, the son of the *hazan* at Bevis Marks Synagogue, who was awarded the Lord Mayor's Scholarship. He was entered to train as a minister. The bad news was that the shortfall in the accounts in 1860 was higher than usual at £150, but in 1861 the donation of 100 guineas from David Salomons kept the books straight.

There was no similar help in 1862 when it was reported that, 'The Council regret that they cannot congratulate the Governors and Subscribers upon the financial condition of the College.'[8] The problem wasn't so much the £150 shortfall as the lamentable total of only 17 guineas (£17.85) which came from donations. The report is frank about the future financial position of the College:

Setting Down Roots

Louis Loewe, Headmaster 1855–58. Reproduced with permission from the Jewish Museum.

Michael Friedländer, Principal 1865–1907. Reproduced with permission from Harris, *History of Jews College*.

> It will usually happen that the majority of those aspiring to the honours of the clerical profession will be of the class little favoured by fortune; and it will therefore be vain to expect from the College students the payment of such fees as would be adequate for defraying the cost of their education.

Typically, in that year, the cost of the salaries of the teachers alone was £670 but the school fees produced only £350. There just weren't enough fee-paying children at the school. Helping to bridge the gap in 1863, Barnett Myers gave the College £30 a year to pay for a music instructor to teach vocal music to those pupils who meant to become *hazanim*. Henry Solomons, one of the Treasurers, paid for a piano for the use of the music class. Barnett Myers also and Adler's son-in-law gave the College a property which produced an annual rent of £35, enough money to support a pupil. It would be called the Barnett Myers' Scholarship.

Another friend of the College set up a trust which would produce £30 a year to pay for the board and lodging for a student. Indeed it was likely to produce more, and the surplus would go towards free pupilships for the sons of Jewish ministers. The Council were very unhappy that many ministers could not afford the school fees, even if their children wanted to follow in their fathers' footsteps. So much for the excellent living Adler had forecast for them a few years before.

Not all the bright children of ministers were lost in this way. Two of the sons of the *hazan* at the Hambro Synagogue in London would become Rabbi Professor Sir Hermann Gollancz (1852–1930) and Professor Sir Israel Gollancz (1863–1930). Sir Hermann recalled Jews' College in his early days:

> At the age of 9 I entered Jews' College School. Before I was 13 I was permitted by the Council to attend the Talmud Class of the College proper. I matriculated in 1869 and took my first BA with Honours in 1878. Owing to the fact that my father required my assistance at the Hambro Synagogue, I continued my studies only at the College and kept up secular work privately.[9]

Hermann Gollancz became the Minister of a Manchester synagogue and particularly admired Professor Tobias Theodores, who he pronounced the greatest linguist he ever knew. It was Theodores who was the main protagonist of German Reform as well as advocating the diminution of the powers of the Chief Rabbi, but the religious arguments did not cause a rift with Gollancz.

He remembered, 50 years later, that when the Shah of Persia visited Manchester, Theodores was the only person who could speak to him in his own language. Hermann later became the minister at the Bayswater Synagogue from 1892–1923 when he was knighted. He was one of the main proponents of the use of the rabbinic title if *semicha* had been granted. As he remembered in 1912, 'From my college days I always felt that Jews' College was deficient in that it allowed its students possessing all the qualifications to leave its walls without the hallmark of the rabbinical degree. And for years this crying injustice rankled in my breast.'[10] It was a very natural reaction, but it didn't address the main problem Adler had, of retaining to himself the ultimate spiritual authority to ensure the community remained Orthodox. Hermann Gollancz was the first Jew in Britain to be awarded a D.Litt and eventually became Professor of Hebrew at the University of London from 1902–24.

Sir Israel Gollancz became the Professor of English Language at Kings College, London from 1912–30. He was also the first secretary of the British Academy, and there is still in existence the Sir Israel Gollancz prize, offered by the British Academy, for papers on Early English Studies.

In 1862 Moses Montefiore provided an endowment in memory of his wife, Judith, who had died that year. This would produce £100 a year. There is no question that as long as Montefiore was alive, the College was in no danger of completely running out of funds, but the balance sheet for 1862 still showed a deficit of £60. The school still 'craved the support of numbers'. It was particularly disappointing as they could now point to the children passing the Matriculation exam and the Oxford exam, but there still weren't 50 pupils in all.

In 1860 it had been reported that the instruction of the lower-class students in conjunction with the upper class at the School 'was found to interfere materially with the maintenance of discipline'.[11] To resolve this a Classical Tutor was hired for the College and a principal English and Classical master for the School. This kept the boys apart but there hadn't been that many of them in the first place; thirty-two in the School and three in the College.

The opportunities for further education for the College pupils were enhanced when London University stopped requiring students to regularly attend one of its colleges before being admissible for a degree. It was very welcome to record that Samuel da Sola had now been appointed a minister at Bevis Marks at so young an age. He went on to become the *hazan* in succession to his father but, unhappily, died at 26.

In 1862, after Louis Loewe had left at the end of his contract, the responsibilities of the headmaster were split between Rev. Barnett Abrahams as Principal of the College and J.S. Benifold as Headmaster of the School. It would emerge that Benifold was either unaware, or chose to ignore, the school regulation that there would be no corporal punishment. As Benifold wasn't Jewish, Abrahams was responsible for the religious education of the pupils.

Barnett Abrahams was only 27 when he succeeded Louis Loewe:

> He became one of the most remarkable men of his time, and such a force for good as made him an ideal head of an institution which had to train students for the sacred vocation of minister. His enthusiasm for the cause of religious education was unbounded ... with the utmost simplicity and humility he gave himself and the little that he possessed to others ... [His] saintly character impressed itself alike on his pupils and on all who were brought under his influence.[12]

Official reports are all very well, but personal reminiscences give a far better picture of what life was actually like for the students at the College. Rev. Isidore Harris (1853–1925), was there between 1863 and 1874. He was first a pupil of the School and then a student of the College.

'The building itself was but ill adapted for the accommodation of so many scholars. One particularly felt the need of a playground. A large front kitchen had to serve this purpose in my time; and it was there that we were drilled by the resident porter of the institution, Sergeant Miller, after Michael Henry – the most fervent advocate in his day of muscular Judaism – introduced drilling into the School. Certainly a minute of the 12th January 1869, records that Sir Benjamin Phillips obtained from Colonel Wilson the kind concession of a portion of the Artillery Ground 'for the use of the pupils of the College'; but I have no recollection of any such concession having been utilised. The back of the College looked on to the Artillery Ground, and my only memories of this fine open space are connected with the Militia practice for which it was used several weeks in the summer. Those of us who occupied the classroom facing it were, I fear, more interested in these military evolutions than in the lessons to which our distracted teachers tried to compel our attention. And there were the annual sports which took place on a certain Saturday afternoon in the summer, which we watched from the leads, or were admitted to the ground to witness. But for the scholars themselves there were no opportunities of athletic exercise in our day.

A very strict discipline was maintained in the School, and corporal punishment was freely resorted to. While we small schoolboys stood in mortal dread of the caning proclivities of the headmaster, Mr Benifold, a more pleasing impression is retained of the pedagogy [how best to teach] of the second master, Mr Roberts, the author of *Arithmetic by Common Sense*. He made the subject delightful to us, and must have been one of the best elementary teachers of his day. The arithmetical teaching of the Rev. John Chapman[13] was also made exceedingly interesting. His lessons in mental arithmetic will never fade from the memory of his pupils. He contrived to make us calculate with lightning rapidity. Mr Chapman's mental arithmetic lesson – taken standing in a circle – was looked forward to as a pleasure. In other subjects, too, his teaching impressed us by its lucidity, and as he had none of the infirmities of temper that characterised some of the other masters, he was our favourite teacher. Another genial master was Prof. Hartog, who likewise possessed the secret of interesting his pupils, and who taught French capitally. I cannot remember who was responsible for bookkeeping, but it was well taught, and proved of use to some of us when, on leaving the College, we had to combine secretarial duties with our ministerial vocation. Mr Benifold's successor was Mr Maconachie, a dear old gentleman, whose strong point was Latin, but who was less sound than could be desired in his Greek.

One feature of our school days of which I have a vivid remembrance was the monthly evening lectures, which became so popular, and formed such a pleasant break in our school life. These lectures were followed by recitations which the pupils gave in English, French, German and Hebrew. Some of us were able to recite the whole of Schiller's 'Glocke' from memory ... Gradually these recitations developed into dramatic representations. Scenes from Shakespeare and Molière were acted by the pupils with the aid of some of the older College students; and even at this distance of time it is possible to recall the excellent impression made by Mr Singer's [later of the Singer Prayer Book] elocution in a scene from Julius Caesar ... Less credit, however, attached to a performance from King John, in the scene where Arthur prays Hubert to spare his life. 'Have you the heart?' he asks in his famous appeal. But the lad who was to recite this speech had the misfortune to drop both his 'h's. ''Ave you the 'art?' he asked, to the consternation of Mr Benifold who promptly rang down the curtain.

Of the College class, to which those of us who were studying for the ministry were in due course promoted, recollections are naturally more keen. Here our two principal teachers were Dr Friedländer and Dr Hermann Adler. Dr Friedländer impressed us by his encyclopaedic knowledge, among many other things. One hour he would be teaching us Hebrew or German, and at another he would be construing Homer or Horace. On another occasion

Finsbury Square, the first home of the College. Reproduced with permission from Harris, *History of Jews College*.

he would be conducting us through the mazes of the Higher Mathematics, from which he would pass quite easily to the performance of experiments in Chemistry and Natural Philosophy. Nothing in the curriculum seemed to come amiss to this 'Admirable Crichton'.

Dr Hermann Adler's range of subjects was also exceedingly wide, including, as it did, Talmud, Shulchan Aruch, Homiletics [the art of preaching], English Language and Literature, and English History. And he gave us the full benefit of his varied reading in all these departments ... The character of his teaching may be summed up in one word: it was inspiring. Dr Adler was full of a loving enthusiasm for knowledge, which it is to be hoped, he succeeded in imparting to his scholars ... The Saturday morning services, in which the College students took regular part, formed, as has been said, a valuable feature of our ministerial training ...

And there was another member of the Council who made the deepest and best impression upon us all – the Chief Rabbi and President of Jews' College, Dr N.M. Adler, whose dignified and venerable figure we saw constantly, and whose devotion to the interests of the College seemed the master passion of his life. Hardly a day passed that he did not visit the institution. The Council minutes show that he was rarely absent from a meeting. He lived opposite the College, or he could not have spared us so much of his precious time. As College students, he frequently examined us to see what progress we were making in his favourite subject, the Talmud. His interest in us personally manifested itself in so many gracious attentions, as when a student who had matriculated would be invited to spend a weekend with him at the seaside – an honour, the pleasure of which was only marred by the consideration that Dr Adler's student-guest was expected to conduct the whole of the Sabbath service which he held in his house.[14]'

It was a tragedy that Barnett Abrahams, the Principal after Louis Loewe, died in November 1863 when he was only 31. He had already been made a Dayan in the Sephardi community and was very highly regarded by the governors. He was also the founder of the Association for the Diffusion of Religious Knowledge. His death from rheumatic fever was totally unexpected and he left a pregnant widow and five small children.

A memorial fund soon raised £2,000 for the family – which is about £170,000 today – and the College gave his wife a pension of £30 a year as well (about £50 a week today). There was no question, however, that Abrahams' death left a big gap at the College which Hermann Adler, the Chief Rabbi's son, and Rev. H.L. Harris, the minister of the Hambro Synagogue, endeavoured to fill.

Hermann Adler had just returned from Prague where he had received his *semicha* from Rabbi Rapaport and had studied at Leipzig University at the same time. As a young rabbi he may have been considered inexperienced to be in charge of the College's religious teaching, but the choice of rabbis in Britain remained very limited.

The Annual Report referred to his 'profound learning' and he had been thoroughly taught from an early age by his father. As Isidore Harris recorded, he was able to inspire the pupils, which is the finest attribute of a schoolteacher. The fact that his father had not thought the College worthy to train his son to a *semicha* standard was diplomatically overlooked.

Eventually a first class academic was imported to London to head up the School and College. Dr Michael Friedländer was an excellent choice. He was a Prussian who came from the Talmud Association School in Berlin and would serve as Principal from 1865–1907. A child prodigy, his father was a fine Talmudist and his mother the daughter of a rabbi. The extraordinary thing about Friedländer was the range of his abilities; he was not only an expert Talmudist but also a first class mathematician and a Classical scholar. His thesis for his degree was a Latin work on the Persian Kings – *De Veteribus Persarum Regibus*. It wasn't surprising that the seminary in Berlin tried to get him back, but Friedländer would spend the next forty-two years developing the College.

He was a man who earned affection from his pupils and in private life, together with his wife Bertha, he presided over what became a literary, intellectual and social salon in Anglo-Jewry. He took a keen interest in every Jewish literary society and wrote several important books on subjects like Maimonides' *Guide to the Perplexed*. The Friedländers had one daughter, Lucy, and she would marry Moses Gaster, the Sephardi Haham in the latter part of the century. So another German educationalist joined the Chief Rabbi to bolster the British community.

Hermann Adler was able to leave the College to Friedländer, but he continued to teach Theology and prepared the students for their English exams at the University of London. Benifold resigned when Friedländer had been in office for a couple of years and was not much missed.

A new French teacher was Alphonse Hartog whose son, Numa, was the first Jew to be Senior Wrangler in Cambridge. He also paved the way for Jews to be able to gain Fellowships, because the Senior Wrangler automatically got a Fellowship and, as a Jew, the University couldn't give one to Hartog. So they had to change the rules. It was another tragedy that Numa Hartog died at 25.

In 1864 the number of school pupils had risen to 77, double the number of a few years before, and the income from fees was a more acceptable £517. There was still an overall loss of £50, but an extra class was now deemed necessary. With two exceptions, the College students were all receiving free education. One would be supported by Albert and Sassoon Sassoon who gave £1,000 to fund the David Sassoon Free Studentship in memory of their father. The Treasurers of the College, Henry Solomon and Joshua Alexander, were meticulous in their account of the College's finances. In 1866 they had to report the loss of £15 due to "defalcations [theft] by the late Beadle".

In a happier vein the College was able to report a trickle of its students obtaining posts as ministers with congregations. One, John Chapman, was also a Clerical Visitor to Portsmouth Prison.[15] Another was in post in Louisiana in the Southern States of America. The objective of the College was to provide learned laymen for communities as well as ministers. 'The great aim of your institution is to train not only Jewish ministers and Teachers, fit interpreters of the Divine Word, who shall bid it discourse in the current language of men [English], but also a community that shall lend a willing and an understanding ear to the holy lessons such Ministers shall teach.'[16]

To provide more information about the quality of studies the pupils were undertaking, the Annual Reports now started to include extracts from their graduation examinations. Typical questions were: How do you explain Isaiah chapter 53? What was the state of the parties in Judaea immediately after the death of Judah the Maccabee? What were the principal events in the reign of Alexander Jannaeus? In addition, there were extensive papers on Greek and Latin. In the secular examinations were questions on Euclid and book keeping. It was a wide curriculum which might well stretch students even today.

New expenses appeared of an alarming size. In 1867 £260 had to be spent on repairs to the structure [at least £20,000 today]. It was fortunate that a developer wanted to put up a building near the College at the same time. This would take away some of the light from the College structure and compensation would, therefore, have to be paid for the loss of what is known as Ancient Lights. The agreed figure was £250, which matched the cost of the repairs, but such fortuitous occurrences could not be guaranteed every time there was a financial crisis. The adverse balance for the year was still £100. One saving could be made when Hyman Montagu volunteered to be the College Secretary without receiving a salary. Another lifeline arrived when Sassoon Sassoon died and left the College £200.

While fighting the waves of potential insolvency the College continued to teach in the calm harbour of academia. The venerable George Maconachie arrived to assist Dr Friedländer as Headmaster of the school, but that experiment only lasted a few years. In 1871 there was another challenge. A new school opened nearby and threatened to take the School's pupils. Fees were, therefore, dropped and a new younger class was started. The reaction was positive and the school roll reached nearly 100. The Annual report was reassuring for the class-conscious governors: 'Although it might be apprehended that the reduction of the school fees would deteriorate the social calibre of the establishment, it is pleasing to record that no such result has appeared.'[17]

In 1874 there were ninety pupils of the School and seven students of the College. The Council decided to try to spread its influence wider. It started Hebrew classes in Portman Square in the West End. It took advertisements in the press and the Council members did their best to promote the new venture among their friends. There were, however, only fourteen pupils in the first term and twenty-five in the second. The financial loss was nearly £100, the situation didn't improve in the next year and the experiment was ended at that point. The Council reported with dignified regret: 'They were organized to supply a great want, but they have not received from the heads of the Jewish families resident in the district, for whose benefit these classes were established, the support and encouragement which they deserved.'[18] Nobody could say the College Council wasn't constantly trying, but the magic formula for success continued to elude them.

In 1872 Mrs Lyons of Sheffield died and left the College £100, and of the now nine students in the College, eight did not pay fees. The Chief Rabbi was concerned to find some way of supporting those who usually had to survive by giving private lessons, but the Council couldn't see how they could do more than give them a free education.

The annual budget, which was £1,183 in 1866, had now risen to £2,404. The Treasurers sold the Consols [gilt edged stock] they had been given originally for £950. They used £250 of the proceeds to pay back borrowings and then invested £545 in East India Railway Stock. Consols paid $\frac{31}{2}$ per cent interest but the railway stock nearer 5 per cent. Every little helped.

In 1875 the students decided to produce their own magazine, *The Jews' College Journal*. The joint editors were Israel Abrahams, Delissa Joseph, Aaron Green, Herman Cohen and Elkan Adler, all of whom would make their mark in Anglo-Jewry in the years to come. There were, however, other demands on their time and pockets, and the journal only lasted six months.

The main objective of the College was, however, slowly being realized: graduates were beginning to benefit the community. Isidore

Harris became the minister at the North London Synagogue and Morris Joseph the minister at the Liverpool Old Synagogue. Simeon Singer would soon be appointed the minister at the New West End Synagogue, and Hermann Gollancz the minister at the Bayswater Synagogue. By 1876, however, the School roll was down to fifty. Progress was very slow because, after twenty years, the original concept of creating a School and a College wasn't working.

The idea had been that middle-class youngsters would go from the School to the College and into the ministry and teaching. The reality was that most of the boys at the school did not go into either. What was more, the College students still usually emerged from poor families, rather than middle class, couldn't afford the fees and had to be given free tuition.

The situation got worse; living in the City was becoming less popular with the well-to-do. They were moving into the West End and, therefore, getting the children to and from school was becoming more of a problem. It had also been the aim of the founders to provide the College students with a good secular education, but the cost of creating the infrastructure for it was prohibitive when there were no College fees. It was appreciated that it would be better financially to have the students given their secular education at University College, but the Finsbury Square location was a long way away from Gower Street, where UCL could be found.

There was another factor which had an adverse effect on recruitment. Where good schools for Jewish children had been in short supply, the situation had now changed. The City of London and University College schools were happy to take Jewish children and, if the curriculum didn't include Judaism, there were always Hebrew teachers available for middle-class homes. Too many of the families Jews' College had hoped to attract continued to feel that a public school education was more in keeping with their ambitions for their children than a Jewish one. This conviction would continue to be the case until at least the latter half of the next century.

Even for those who didn't reject the idea, there were now more Jewish schools being started in other parts of the metropolis. Hyman

Hurwitz had his school in Highgate even before the Jews' College School, and now Henry Solomon had started one in Edmonton, Leopold Neumegen at Kew and Rev. Abraham Mendes in St Johns Wood.

There is a first hand account of the last years of the School from Rabbi Harris Cohen, who was there for five years as a youngster and wrote of his memories sixty years later.[19] Cohen was the son of Dayan Susman Cohen, Hermann Adler's right hand man when he became Chief Rabbi. He was particularly fond of Dr Friedländer: 'He was an angel on earth ... but the master we loved most was Israel Abrahams. He was the friend of every one of us.'

When they eventually moved to Tavistock Square, Abrahams would take them to Regents Park on a Friday afternoon to play cricket. Not all the masters were popular: 'The master we liked least was the French teacher ... he came in in a temper, remained angry during the lesson and left in a temper. He was very small and very fat and could hardly climb the high chair behind his desk.'

Cohen remembered that not all the students went into the ministry, though he, personally, would serve the Stoke Newington community for thirty-one years. The brothers Bendet and Victor Saul, for example, would become distinguished doctors. As could be expected among Jewish academics, there was a good deal of mordant humour; Harris remembered Aaron Green talking of a Jewish girl who wanted a job where she could have Saturday off. 'I have asked every member of the synagogue who keeps Shabbos and they both refused!' Or Dr Friedländer responding to a leaving student's thanks for all he had learned at the college: 'Oh please. Don't mention such a trifle!'

Much still depended, of course, on a teacher's ability to inspire, and Cohen particularly remembered Solomon Schechter, who was 'a tall, imposing, fascinating, dynamic personality'. Cohen enjoyed his years at the College and became a minister at the Merthyr Synagogue when he was only 19.

London had always been the centre of the Jewish community in Britain and, in 1870, the Chief Rabbi had been able to prod the three main synagogues, the Great, the Hambro and the New, into amalgamating. The new body, named the United Synagogue, recognized the need for that flow of English ministers that Adler had been so anxious to produce, but never accepted its responsibilities to underwrite the College. It would make a limited annual contribution and have representatives on the Council, but otherwise it left the College to solve its own financial difficulties.

Moses Montefiore was now in his mid-80s and an Ashkenazi equivalent of his philanthropic leadership was needed. Cometh the hour, cometh the man, and the man was Charles Samuel (1820–1903). Nobody ever had a bad word to say about Charles Samuel. He had built a firm of wholesale clothiers, called Samuel Brothers, into a major concern and was both religious and extremely generous. Few Jewish charities and associations failed to be the beneficiaries of his support. He was also passionate about Jewish education and for twenty-five years he was going to be, effectively, the lay CEO of Jews' College.

At the United Synagogue he had been elected Treasurer and, in 1878, he would take on the same role at the College, five years after joining the Council. It was Samuel who initially persuaded the United Synagogue Council to support Jews' College, over determined resistance by some of Jewry's most important leaders.

At the Council meeting to discuss giving the College some substantial financial assistance, the Chairman, as well as Samuel Montagu who created the Federation of Synagogues, and Sir Nathaniel de Rothschild, all opposed the idea. Rothschild's view reflected that of many: 'If they wished to have popular, cultured gentlemen as Jewish ministers they should not have them brought up in a semi-monastic institution presided over and more or less controlled by the Chief Rabbi.'[20]

Where they were to be brought up differently, Sir Nathaniel didn't specify. He was representing the attitude of those who felt that Jewish ministers should, in reality, be more vicars than Talmudic scholars. It was also suggested that the Jews' Free School had produced more ministers than the College, but its defenders pointed to the core problem which was the lack of support the College had received from the community. Furthermore, the Jews' Free School was over 2,000 pupils strong. It was obvious that some of the JFS school roll would have a vocation for the ministry and a number of them moved on to Jews' College anyway. Charles Samuel had proposed the motion to support the College, at the United Synagogue, summed up, and saw the final vote come down in favour of his proposal by 22-13.

Samuel's plan was to tackle the annual financial problem once and for all. As their Treasurer, he persuaded the Jews' College Council to close the School and concentrate on the College. The School wasn't producing candidates for the College and the school roll was now dropping and likely to diminish further as families moved out of the district.

The Chief Rabbi and Dr Friedländer were, as could be expected, very much against the idea, hoping against hope that things would improve. The financial figures were against them, though, as was the failed original philosophy. In addition the Chief Rabbi was ill and, even when he recovered, was very much a spent force. On 25 June 1879 it was resolved to close the School at the end of the term.

NOTES

1. Jews' College Annual Report. Available from Jews'College. Hereafter JCAR.
2. Rabbi Raymond Apple, a paper on *Jews' College and the Jewish Ministry*.
3. JCAR
4. *Jewish Chronicle*, 24 November 1855, p.387.
5. JCAR.
6. JCAR.
7. The diacritical marks, or vowels, in Hebrew are placed above and below the letters, except in a Sefer Torah, the scroll of the five books of Moses, where they are left out.
8. JCAR.
9. *Jewish Chronicle*. 29 November 1912, p.20.
10. Ibid.
11. JCAR.
12. Rev. Isidore Harris, *History of Jews' College 1855–1905* (London: Luzac & Co., 1906), p.xix.
13. Rev. John Chapman was born in 1846. He was a student at the College and taught there from 1866-67. He became its Secretary from 1884-1909. He was also the Assistant Minister at the Western Synagogue and Headmaster of the Jews' Hospital and Orphan Asylum from 1868-78. From 1881 he was Headmaster of

    the Great Ealing School, founded in 1698, and described at the best private school in England. It rivalled Eton. Cardinal Newman was a pupil and Chapman taught a large number of boys from the ranks of the Jewish middle classes.
14. Ibid., pp.xlii-xlvii. A lot of the information in the chapter also comes from the Annual Reports of the College which have survived.
15. *Jewish Chronicle*, 8 October 1948, p.13.
16. JCAR.
17. JCAR.
18. JCAR.
19. *Jewish Chronicle*, 10 May 1878, p.7.
20. Harris, *History of Jews' College 1855–1905*.

CHAPTER THREE

The Michael Friedländer Years

The closing of the School led to a rethinking of the purpose of Jews' College. The original idea to train Jewish leaders for the benefit of the community was now dropped: 'It was in future to be restricted to the education of theological students who intended to enter the Jewish ministry or teaching profession.'[1]

To enable students from poor families to attend University College, they needed sponsorship. In 1874 Baroness Mayer de Rothschild had undertaken to look after two students, 'likely to fulfil, by the promise of their youth, the generally entertained desire for a liberally instructed and properly trained Jewish clergy'.[2] Charles Samuel was paying for another six students and also promised to give the College £200 a year if it moved out of the City and nearer UCL.

The change and subsequent move came at a time when the old guard was retiring. The Chief Rabbi had moved permanently to Brighton; Sir Moses Montefiore, the Vice President, stood down because he was approaching 100 years old; and Moses Picciotto, a member of the Council, passed away. Joshua Levy came in as Hon. Secretary together with Rev. Aaron Levy Green. The faculty was, however, strengthened by the appointment as teacher and senior tutor of Israel Abrahams, a talented Hebraist who had been a student at the College and remained in post until 1902. He is best known as the author of *Jewish Life in the Middle Ages*, published in 1896.

Sir Barrow Ellis became the new Vice President in 1882, replacing Sir Moses Montefiore. Ellis was a former very senior Civil Servant in India and when he came back to London he was not only given the KCSI (Knight Commander of the Star of India) but was also made a member of the Indian Council where he wielded considerable influence. He was unmarried and gave a lot of time to the College.

Now, under a new constitution passed in 1879, 'the objects of Jews' College were the educating and training of Ministers, Preachers, Readers and Teachers of Religion, for Jewish congregations whose vernacular is the English language'.[3]

At the back of the Council's mind remained the perceived need to produce ministers who had the same image as vicars of the Church of England. Not just Talmudically knowledgeable rabbis, but men who looked the part, spoke Oxford English and could boast of university degrees. To further the transformation *hazanim* became known as precentors, *parnasim* became wardens and the *shammash* was now the beadle or sexton. Yiddish was widely frowned upon by the community's leaders. It was associated with poverty-stricken immigrants and was, therefore, behind closed doors, roundly condemned as common.

Ministers now started to wear vicar's dog collars, which had been invented by a Presbyterian Scottish clergyman in 1840. Hermann Adler, as Chief Rabbi in the future, would occasionally be seen in bishop's gaiters. The *din* is that, as clothing is not doctrinal, there is no prohibition against the uniform of other religions being adopted by Jewish clergy. A historian for the United Synagogue suggested in 1970 that David Tevele Schifff, who had been Chief Rabbi in the eighteenth century, was the first to wear a distinctive costume.[4] This new approach was known as *Minhag Anglia*, although the expression doesn't occur in the *Jewish Chronicle* until 1924. *Minhag Anglia* was often considered the Jewish British way of doing things. However, it only applied to the Orthodox Ashkenazim and the whole *minhag* had been firmly based on the Hamburg ritual of the Jews, from the time they had started to arrive in Britain around 1660–1700.

Minhag Anglia referred to minor changes in the form of prayers. For example, prayers after *Aleinyu* at the end of the Shabbat service used to have added verses originating from the Book of Esther. These were now abandoned. There was a prayer called *Av Harahamim*, said after the prayer for the Royal Family. Where it used to be said every week, it was now agreed that congregations could, if they wished, only

A.L. Green, Honorary Secretary 1852–83. Reproduced with permission from Harris, *History of Jews College*.

Henry Solomon, Treasurer 1855–91. Reproduced with permission from Harris, *History of Jews College*.

sing it on the Sabbaths preceding Shevuot and Tisha b'Av, which shortened the service a little.

Nathan Marcus Adler was often under pressure to make changes in the ritual, but had resisted all but a tiny number of these unimportant alterations. What would be more in keeping with the concept of *Minhag Anglia* was the presentation of the first prayer book to be almost universally used throughout the community. The first edition was exactly the same size and colour as the Church of England *Book of Common Prayer*. It was this attempt to bring, effectively non-essential elements of the faith more into line with the church, which the Principals of Jews College had to ensure did not undermine the *din*.

They stood between their students and the lure of greater social acceptance, with the arguments of the Secessionists (the future Reform movement) an additional temptation. Many considered that the mental effort Adler had to make to resist their recommendations – one was to reduce the number of men required for a *minyan* to three Jews rather than ten – played a part in his eventual poor health.

The other attempt to mirror church services was the emphasis on decorum. With this Adler was fully in agreement, as have been all ministers for centuries past, but a synagogue is a place of meeting as well as prayer, and old habits die hard.

Recreational activities at the College had been largely confined to the students. Now, in 1882, the Jews' College Literary and Debating Society was formed. The public was welcome to attend its meetings and the quality of the speakers illustrated the respect that was held for the College in academic circles. Among them were Dr Neubauer from the Bodleian, Moses Gaster, the Haham, and Dr Henry Behrend, the physician and medical writer. Lectures were also given by Solomon Schechter, Joseph Jacobs, whose speciality was Jewish folklore, and Major Claude Condor, the Palestinian archaeologist. Sir Sidney Lee, the Editor of the *Dictionary of National Biography*, spoke, as well as Lucien Wolf, the Anglo-Jewish historian, Sir Israel Gollancz and Claude Montefiore, the theologian and philanthropist. In the first series, subjects included the life and writing of Kalir, witchcraft in the Bible, the Midrash, music in the Bible and the synagogue in the time of the

Talmud. The lectures continued to attract audiences for the next quarter of a century.

It was after 1881 that the pogroms in Eastern Europe began to trigger the vast flow of oppressed Jews to America, with smaller numbers swelling the British community ten times over. Within their numbers were many rabbis with *semicha*, but who were invariably impoverished. One way for the newcomers to maintain their self-respect, by comparison with the wealthy Jewish leadership, was to criticize the level of well-to-do Orthodox observance. Observance, like wealth in other societies, could become a yardstick for status in the East End. The migrants could, in reality, make a good case for their superior level of compliance with the *mitzvot*, but the core community still considered them second class, and many of them weren't citizens either.

With the closure of the School and the shift from living in the City to settling down in the West End, a new building had to be found. This took till the end of 1880 and houses in Euston Square, Upper Bedford Place, Gower Street and Endsleigh Gardens were all considered, but eventually rejected. In December 1880, however, the Building Committee was able to report that the purchase of Tavistock House in Tavistock Square had been completed. It was an iconic building. Charles Dickens had lived there in the 1850s and Hans Anderson had written about it when he visited the house: 'This and the strip of garden in front of it are shut out from the thoroughfare by an iron railing. A large garden with a grass plot and high trees stretches behind the house, and gives it a countrified look in the midst of this coal and gas steaming London.'[5]

The house had a basement and was on four floors. The housekeeper lived in the basement, the ground floor housed the Library and the Council Room, the first floor had two large schoolrooms and the two top floors were a flat for Dr Friedländer. It was described as a commodious, clean and comfortable building and much better than Finsbury Square.

It cost £3,000 to buy Tavistock Square, (over £250,000 today): 'In order to render the move possible, a building fund had to be raised and three thousand pounds were obtained for this purpose without undue difficulty.'⁶ That was the official version, but the Council was still appealing for contributions as late as June 1881 in the *Jewish Chronicle*. When all else failed, though, core supporters like Charles Samuel usually came to the rescue. The United Synagogue Council met to consider the size of their support for the Building Fund. Although they were substantial beneficiaries of the graduate products of the College, the suggestion that they give £1,000 out of the total £3,000 a year needed was only passed by 23 votes to 17.

The new building was opened on 27 June 1881 with a religious service and the choir of the Great Synagogue. The main speech was by Sir Barrow Ellis who said that the cost of the move was still not paid for, but that, 'all present would concur with him in the opinion that Jews' College had done good work in the past, and that there was every prospect of its doing still more in the future'.⁷ Since all those invited were staunch supporters of Jews' College, Sir Barrow was on safe ground there at least. Rev. Aaron Green supported his Chairman realistically and suggested that, 'those present that evening could show their appreciation of what the College had done not merely by clapping their hands, but by putting their hands into their pockets and liberally contributing towards its maintenance'.⁸ Rev. Green did not seem overfond of the delicate approach. Unhappily, Green died in 1883 and John Chapman became the sole Honorary Secretary. He remained in office until 1909.

Arthur Cohen, a noted barrister, spoke after Rev. Green. His rationale for Jews' College was that Christians were now taking more notice of Judaism and good ministers were needed to present Judaism's case. That better educated Jews needed better educated ministers, and that they were also needed to present the counter-arguments to anti-Semites.

There still had to be different classes in the new form of College; Junior and Senior. The former was for boys aged 16–20. In case there weren't enough of them, though, an Elementary class was formed for 13–16 year olds who were to work for the London Matriculation exam. To that extent the School was still in existence, but only for prospective ministers. The students themselves had to pass an examination in

The Michael Friedländer Years 59

John Chapman, Honorary Secretary and distinguished teacher. Reproduced with permission from Harris, *History of Jews College*.

Chief Rabbi Hermann Adler, teacher and President. Reproduced with permission from Harris, *History of Jews College*.

Jewish subjects and to have successfully matriculated at the University of London. The institution was to be far more akin to a university college than a yeshiva, and this approach emerged in one way, in a less austere atmosphere.

The fees were £30 a year for the Students and £10 a year for the younger pupils, but parents who could pay for the education of their children beyond the age of 13 were still thin on the ground. Only £30 in fees supported the balance sheet in 1890, though some of the Students taught the Elementary Class on occasions, which would have saved some costs in teaching salaries.

In the absence of the School acting as a feeder institution for the College, there was a partial alternative in school children coming from Aria College in Portsea, which is part of Portsmouth. Lewis Aria had endowed it in his will as a Jewish school in 1874, but its development was somewhat restricted by the size of the endowment and the condition that preference should be given to Hampshire children.

The new Jews' College constitution recognized the problems the students faced: 'The Council shall provide maintenance, board and clothing, or any of them wholly or partially, for Students of the Foundation, whose means of subsistence are insufficient.'[9] In return, parents would have to agree to repay the College up to £50 if their sons did not enter the ministry, but it is never recorded that this actually happened. What did make the columns of the *Jewish Chronicle* was the complaint of students that they had to pay the UCL examination fees before they sat their papers, and they were only reimbursed if they passed. The Annual Report was not noted, however, for talking about the views of the students.

At the same time, at the conclusion of their course, senior students could be given certificates of qualification to be ministers. They indeed were making their mark in the wider community. When there was a vacancy for the minister at the prestigious Bayswater Synagogue after Hermann Adler had become Chief Rabbi, all four candidates had been trained at Jews College.

Students were also moving on to higher education, with Joseph Polack and Herman Cohen gaining admission to Oxford. Those who had ambitions to be *hazanim* were now taught music by Marcus Hast, the *hazan* at the Great Synagogue in the City. Another new academic appointment was George Washington Kilner, who would teach classics at the College for the next 53 years. Kilner was such an able tutor that he was appointed Lecturer in Classics at New College, London, which trained nonconformist ministers. He was recognized as an Official Lecturer by the University of London, the first member of the Jews' College staff to hold such a qualification.

The students started working for the community early in their studies. In 1890 David Wassersug and a colleague conducted religious services in Holloway Prison and Portsmouth Prison, 'thus bringing spiritual consolation and edification to the inmates'.[10] It was recognized, however, that the convicts were not the only ones who needed support, and the Council now approved the idea of appointing advisers for the students to help them with any personal problems.

Under the new academic curriculum, there were to be three classes of diploma which could be earned at the College. These were Probationary, which certified that the student could be a *hazan* and teach Jewish Studies; Associate, which certified that he could preach in synagogue and, effectively, be a minister; and Fellow, which meant that he had been given *semicha*. It was a cause of resentment that the first Fellow awarded *semicha* would not emerge until 1896, after at least a decade and, perhaps not coincidentally, when the Sephardi seminary in Ramsgate was about to give *semicha* to two former Jews' College pupils.

The whole subject of the title of Rabbi was a running sore for many years. Yet when the community needed administrators to keep congregations together, it was understandable that the view might prevail that concentration should be on teaching bureaucratic abilities, and not on producing expert Talmudists.

When the title of Rabbi was discussed, another consideration was that opposition to the Chief Rabbi's hegemony as spiritual leader of the community came for some years from the Hungarian Rabbi Solomon Schiller-Szenessy in Manchester in the 1850s. His rabbinic title could be seen to give him prestige. There was, therefore, a

THE JEWS' COLLEGE JOURNAL.

"Folio of four pages, happy work!
Which not even critics criticise."
— Cooper.

| No. 1. | April, 1875. | Vol. I. |

The Sir Moses Montefiore Testimonial Fund.
By Joseph Polack.

One of the most beneficial results of the advance of civilization, and one which interests Jews most, is the spread of religious toleration. Gradual in its growth, but prosperous where it was exercised it has at last after a long struggle with superstition and prejudice, come to be universal, wherever civilization sheds its radiant lustre. The condition of the Jews therefore at the present time contrasts favourably with their condition a century or two ago. But alas! there are countries and states, which are yet involved in ignorance and semi-barbarity, and where our brethren who are very numerous, are oppressed and ill-treated with the severity arising from popular prejudice. When a dishonest act is committed, when a murder is secretly perpetrated, the Jews are accused and often a popular rising takes place and the Jews are massacred in large numbers.

One of those high-minded men who strive with all their power to prevent these occurrences, whose highest aim is the rooting out of religious intolerance is Sir Moses Montefiore. He has spent his time his energy, his talents for the amelioration of the condition of the Jews in all countries where the trammels of oppression yet linger; he may well be styled the "Champion of Humanity". To attempt even the slightest sketch of a life spent in the relief of his brethren abroad, and yet marked with acts of the highest liberality and generosity at home would be far beyond the limits of this paper; such a task must be left to the biographer, and may well occupy more pages than this does words, suffice it to say that the name of Sir Moses Montefiore is as a household word in the whole civilized world. Whenever he travelled to other countries for the purpose of bettering the condition of his brethren and of interceding on their behalf, he was met at all the towns through which he passed, with addresses and blessings; kings bowed at his word and governments felt respect for the man, whose object was the spread of religious toleration.

But the highest aim of Sir Moses was and is the elevation of the Jews in the Holy Land from their present destitute state. Eight journeys have been undertaken by the venerable Baronet, to the land whence his heart yearned, time after time has he sent large monetary gifts to the Jews of Jerusalem, but notwithstanding the unbounded beneficence of Sir Moses, seconded by large sums of money from the Jews of all countries of Europe, the condition of the Jews of Jerusalem and other towns of Palestine is still most unsatisfactory. They are without the means of gaining their livelihood, and consequently, famine and drought often overtake them and reduce them to a state of beggary.

To remedy this dismal aspect of affairs a project has been set on foot which has the full approbation of the great philanthropist himself; and if carried into effect, will be the fulfilment of the wish for the gratification of which he has spent his long and useful life, it is proposed to collect a large sum of money from all parts of the world, which is to be utilised in the founding of a scheme for promoting agriculture or some other industrial occupation for the Jews of the Holy Land, which will provide them with the means of earning their own bread; and thus to establish a testimonial to Sir Moses which will at once be

The Victorian Student Journal. Reproduced with permission from Harris, *History of Jews College*.

perceived case for not creating new *rabbonim* who might become the focus of dissent; after all, in Germany and America the Reform movement was making great strides and Nathan Marcus Adler's overriding and primary concern was to keep the British Jewish community Orthodox.

It caused a great deal of aggravation. Adler sent Hermann to Eastern Europe to get *semicha*. A few others followed: Simeon Singer, who would get the credit for the iconic Singer's Prayer Book (it was really the Adler Prayer Book) got his *semicha* abroad, as did Hermann Gollancz, who would be the first British rabbi to be knighted.

The College soldiered on without producing home-grown rabbis. The Council chairman and vice-president, Sir Barrow Ellis, died in 1887 when he was 64. He left the College £1,000. With his affection for India it was not surprising that he also left £2,500 to help the poor of Ratnajiri.

The College settled down in its new home and normally had about 10–15 students and 25–30 in the Elementary Class. The standards remained very high under Dr Friedländer, even with extra-curricula activities; in the Literary Society, the lecture subjects ranged from 'Children in Jewish Literature' to 'The attempt of Anton, Speidel, Haupt and Arends to reconstitute the psalmestry of the Ancient Hebrews'. The hours in the classroom were extensive for the time; in the Elementary Class it was two hours on Sunday, and an average of five and a half hours on the other five working days of the week. The older students put in over thirty hours a week, apart from homework and the voluntary support many of them gave London synagogues and schools. In 1891 Friedländer wrote *Jewish Religion* which was to be reprinted again and again. He also held open courses in Rabbinics outside the college which anybody could attend.

The faculty was improved still further when Solomon Schechter, a noted academic, joined the staff, but he left again to become the Reader in Hebrew and Rabbinic Literature at Cambridge. Schechter was one of the lecturers because he felt strongly that the need for ministers was undermining the need for scholars in the community. As he remarked: 'Occasionally rumours spread about some minister that he neglects his duty to his congregation through being secretly addicted to Jewish learning, but such rumours often turn out to be sheer malice.'[11]

When Schechter went on to head up the Jewish Theological Seminary in New York, Jewish learning would be prominent in the curriculum. Although the move towards the Conservative academy it is today started with very minor alterations in Schechter's time, he remained firmly in the Orthodox camp. His close friends included the man who would become Chief Rabbi in Britain in 1913, Joseph Herman Hertz. Indeed, at Hertz's wedding, Schechter was chosen to act as the *Unterfuhrer* for the bride.[12]

Due to a mix-up, the United Synagogue passed a motion totally abolishing their contribution to the College and although it was reinstated at £100 a year, it was some time before it became £200 again. The Secessionist synagogue, Upper Berkeley Street, also stopped its annual contribution and Charles Samuel needed to go the rounds again to fill the gap. In 1885, however, Lewis Mayer Rothschild – no relation to the banking family – who had done so much to strengthen the Library, passed away. He left one third of the residue of his estate to the College which was a massive £8,000 (£750,000 today).

In the same year another new member of the Council was Sir Philip Magnus, who had originally been a theology student in Berlin and had been appointed the Assistant Minister at The Secessionist Upper Berkeley Street. Magnus would stay on the Council for fifty years, which illustrates the narrow gap that existed between the Orthodox and Reform communities in his time.

When in 1893 a staff member, Morris Joseph, a former student, was appointed minister at Upper Berkeley Street, there was praise for his teaching of homiletics at the College. This was in spite of the fact that the President, Chief Rabbi Hermann Adler, had refused Joseph a certificate to be the minister of the Orthodox Hampstead Synagogue in 1892. The sticking point had been that Joseph had decided he would not say the prayers for the sacrificial rites in the Temple to be restored, although these had always been part of the Orthodox service. The dispute might have been portrayed as being over the prayers for the restoration of the sacrificial rites, but the principle underlying the

Tavistock House, the second home of the college. Reproduced with permission from Harris, *History of Jews College*.

argument was far more a contemporary issue. The question was whether a minister could make up his own mind on what was appropriate, or whether that responsibility lay solely in the hands of the Chief Rabbi.

When rabbis wanted to make their own decisions – Schiller-Szenessy, Joseph and, sixty years later, Louis Jacobs – the Chief Rabbi either had to insist that the responsibility was solely his, or allow traditional practices to be altered within different congregations. It could be argued that the rabbis had often had differences of opinion in the past, but the fact was that the British Chief Rabbis had always maintained their overall control.

Philip Magnus, at the West London Synagogue, did not acknowledge the overriding authority of the Chief Rabbi. Nevertheless, he did manage to obtain financial support for the College from his community. The Council commented: 'To the West

London Synagogue at large and to those gentlemen in particular, the warmest thanks of the Council are due. So striking an act of true communal brotherhood is a notable event in Anglo-Jewish history, full of significance for the present, and bearing the promises of happiest augury for the future.'[13]

Magnus was a great educationalist and the founder of the City and Guilds Institute, which provided practical vocational courses rather than purely academic ones. He was a Liberal MP for many years and always a great supporter of the College. The future, however, would bring increasing separation of the Orthodox from the Progressive communities.

It was up to the Treasurers to decide how to invest the money the College had been given as bequests and for Scholarships. The safe investment was Consols, government gilt edged stock, which paid a 3 per cent dividend. In 1888 though it was reduced to 2¾ per cent, and then 2½ per cent, so the Treasurers tried to do better and invested in a number of overseas stocks; New Zealand 4%, East India Railway Co., New South Wales stock, Madras Railway, Great Indian Peninsula Railway and Canada 3½ per cent.

It was a pity that nobody thought, or was able to persuade, the Rothschilds themselves to take over the control of the College's investments. When Disraeli borrowed £4 million from the bank to buy shares in the Suez Canal company, there could well have been more stock available on the market. By 1935 the £4 million had become £93 million. The College could have solved all its financial problems if they had followed the government's lead as had the Jews' Free School. It has been estimated that the family gave up to £20,000 a year to the JFS throughout the nineteenth century, and acted as the school's bankers.[14] These decisions were never discussed in the Annual Reports, which confined themselves to thanking the Treasurers for their hard work, but Consols were the absolutely risk-free option.

In 1891, the last of the Founding Officers, Henry Solomon, the co-Treasurer, died. His son, James took over. Charles Samuel lost his wife in the same year and gave £1,000 for the Marianne Samuel Scholarship in her memory. The money was invested in 4% Industrial Dwelling

Sir Barrow Ellis, Chair of Council 1879–87. Reproduced with permission from Harris, *History of Jews College*.

Charles Samuel, a friend in need. Reproduced with permission from the Jewish Museum.

Company shares, a project of the Rothschilds to provide decent housing for the poor, and with little potential for an increase in the capital value.

It wasn't only the poor who were in need of better housing though. The report for 1891 pointed out that: 'The College premises are in a most dilapidated condition and there are no means available for their restoration.'[15] A large appeal followed and Simeon Singer, now a member of the Council, got eight of his friends to put up £100 each in donations and subscriptions. In all £1,300 was raised but once the old bills had been paid, there was only £400 left for working expenses.

The irritation of the Council at this state of affairs was understandable. They could point to 80 per cent of Jewish pulpits being filled by Jews' College graduates, though if the twenty-eight ministers identified were that large a proportion, then there were only thirty-five Jewish communities in the country, which seems a little low. Even allowing for slight exaggeration, though, the congregations were getting good applicants without being prepared to contribute meaningfully to the cost of their training. It was at this time that Jews' College started being referred to as the Cinderella of Jewish Charities in Britain.

In 1893 the College offered its teacher's training course to women for the first time. Claude Montefiore, a member of the Council, also wanted the Student's curriculum to be extended to cover the Social Sciences, including Economics and the relations between capital and labour. His argument was that ministers would be dealing with the problems of working people and should be educated accordingly. Time spent on such subjects, however, would detract from that available for religious studies. As regularly as clockwork and from all sorts of quarters over the years, the attempt to undermine the importance of Talmudic study was a threat to the College curriculum, and all that its principal officers held dear.

When the Chief Rabbi died in 1890 there began discussions on the possibility of closer cooperation between Jews' College and the Sephardi Seminary on the South Coast. It was in the following year that Haham Moses Gaster accepted the role of Principal at the Judith Lady Montefiore College in Ramsgate.

Jews' College might have had innumerable administrative and financial problems, but it was not until now that it started to get competition from another institution. When Sir Moses' wife died in 1862 he had first thought to perpetuate her memory by building a theological college in Jerusalem. He then changed his mind and built it at his home in Ramsgate instead.

The idea was to provide ten elderly retired scholars with the opportunity to study in their retirement. It was somewhat difficult to find candidates, though, even for such generous conditions, because texts were specified for study every hour of the day. Work was meant to start at five in the morning and go on till midnight, when the *tikkun* prayers would be recited. Louis Loewe was the first Principal. It was an exhausting schedule.

After the deaths of Sir Moses' in 1885 and Louis Loewe in 1888, the Sephardi Elders decided to convert the college into a theological college to train rabbis, *hazanim* and Jewish teachers. Moses Gaster, the new Principal, was the only Ashkenazi ever to be appointed Haham of the Sephardim in Britain. He was brilliant on many levels, but he was also an individualist. He would be just about the only Jewish leader in Britain who would chair a meeting for Theodor Herzl, when he came to London to promote his Zionist concept towards the end of the century. Gaster, as spiritual head of the Sephardim, was only second in importance to the Adlers as a Jewish religious leader, but this was not a position he relished. He disliked the fact that he was always placed second in community matters after the Chief Rabbi. He was forever Deputy this and Vice that.

He would have liked to establish his equality or even superiority and, academically, he was more able than Hermann Adler. If he could find a weakness in Jews' College by adopting an opposite course, he felt he would compare more favourably with the older and larger establishment. Such a gap could be made to exist in the educating of *rabbanim*. It had been stated by both sides, however, that the 'two colleges should work together in perfect concord'.[16] They had also agreed not to poach each other's students. If a student at Jews' College wanted to transfer to Ramsgate, it was arranged that the assent of the

Council would be necessary.

To obtain *semicha* a student absorbs different subjects. The four most common are, first, *Basar v'Chalav*. This covers kashrut. Then Shabbat. Then *Taharat Ha-Mishpachah*, which is the law relating to family relations, and the Mikveh. Fourth, Kiddushin, which is about marriage. The *semicha* qualification is called *Hattarat Haraah* which means licensed to give rulings. If the student wants the qualifications to become a Dayan, this is called *Yadin Yadin* (licensed to give comprehensive judgment) and involves a much wider curriculum.

Those English ministers who earned *semicha*, did so abroad, and officially they were not permitted to be called by any other nomenclature than Reverend. The ubiquitous Singer Prayer Book is still described as being produced by Rev. Simeon Singer, ignoring his *semicha* from Rabbi Isaac Weiss in Vienna in 1890.

Gaster determined that he would grant *semicha* at Ramsgate to suitable candidates. The two students he eventually decided would be good enough for the award came to Ramsgate, ironically, from Jews' College; Henry Barnstein and William Greenburg arrived, presumably, with the Council's approval. They had done well at the College; both had scholarships: Barnstein's was worth £30 a year and Greenberg's £15, though that was raised to the same £30. Both had obtained Senior English Certificates in 1888. Barnstein had a first class diploma in English Literature from UCL. Greenberg won the Eleazar Magnus prize at the College. Greenberg had been teaching at the Chicksands Street Board School and working at the Convalescent Home. Barnstein at the Settle Road Board School. All of this was mentioned in the College's Annual Report for 1889. Their ambition, however, was *semicha* and so they switched to Ramsgate. In 1895 Gaster considered they were sufficiently knowledgeable to receive the award and there was a ceremony to present it to them.

At which point one of their teachers said publicly that their behaviour in their personal lives made them unfit to be rabbis. It quickly became a cause celebre. The *Jewish Chronicle* ran the story in lurid detail every week for the next six months, first supporting one side and then the other. Eventually, after a massive row, the Elders tried to get

Sir Adolph Tuck, the financial supporter after Charles Samuel. Reproduced with permission from Harris, *History of Jews College*.

Gaster dismissed, but to their chagrin the ordinary Sephardi members refused to vote in favour of the proposal. He was the first Haham the ordinary members had been allowed to elect and they weren't going to go back on their decision. So Gaster stayed, the Elders were furious and went so far as to close the seminary down.

Barnstein and Greenberg both accepted calls from congregations in America and became Reform rabbis. Their accuser finished up discredited and nobody lived very happily ever after. There does seem a possibility, however, that what was acceptable behaviour in the laissez-faire atmosphere of Jews' College may have been seen as inappropriate

Simeon Singer, of the Singer Prayer Book. Reproduced with permission from the Jewish Museum.

in students at the Ramsgate Seminary; though this would not have applied to some of the more lurid accusations made against them.

When Louis Loewe was the Principal in Ramsgate, the curriculum had been extremely rigorous and the elderly scholars in his time were unlikely to want much of a social life. Gaster had softened the curriculum to cater for what students now coming from Europe would expect, but the Loewe legacy would remain in the background. Many years later, students coming to Jews' College from the twentieth-century seminary in Gateshead would also note the difference between an almost monastic and a semi-university life. Judgements are difficult; one man's monastery may be another's man's holiday camp.

The granting of *semicha* at Ramsgate galvanised Hermann Adler into following suit and Solomon Levy was the first to gain the qualification from the College in 1896. It was certainly not a necessity for getting a job at the time, but it looked very good on a CV. Although no student up till then had passed the third grade of the examinations formulated in 1883, the Jews' College alumni were still being welcomed as ministers in congregations far and wide.

In 1895 Solomon Levy was already the minister of the New Synagogue in the City, Joshua Abelson in Cardiff and Zachariah Lawrence in Newport. David Wassersug had moved from Cardiff to Port Elizabeth, and would be a colleague in South Africa of the future Chief Rabbi Hertz. When Wassersug had exhausted himself in the turbulent Boer War period, he retired to the peace and quiet of Dalston Synagogue in London where he served for many years. In 1896 D.I. Freedman was elected the minister of the Perth congregation in Australia.

Jews' College was now producing spiritual leadership for congregations at a fair pace. In 1897 Gerald Friedlander became the minister at the Western Synagogue in London, and in 1898 Goodman Lipkind took up a post in Brighton, while Walter Levin was appointed at the North West London Synagogue and Abraham Wolf went to Manchester. Asher Feldman took New Dalston, Benjamin Michelson, Newport and Moses Cohen went to Bulawayo.

The effect of the graduates is well documented by an account of a sermon by Moses Cohen in South Africa on the first day of Succot in 1900. The minister: 'described the scene in ancient Jerusalem during the festival. There is no doubt that informative, descriptive sermons of this sort please and interest far more than abstract philosophical disquisitions.'[17] There were 200 listening to his sermon next day.

In 1896 there was a lunch at the Central Synagogue for Honorary Officers, Council Members, staff and Senior Students, 'as an acknowledgement of the services rendered by the Senior Students of the College as Occasional Preachers in Metropolitan Synagogues', but it is the only recorded occasion when the valuable contribution of the Students was officially recognized. In fairness, they were probably paid for conducting High Holyday services or teaching synagogue religion classes. Nevertheless, to the study schedule had to be added the time they needed to spend just on supporting themselves. It was not surprising that some of them failed to stay the course.

Hermann Adler gave other candidates *semicha* in 1898 – Asher Feldman and Abraham Wolf, followed by Benjamin Michelson in 1899, Michael Adler in 1900 and Maurice Simon in 1901. In the ministries they took up, they were still referred to as Reverend, but Hermann Gollancz insisted on being called up to the Reading of the Law as 'Ha Rav'. They wouldn't accept this in his own London pulpit, so once a year he would take himself to the synagogue in Leeds, which was more accommodating.

When the dust had died down and the Elders had closed Ramsgate, they lent its Montefiore Library to Jews College, together with a substantial donation. The staff at Ramsgate found other posts, but experts like Dr Hartwig Hirschfeld might have looked askance at finding himself appointed sub-librarian at Jews' College.

The ranks of British Jewry were still more cohesive than they would become in the future. Back in 1895 the Council invited Claude Montefiore to preside at the annual distribution of the prizes. Montefiore was the great nephew of Sir Moses and had been raised to be strictly Orthodox. When he grew up, however, he left the Sephardim and joined Upper Berkeley Street. This hadn't prevented him being co-opted onto the Council in 1888, though when he was invited to preside in 1895, it was considered a revolution by some. Montefiore was keen not to be controversial on this occasion though, and suggested that his invitation demonstrated the College's position was: 'as between and among the various sections of thought in our midst, is universal and unsectarian'.[18] Which it certainly wasn't but the differences were much smaller. Montefiore's main message was that the College should move to Oxford – he had been at Balliol – and work in friendly rivalry with Mansfield College, the home of the Congregationalists, and Manchester where the Unitarians could be found. He further told his audience:

A young man of twenty four who knows his Maimonides, but does not know his Aristotle, who knows his Graetz, but does not know his Gibbon, is like a doctor who might know something of the ear or throat, but nothing of the human organism as a whole. Just as the English Jew should learn two histories, the history of England and the history of the Jews, so should a Jewish theological student have a double aspect to his training. The young men who issue from this College are to be ministers of English Jews. And therefore they must help them and lead them, aye, and if need be, reprimand them, not merely as Jews but also as Englishmen.[19]

It would seem a bit far-fetched to expect a synagogue minister to reprimand a congregant for not applying the lessons of Graetz or understanding the complexities of the *Decline and Fall of the Roman Empire*, but the emphasis on higher English education would have sounded very upper class and resonated with his audience.

Montefiore was typical of those who dismissed Talmudic knowledge as outdated. Not even to be a partner in Anglo-Jewish curricula. As he said at the prize giving:

I should not mind the stigma attaching to Jews' College that no single student has received the Rabbinical Diploma at its hands. I should not mind the stigma if it be frankly said, the Rabbinical Diploma cannot be given without the acquisition of a mass of knowledge which has now become obsolete.[20]

So the dual demands of the learning of Judaism and the absorption of British culture was still exercising minds, but then Orthodox Jews had the same problem in ancient Greece, and were thankful that enough of them in those days had concentrated on keeping Jewish culture and learning alive, to enable the religion to survive. Which was more than could be said of the Greek Empire.

There were many issues to resolve in 1896. The lease on Tavistock House was due to expire in 1897 and the landlord, the Duke of

Bedford, would not renew it. The discussion on working with the Montefiore Seminary was overtaken by the decision to close it. A union between Ramsgate and the College had been mooted, but the rules of the Montefiore Endowment did not allow it.

So, eventually, the Sephardi Elders decided to give the College £1,000 a year in exchange for substantial representation on the Council and an agreement to teach both the Sephardi and the Ashkenazi ritual. The payment would be annual rather than permanent, but there was no reason why it should be withdrawn. The representatives of the Elders were welcomed to the Council in October 1897. The Council was now a somewhat unwieldy body, thirty-nine strong.

The search for a suitable replacement for Tavistock House dragged on. Charles Samuel offered over £3,000 for one property, raised it to £4,000 and it still wasn't enough. Eventually the Presbyterian College in Queens Square became available as it was moving out of town. The only difficulty was that there was only twenty years left on the lease, but Samuel managed to get that increased to fifty years at £150 a year, and provided £5,000 to secure the purchase. It was the right building for the College, but it would need a lot of redecoration and alterations. It would be renamed Queens Square House and remodelled by a very well known Jewish architect, Delissa Joseph, a former pupil at the College, who was a prime protagonist for higher buildings for London.

It was opened in May 1900, with the Principal's flat on the ground floor alongside the Senior Tutor's Room, occupied by Israel Abrahams. The Great Hall on the first floor was impressive, but normally too large for purpose. On the second floor were two classrooms and three common rooms for study. As you came through the pilloried entrance and compared the building with Tavistock House, it was a great improvement:

> When one recalls the conditions under which the College has hitherto worked, its cramped finances, its inadequate premises, its undeserved obloquy, one stands amazed that it has attained the successes that have fallen to it. Jews' College has triumphed over neglect; it has produced a clergy of which the community may feel proud.[21]

All kinds of gifts came in to help furnish the new College centre. There was a new lawn mower and a tennis set. Someone gave Physical Training equipment and another benefactor, a small piano. A garden hose and appliances were useful, plus a clock and a neo-cyclostyle machine. This last was the gift of David Gestetner, and it was, indeed, an early copying machine. Charles Samuel gave another £200 to fit out the classrooms and Claude Montefiore provided the Science Laboratory. It was still very much hand-to-mouth.

It was appropriate that the College was registered with the Charities Commission. There were about thirty students of one kind or another, and it was still the case that only a few could pay the fees. Staff costs alone were over £1,300 in 1899 having gone up 25 per cent in the last five years. The yearly outgoings in 1901 would be over £4,000 and there were only eleven scholarships to support the students, though there were some bedrooms in the new property for the students to lodge in.

Three of the scholarships were vacant at this time; the Lord Mayor's Commemoration Scholarship, the David Sassoon Free Scholarship, and the Marianne Samuel Scholarship. The others had been awarded: the Barnett Meyer, the Judith, Lady Montefiore, the Resident Scholarship, Edward Henry Beddington, Abraham Solomon Palmer, Isaac Moses Marsden, the Michael Samuel and the Jacob A. Franklin. The endowments were all invested in gilt edged stocks.

The College also had an endowment fund to which David Davies of Blackheath contributed £50 every year. By 1900 it amounted to £1,200. It was exactly the kind of support the College needed, but benefactors like Mr Davies, the Rothschilds and Frank Samuel were still few and far between. In fifty years, the legacies and bequests to the General Fund would only amount to under £6,000.

In return for the financial support of the United Synagogue, it was agreed that the Senior Students would be given time to work in the East End, where the needs of the vast, new immigrant Jewish community were manifold. The students would visit the poor, give sermons, attend meetings of the Beth Din, supervise Jewish clubs for youngsters, and teach religious subjects in the Board Schools. The

United Synagogue were getting the additional staff very much on the cheap.

At the turn of the century, however, Jews' College could produce a report on the contribution it had made to manning the pulpits of synagogues and providing teachers for the religious education of Jewish youngsters. It not only covered the British synagogues but many overseas congregations as well. As the Council set out:

TABLE 1. The following synagogues, schools and public institutions obtained Ministers, Readers and Teachers from among the students trained at Jews' College between 1855 and 1900.

Bayswater Synagogue, London	Rev. Dr Herman Gollancz
Bevis Marks Synagogue, London	Rev. Samuel de Sola
Borough Synagogue, London	Rev. Simeon Singer
	Rev. Berman Berliner
	Rev. Francis Cohen
Dalston Synagogue, London	Rev. Hermann Gollancz
	Rev. Moses Hyamson
East London Synagogue	Rev. Joseph Stern
Hambro Synagogue, London	Rev. Woolf Esterson
Hammersmith Synagogue, London	Rev. Michael Adler
New Synagogue, London	Rev. Solomon Levy
New Dalston (Stoke Newington) Synagogue	Rev. Asher Feldman
New West End Synagogue, London	Rev. Simeon Singer
North London Synagogue	Rev. Morris Joseph
	Rev. Isidore Harris
North West London Synagogue	S. Friedman
	Rev. Woolf Esterson
	Walter Levin
St Johns Wood Synagogue, London	Rev. Hermann Gollancz
	Rev. Berman Berliner
Upper Berkeley Street, London	Rev. Isidore Harris
	Rev. Morris Joseph
West Hampstead Synagogue, London	Rev. Aaron Green

Western Synagogue, London	Rev. John Chapman
	Rev. Gerald Friedlander
Aldershot Synagogue	Rev. Montagu Cohen
Brighton Synagogue	Rev Goodman Lipkind
Bristol Synagogue	Rev. Berman Berliner
	Rev. Joseph Levy
	Rev. Moses Hyamson
	Rev. Louis Mendelsohn
	Rev. Joshua Ableson
Cardiff Synagogue	Rev. J.H. Landau
	Rev. David Wasserzug
	Rev. Joshua Abelson
	Rev. Philip Wolfers
Dublin Synagogue	Rev. Francis Cohen
	Rev. Louis Mendelsohn
Glasgow Synagogue	Rev. Eleazar Phillips
Hanley Synagogue	Rev. M. Rosenbaum
Leeds Synagogue	Rev. Moses Abrahams
Leicester Synagogue	Rev. Adolf Chodowski
Liverpool Old Synagogue	Rev. Joseph Polack
	Rev. Isidore Harris
Manchester (Sephardi) Synagogue	Rev. J.H. Vallentine
Manchester (South) Synagogue	Rev. Hermann Gollancz
Merthyr Synagogue	Rev. Harris Cohen
Middlesborough Synagogue	Rev. M.E. Davis
Newcastle-on-Tyne Synagogue	Rev. Louis Mendelsohn
	Rev. M. Rosenbaum
Newport (Mon) Synagogue	Rev. Z. Lawrence
	Rev. Benjamin Michelson
Nottingham Synagogue	Rev. Harris Cohen
Oxford Synagogue	Rev. Israel Abrahams
Portsea Synagogue	Rev. Isaac Phillips
Sheffield Synagogue	Rev. Aaron Green
Sunderland Synagogue	Rev. Aaron Green
	Rev. Z. Lawrence

Swansea Synagogue	Rev. Moses Hyamson
	Rev. Philip Wolfers
Wolverhampton Synagogue	Rev. Isaac Aarons
Barberton, South Africa, Synagogue	Rev. Philip Wolfers
Brisbane, Australia, Synagogue	Rev. George Chodowski
Bulawayo, Rhodesia, Synagogue	Rev. Montagu Cohen
Christchurch, New Zealand, Synagogue	Rev. Adolf Chodowski
Dallas, USA, Synagogue	Rev. Edward Chapman
Dunedin, New Zealand, Synagogue	Rev. Adolf Chodowski
Johannesburg, South Africa, Synagogue	Rev. Philip Wolfers
	Rev. David Wasserzug
Kimberley, South Africa, Synagogue	Rev. A. Ornstein
Melbourne, Australia, Synagogue	Rev. Joseph Abrahams
Perth, Australia, Synagogue	Rev. D.I. Freedman
Philadelphia, USA, Synagogue	Rev. Joseph Levy
Port Elizabeth, South Africa, Synagogue	Rev. David Wasserzug
St Kilda, Australia, Synagogue	Rev. J. Friedlander
Sacramento, USA, Synagogue	Rev. Joseph Levy
	Rev. Barnet Elzas
Sydney, Australia, Synagogue	Rev. J.H. Landau
Toronto, Canada, Synagogue	Rev. Barnet Elzas
	Rev. A. Lazarus
Victoria, Canada, Synagogue	Rev. Montagu Cohen

Head Masters and Teachers

Borough Jewish Schools, London	Rev. Berman Berliner
	B. Lewis
Clifton College, Bristol	Rev. Joseph Polack
Dalston Jewish Schools, London	Rev. Moses Hyamson
Jerusalem Von Lammel School & Orphan Asylum	Ephraim Cohn
Jews' College, London	Rev. John Chapman
	Rev. Morris Joseph
	Rev. Simeon Singer
	Israel Abrahams

Jews' Free School, London	Rev. Michael Adler
Jews' Hospital & Orphan Asylum, London	Rev. Francis Cohen
	Rev. Morris Joseph
	Rev. John Chapman
Jews' Infant Schools, London	Rev. Asher Feldman
	Rev. Joseph Simmons
Nicosia, Cyprus	R. J. Solomon
Shaare Tikvah, London	Rev. Julius Gouldstein
	Rev. Joseph Simmons
Stepney Jewish Schools, London	Rev. Aaron Green
	Rev. Julius Gouldstein
	Rev. Moses Abrahams
	Walter Levin
University College, Liverpool	Rev. Joseph Polack
University College, London	Rev. Abraham Wolf
University College School, London	Rev. Gerald Friedlander

Teacher Training Classes (Jewish Religious Education Board)

Jews' College, London	Rev. Michael Adler
	Rev. Asher Feldman
Kings College, London	Israel Abrahams
Toynbee Hall, London	Rev. Asher Feldman
	A. Levy
	Leonard Pass

Sabbath Schools of the Jewish Religious Education Board

Berner Street Board School, London	Numerous College Students
Chicksand Street Board School, London	have served on the staff of
Dalston (Poets Road), London	the Religion classes in those
Hanbury Street Board School, London	schools
Old Castle Street, London	
Settle Street Board School, London	

This was the real rationale for Jews' College. Each man who kept to the vocation, spending his life nurturing communities, performing good works and being satisfied with far less of an income than he could have received in business. From a congregation's point of view, each one should have been recognized as a hero.

NOTES

1. Albert Hyamson, *Jews College, London, 1855–1955* (London: Jews College, 1955), p.49.
2. JCAR.
3. Ibid.
4. Phineas May, *Jewish Chronicle*, 25 September 1970, p.8.
5. Isidore Harris, *History of Jews' College 1855–1905* (London: Luzac & Co., 1906), p.lxiii.
6. Hyamson, *Jews College, London*, p.52.
7. JCAR.
8. JCAR.
9. JCAR.
10. JCAR.
11. *Jewish Chronicle*, 26 November 1915, p.16.
12. The *Unterfuhrer* takes the place of the bride's father if he is no longer alive.
13. JCAR.
14. Gerry Black, *JFS: The History of the Jews' Free School, London, Since 1732* (London: Tymsder Publishing, 1998), p.56.
15. JCAR.
16. JCAR.
17. *Jewish Chronicle*, 7 December 1900.
18. JCAR.
19. JCAR.
20. JCAR.
21. *Jewish Chronicle*, 4 May 1900, p.13.

CHAPTER FOUR

The Adolph Büchler Years

The vexed question of granting *semicha* to students of the College was under consideration throughout 1901. The most persistent advocate was Israel Gollancz. The Council decided that it should, 'take the necessary measures to obtain the Rabbinical Diploma, as a result of an examination conducted within the College, for students who are worthy of the same, by reason of their religious and moral life and of their learning'.[1] The reference to their moral life was obviously to avoid the problems which had occurred with the granting of *semicha* to Rabbis Barnstein and Greenburg at Ramsgate.

The importance of Jews' College granting the *semicha* was that it changed the existing system by which the Chief Rabbi alone had the right to approve the diploma. The fact that Jews' College had not done so before, even though the candidates had been trained at the College, had been widely criticized in the Jewish press for some years. The congregations where the rabbis officiated would also have welcomed the additional status for their minister.

What had brought the matter to a head was the determination of Gollancz's brother, Hermann, to obtain *semicha*. He went to the Continent and after studying under several notable rabbis, was awarded the diploma in 1897. Even with their certificate, however, he was unable to use the title in Britain. Now, however, as Gollancz wrote later:

> The acquisition of these 'Certificates of Competence' known as *Hattarat Horaah*, from ... outstanding ecclesiastical authorities abroad, gave rise to a storm in the hierarchical Chair which practically ended an anomalous and unsatisfactory state of affairs

> – there was no *system* – in the Jewish community here, and in reality, revolutionised the entire status of the Jewish ministry in England. Once and for all there were defined, by means of a clear-cut Syllabus, the requirements in Hebrew and Rabbinics necessary to obtain the Diploma of Rabbi in this country, which had hitherto not been granted – a stronger term might be used – to any student or scholar, however competent.[2]

The Chief Rabbi gave up the sole prerogative with reluctance. A special committee was 'appointed to consider the curriculum as well as the rules and regulations of the Examination, and such changes, if any, as may be necessary in the present scheme of Examination at the College (Constitution Section xxxiii) and to report its recommendations to the Council at as early a date as possible'.[3]

The Committee included clergy like the Chief Rabbi and Simeon Singer, academics like Dr Friedländer and the Senior Tutor, and laymen like Israel Gollancz and E.L. Mocatta for the Sephardim. The result was the Rules and Regulations and subjects of examination to obtain the Diploma of Rabbi (see Appendix C). The quality of the curriculum was high.

Students could, of course, have gained *semicha* for the last fifteen years. There had been the examination for a Fellow of the College since 1883, which gave successful candidates their *semicha*, but it had still not produced any students considered worthy of the award until 1896 and Solomon Levy.

There had also been a level of resentment that the panel of examiners designated to make the award had not included the Principal of the College who had been responsible for all the hard work of educating the candidate. This was now corrected. The agreement reached was that the examiners in the future would consist of the Chief Rabbi, the Haham and a member of the Beth Din, together with the Principal and the Theological Tutor. In the event of a tied vote, the Chief Rabbi would have a casting vote. The first examination under the new system was held in 1908, when Barent Cohen, the minister of the Sheffield Hebrew Congregation, was approved.

The College would have liked their students to have qualifications from the University of London, and when the university introduced Bachelor of Divinity and Doctor of Divinity degrees, discussions took place to try to make these obtainable by the College students. The problem both sides faced, quite naturally, was the knowledge the students were supposed to possess of the New Testament, but the University considered this element of the course essential and so the negotiations were broken off.

In February 1902 the Chief Rabbi decided to strengthen his Beth Din and made Asher Feldman and Moses Hyamson Dayanim. There was an immediate uproar in the East End where a meeting attended by over 500 people passed a motion expressing their disapproval. They complained that they had not been consulted, that they had Russian rabbis within their communities who were far better qualified, and that the new dayanim were too young and too inexperienced. As both had earned their *semicha* after studying at Jews' College, it was a serious criticism of the standard of the teaching.

In fact, Feldman had been born in Russia and Hyamson in Russian Poland. Hyamson was 39 and would go on to teach Codes at the Jewish Theological Seminary in New York. Admittedly, Feldman was only 29 but he was a very fine student and served as a dayan for over thirty years. The installation ceremony in May at the Great Synagogue was crowded and the College took pride in its contribution to the office of the Chief Rabbi. The Beth Din, which had met only twice a week before, now met every day and could tackle far more cases.

Simeon Singer typified the affection so many students had for the College. He had been a student there, the head of the school, a member of the Council, Honorary Secretary and a great supporter of the Endowment Fund. Now he was to become one of the most popular members of the staff. He was born in London in 1848 and the Singer Prayer Book was his lasting memorial after he died in the summer of 1906. He also played a major part in the creation of the Society for the Protection of Women and Children. Rev. A. . Green remembered him from the days when he was himself a pupil at the school:

Queens Square, the third home of the college. Reproduced with permission from Harris, *History of Jews College*.

He was a great teacher and was to us boys what Arnold [Headmaster of Rugby] became to a greater institution than ours. Mr Singer was strict and kind, absolutely just, and always interesting, and the hours spent with him were the brightest of the day. We worked for him because his approval was a prize. He was the very strictest of pedagogues, except for his eyes, the twinkle of which when he withered up some youthful impertinence, somehow told the delinquent that he was appreciated if not forgiven. There was no corporal punishment except of a desultory and wholly unpreventable character, but a look from Mr Singer was more than enough for any self-respecting boy. I can see him now entering the room ... lifting up his eyebrows and saying 'All frivolities stop' and the frivolities stopped.[4]

His work in teaching the boys and editing the prayer book were well known to the community. What would have been less in the public eye was the work Singer carried out as the Jewish chaplain in prisons. On at least two occasions he had prayed with Jewish murderers on the night before their execution and held prayers after their deaths. The strain of those occasions could only have been borne by a man totally dedicated to his calling. Singer's ability as a preacher and religious leader was also recognized by his appointment to be the first minister of the New West End Synagogue in 1879.

The most prestigious graves in a Jewish cemetery are near the chapel and are reserved for the most worthy in the community, rather than the richest. At the Willesden cemetery when you leave the chapel to bury the dead, the first grave you pass is that of Rabbi Simeon Singer.

As the immigrants settled down in the East End of London, many of them remained as dedicated as ever to studying the Torah. There were ample numbers of the very Orthodox to support a yeshiva. Etz Chaim would grow from small beginnings at the turn of the century into a renowned centre for additional learning in all aspects of the faith. One of its main founders was Rabbi Aharon Hyman (1863–1937) who served it faithfully for the first twenty-nine years of its existence.

Its main claim to fame, however, came when a Polish Rabbi escaped with his family from Belgium at the start of the First World War and became the Rosh Yeshivah from 1918–61. Rabbi Nachman Shlomo Greenspan (1878–1961), was a great Talmudic brain. He had been given *semicha* at the age of 18. He was taught by other great Talmudists, like the Sfas Emes (Rabbi Yehudah Aryeh Leib Alter, 1847–1905), and had worked with giants like the Chofetz Chaim (Rabbi Israel Meir Kagan 1839–1933).

As a college for teaching Talmud, the Etz Chaim Yeshiva was every bit as eminent as Jews' College among the Orthodox, but it didn't set out to produce ministers. It existed to enable students to study Talmud and that was all that Rabbi Greenspan concentrated upon. The organization was no threat to Jews' College, but it created a precedent; there could be other yeshivot emerging to satisfy the thirst for knowledge within the very Orthodox communities. It too would have its financial problems, but at the beginning it had the support of Lord Swaythling, the banker, Samuel Montagu, who had done so much to draw the new immigrant communities together.

Jews' College's move to Queens Square House had gone smoothly but it was a costly business. The deficit increased to £600 in 1901 but that was after selling £1,000 of North Western Railway stock. A further appeal had, however, produced more than £600 in donations and £150 in additional subscriptions. If many a mickle makes a muckle, the Manchester community had come up with £10.50 and the Birmingham congregation with £5.25, but it was still a struggle every year.

The start of the Edwardian era was marked by the resignation of Charles Samuel as Treasurer and his death in 1903 at the age of 81. This was, potentially, a serious blow because of the loss of his great generosity, but his replacement by Sir Adolph Tuck provided the College with another major businessman to wrestle with its finances.

Tuck was the second generation of the family firm of Raphael Tuck, who had invented Christmas cards for the masses. Raphael Tuck also persuaded the Postmaster General that letters didn't have to be in envelopes and had postcards made legal; his firm then manufactured 40,000 different varieties! When he died, his son Adolph took over and, in the coming years, the firm went on to popularize cardboard jigsaw puzzles and Valentine's Day cards. Tuck would become Chairman of the College Council and remained in office until his death in 1926.

The College continued to produce the ministers and teachers the community needed. In 1902, for instance, no less than thirty students received their Preliminary Grade Teacher certificates and of these thirteen were women. In the higher Intermediate Grade there were seven awards and six went to women. In 1904 when the University of London held its examinations for a BA in Hebrew and Aramaic, all the candidates were from the College and all passed.

The range of activities at Queens Square House was eclectic. The Literary Society had six lectures on Jewish Romantic Literature, ranging from the romantic aspects of the books of Ruth, Jonah, Esther and Job to Mediaeval Satirical Romances and Modern Hebrew novels. The students also continued to get experience in leading congregations in prayer during the High Holydays, when they were in great demand for overflow services in many parts of the country.

Academically, there were some notable changes. Israel Abrahams, a former student, resigned as Senior Tutor when he was appointed Reader in Rabbinics at Cambridge. He was the son of the ill-fated early Principal, Barnett Abrahams, and the College had generously stood in loco parentis for a number of his children. The teaching of *Hazanut*, which had been the responsibility of Isaac Samuel of the Bayswater Synagogue and Francis Cohen of the Borough Synagogue, now fell to Lionel Geffen, of the New West End Synagogue. Cohen went on to be the Chief Minister of the Sydney Hebrew Congregation in Australia.

After thirty-five years the College decided to stop teaching French and retired M. Antoine, with effusive plaudits but, if Harris Cohen's account is accepted, with probably the full approval of the students. It was also decided that there should be supervision of the overall quality of teaching at the College, and a Visiting Committee was formed to carry out periodic inspections. This originally consisted of two Inspectors of Schools, Alfred Eichholz and Augustus Kahn, Michael Lange, a scholarly layman and Dr Lionel Barnett of the British Museum. It was their recommendation that there should be four theological examinations covering a period of six and a half years, leading to the granting of *semicha*.

It was also significant that a very senior rabbi, Avigdor Chaikin, was invited to join the Council, strengthening its highly expert representation. The quality of a *semicha* is often measured internationally by the reputation of the rabbi who gave it to the student. Thus it was very important that Chaikin, a renowned authority, would be given the task of organizing and taking charge of a class to prepare qualified candidates for the highest examination, the culmination of which was the conferring of the rabbinical diploma.

Avigdor Chaikin had come to Britain from Eastern Europe and was a nominee from the Orthodox East End communities to sit on Herman Adler's Beth Din. He was appointed to ensure that this large body of immigrant Jews should have some representation on the body which settled disputes within the community, and he was not beholden in any way to Hermann Adler. As far as Jews' College was concerned, he provided an additional guarantee that the granting of *semicha* was justified.

Stalwarts like Michael Friedländer and John Chapman soldiered on, but Friedländer was now in his 70s and needed an assistant to take some of the load off his shoulders. The Annual Report highlighted the additional expense, and still found room to thank the donor of 'a pair of parallel bars and other apparatus for the gym'.

When an organization is fifty years old, it is a good time to take stock, and there was no shortage of commentators to give their opinions of Jews' College in 1905. Contrary viewpoints had been aired for some years and among the foremost protagonists in favour of the College was Dayan Moses Hyamson, a former pupil, who would become the head of the London Beth Din and act as Chief Rabbi pro tem after the death of Hermann Adler. In the *Jewish Chronicle* he took the community to task on its attitude to the College:

> Sufficient justice has never been rendered to the good it has undoubtedly accomplished. For the whole of the 50 years it has been in existence, it has been continually subject to a running fire of criticism, much of it carping and unjust. Even the defence set up by its friends has frequently been of a lukewarm, half-hearted, apologetic manner.[5]

Hyamson spread the blame widely. On the staff, who he said were 'content to work steadily, quietly and under difficulties'. On the Treasurers, who 'were not sufficiently pushful', and the Council, who didn't understand advertising: 'The method for raising necessary funds suggested not the sturdy and successful beggar, but the bashful maiden lady in reduced circumstances.'

Holding a fund raising dinner had always been resisted, presumably, because it was not considered sufficiently dignified for the College. When it was finally agreed to have a Jubilee Dinner, it was a great success, but it was very late in the day. Indeed, it was in the 51st year. At the Trocadero restaurant on 13 June 1906, with Lord Rothschild presiding, over £14,500 was raised (about £1.5 million in today's money). Hyamson would have liked to see such events become a regular occurrence.

Even those additional funds were only just over half the £25,000 the College was hoping to raise, but there was an economic slump at the time, so it was a fair result. Major contributions of £1,000 came from Henry Louis Bischoffsheim, the banker and founder of the London Ambulance Service; Adolph Tuck also gave £1,000. £500 came from Jacob Schiff, the leader of American Jewry, and Sir Edward Stern, the builder of much of the London Underground, gave £500. Arthur Sassoon and Salmy Japhet gave £250 each. Hermann Adler couldn't, in fact, be at the dinner because he had recently lost his sister, Minna Israel, but he was well pleased with the result.

The £500 from Jacob Schiff was accompanied by congratulations, for which Hermann Adler later offered his 'high appreciation of the compliment paid to the College by the Theological Seminary of America in sending them an admirably-worded address'.[6] Schiff, a prominent New York banker, was the financial support of the Jewish Theological Seminary. He was a descendent of David Tevele Schiff, the eighteenth-century Chief Rabbi in England, and had recruited Solomon Schechter from Jews' College to head up the New York organization after it had run into difficulties. Although in the years to come the JTSA would become the main College for the Jewish Conservative movement in America, and change to a Reform approach to Judaism, in 1906 the two institutions had a great deal in common.

The *Jewish Chronicle* had supported the College in a number of articles before the dinner. It was equally aggrieved at the lack of financial support from the community: 'And so it has remained in a state of chronic poverty, more or less acute, and more or less detrimental to the sacred cause which it serves.'[7] To make matters

Adolph Büchler, Principal 1907–39. Reproduced with permission from Hyamson, *Jews College, London, 1855–1955*.

worse, it noted that when the United Synagogue wanted to make savings, the first victim of the cutbacks had been the College. The *Chronicle* defended the College against its traducers:

> Knowing as they did the high services which he [Israel Abrahams] had rendered to their literature in his capacity of Reader in Talmud at Cambridge, and as joint editor of the *Jewish Quarterly Review*, who could assert that Mr Abrahams had not richly repaid the expense devoted to his training? Or take Dr Snowman [the

most eminent *Mohel*]: who would grudge the loss to the ministry of such a zealous votary of the healing art?

Another criticism was that all the students were drawn from one class. This was an argument that should not be levelled against Jews' College but against the community, and the College must not be blamed for the fact that whilst, for example, the Church of England had so many prizes, and every curate had a crozier [a bishop's crook] in his desk, the rewards in the Jewish community were few and far between.[8]

When Hyamson turned to the College's scholastic record, he was equally scathing of the opposition. There had always been critics who would piously hope it might become a place of learning in the future. Hyamson held quite rightly that it always had been in the past. He lauded the teachers over the years and pointed out that: 'Nearly all the metropolitan and provincial, most of the colonial and many of the American pulpits are filled with their disciples.' If that was a slight exaggeration – the next Chief Rabbi would be an American from Johannesburg, where his main colleague was a Lithuanian – there was no doubt that many congregations all over the Empire had benefited from the ministrations of Jews' College graduates. While they were expected to welcome ministers trained in other lands, there was warm support for Edward Sassoon when he said at the Jubilee Dinner: 'I am glad to think we are free ... of having office and clerical positions filled by strangers.'[9]

In defence of the present ministry in Britain, Hyamson said it was the fashion to decry it. He pointed out, however, that: 'they conceived and have possessed a broader view of the minister's function than are set forth in their agreements, [which] must certainly be placed to the credit of the Institute that trained them'.

The College had practically forced the graduates to take up ministries in the provinces. This had resulted in far higher standards of education for the children of many communities out of London than before, when the girls were totally neglected and a lot of the boys didn't know even the simplest prayers in Hebrew. Now at least congregations considered both a teacher and a preacher to be vital. As the *Jewish Chronicle* spelt out:

> That the youthful ministers who went as teachers and preachers to the provinces did their duty conscientiously and zealously is proved by the fact that the congregations where they worked have never drifted back to the old conditions, but have ever since looked upon the provision of a qualified preacher for adults, and teachers for the young, not as a mere disideratum, but as a vital necessity of a healthy Jewish community. And it is to the College that they have looked to supply this felt want. And the College has not disappointed the expectation.[10]

There was still, of course, a demand for more graduates but: 'fully qualified rabbis cannot be turned out to order, nor can they be manufactured with the same celerity that jerry-built dwellings are raised.'

Hyamson said it was inevitable that not all those who left the College would go into the ministry. A 50 per cent wastage seems very high today but the Christian Theological Colleges had the same drain. The fact remained that the pupils at the college had all been exposed to a wide swathe of Jewish learning and were the better for it. 'The community is not yet alive to the paramount importance of providing a liberal Hebrew education for the youth who are to be its future leaders and workers'.

Hyamson finally quoted the Bodleian Librarian, a guest at the 1907 Maccabean dinner, who had welcomed the new Assistant Principal, Adolf Büchler, and said, 'They would like him to make Jews' College the centre of Hebrew learning, the focus of Jewish scholarship and produce in the future good books, good scholars and good men.' Büchler hadn't applied for the position. He had been invited to accept the post. He was a Hungarian who had studied at the Budapest and Breslau yeshivot, received a doctorate from the University of Liepzig for a thesis on *The Origins of the Hebrew Accents*, obtained *semicha* at 25, and then spent a year at Oxford.

There he had worked at the Bodleian, under the direction of his uncle, Dr Adolph Neubauer who was a sub-Librarian. He had then spent some years teaching at a yeshiva in Vienna. It was agreed that he would succeed Dr Friedländer, which he did in 1907 and in the meantime would be paid £400 a year. Büchler was a spare, fierce man who radiated energy, determination and very definite opinions. If he was going to meet opposition to his beliefs, he believed that attack was the best form of defence.

So in 1907 Michael Friedländer retired after forty-two years as Principal and the Council decided: 'to confer on him the title of "Emeritus Principal" of the College, with an ample retiring allowance and provision for Mrs. Friedländer in the event of her surviving him'.[11] The cost of pensions went up nearly £200 in the following year.

Friedländer's last prize-giving was typical of his modest approach to life. He said:

> Having now reached the end of my list and having distributed all the prizes, there remains for me only to mention one more name; my own. Today's distribution being the 42nd, it is, I think, time that the part I take in this ceremony be delegated to someone else, and therefore I take this opportunity to announce my intention to retire from the principalship of Jews' College within the present year. You will pardon me that, true to my principle, I do not speak many words on this occasion.[12]

Adolph Büchler moved on from Chief Assistant to take the bridge. Friedländer was also elected Vice-President as a mark of esteem, but the Chief Rabbi resigned the Chairmanship of the Council. James Solomon, the Senior Treasurer also decided to go. He: 'found the burden of office in the more strenuous times inaugurated by the appointment of the new Principal, heavier than he could bear'.[13] What 'the more strenuous times' actually involved was not spelt out, but Büchler had his own agenda. All that the Council would report was that, 'By the advice of the Principal, the duties of the Lecturers have been revised and the Teaching Staff augmented.'[14]

Solomon was succeeded by Otto Schiff, who would do a tremendous amount of good during the First World War in looking after the very large influx of refugee Belgian Jews. After the rise of Hitler he would also be responsible for looking after a flood of immigrants from Nazism, as Chairman of the German-Jewish Aid Committee in the 1930s.

John Chapman also gave up the position of Honorary Secretary, which he had held for twenty-five years, having been working for the College since its inception. Dayan Asher Feldman took his place. The teaching staff were strengthened by the appointment of Dr Samuel Daiches from Sunderland to lecture in Talmud, Shulchan Aruch and Bible. There had been fourteen candidates, so it was obviously considered a prestigious post.

The change from Friedländer to Büchler was the second occasion in the history of the College when a member of the older generation retired and gave way to a younger man. It is seldom the easiest of situations because new brooms often like to sweep clean, and there are different academic approaches. The change from Friedländer to Büchler was no exception.

To begin with, Büchler wasn't at all sure he wanted the job. He came from an austere regime in Vienna and the reputation of the British community on the Continent was of a more relaxed approach to the observance of the minutiae of the religion.

> It was with considerable hesitation that Dr Büchler accepted the invitation and the negotiations were somewhat prolonged ... if he entertained any misgivings it was that the state of English Judaism would not provide a particularly congenial environment for one of his rigid Orthodoxy and devotion to Jewish learning.[15]

It was the difference between the attempt to produce English ministers cum congregational office managers, as against the overriding objective of studying Talmud and obtaining *semicha*. Only seven men received *semicha* at Jews' College in Friedländer's forty years as principal, but Büchler would only improve on this slightly, with twelve in his thirty-three years.

Büchler was also accustomed to a system by which the head of a Yeshiva had no superior. At Jews' College, which was not set up as a Yeshiva, both Nathan Marcus Adler and Hermann Adler took a great interest in the College and had the overall responsibility for its operation. This had not been a problem for Friedländer, under whom Hermann Adler had worked for many years in his youth, but it certainly was for Büchler. There would be occasions in the future when he would criticize the Chief Rabbis for their actions, even on the occasion of prize-givings.

At the same time, Büchler was a totally dedicated scholar. He wrote a large number of learned articles and books in his lifetime and took immense care over his lectures. He might not suffer fools gladly among his students but his zeal and enthusiasm rubbed off on many of them. He was an expert in Jewish history and ritual, a fine mathematician and highly regarded internationally. Many Christian clergy would consult him; their problem was the interpretation of rabbinic Judaism where they hadn't studied the books with the same diligence as Jewish scholars. Büchler was always happy to go into the texts with them in detail.

Büchler's greatest contribution in this area was on the question of the authenticity of the Talmud and the Midrash, if there was contradictory material in Greek and Roman sources. Before Büchler it had been axiomatic to accept the evidence of the Greeks and Romans rather than the Talmud. Eminent non-Jewish historians had put forward this assessment and Büchler proved there was no justification for it.

He also proved the Talmudic data more reliable as evidence, particularly in the centuries immediately before and after the rise of Christianity. He established, for example, that there were two Sanhedrins at the time, one of which was influenced by Rome, as in the trial of Jesus, and the other – the Great Beth Din – which was purely religious and the only overriding authority for the Jewish community. His influence was felt well outside the College precincts. Nevertheless, from the time he left his home, punctually at 7.55 every morning, he was devoted to the interests of the College. He set out to get more of the students to work for degrees and he introduced higher standards for teaching diplomas.

One new arrival onto the faculty was Samuel Daiches (1878-1967) who became a lecturer in Bible, Talmud and Codes at the College in 1907. He was the first rabbi to be called to the Bar and his special field was Assyrian Studies, on which he wrote widely. He became very popular with the students and when he completed twenty-five years at the College, the Chief Rabbi said of his record: 'A perusal of its contents can only deepen our admiration for Dr Daiches as a spiritual influence.'[16]

It had been almost a clean sweep of the old guard. Another sign of change was a resolution that in future the Jewish press would be invited to attend the meetings of the Council. This motion was put forward by the representatives of the Elders of the Sephardi community on the Council. They had agreed to the press being at their own meetings ten years previously, and they probably saw the change as a way of avoiding undue pressure being put on them in closed assemblies. They certainly weren't happy with the way the Council was coming to decisions.

> The remarks of the Elders ... were emphatic, in some instances almost forcible. They protested against what they termed the dictation of the Chairman – then the Chief Rabbi – at the meetings of the College ... The resignation of Hermann Adler of his Chairmanship of the Council was certainly in part a consequence of that resolution.[17]

Hermann Adler resigned less than a year after Büchler's appointment. He was accustomed to getting his own way. As the son of the old Chief Rabbi, he had been brought up in a world where his father was in charge of spiritual matters. He had *semicha*, which very few of his contemporaries could match, he was related to some of the richest families in the Jewish community and he was held in high esteem at Court. He was made a member of the Victorian Order and had his suits specially made so that the ribbon of the order was seen, but the cross that went with it was concealed under his coat. His negotiating skills in the world of fund raising were also finely honed.

Adler knew his weaknesses. He had a guttural accent he couldn't shake off and he couldn't relate to the arrival of so many poor Jewish immigrants in the East End. His authority was under fire from the religious members of that influx who complained that Anglo-Jewry was not Orthodox enough. The criticism descended to posters in the East End attacking the Orthodox Beth Din's rulings. There was even a court case in Liverpool in 1904 because of a suggestion that the United Synagogue authorities were said to have held that there was bribery involved in the working of the ultra-Orthodox Board of Shechita.

The case was a public relations disaster for the community. The spokesman for the ultra-Orthodox, after eleven years in the country, still couldn't speak English. The court had to appoint a German-speaking judge. Typical of the exchanges reported in the press was

Witness: The rabbi does not grant divorce. It is the husband who divorces.
His Lordship: Oh, really! (Laughter).[18]

The relationship between Adler and Friedländer had been more harmonious. Adler had taught at the College for many years when Friedländer was Principal, and their friendship survived. Michael Friedländer died in September 1910. He had been more successful than Adler in many academic areas; there was his four volume translation of the works of Ibn Ezra and his voluminous translation of Maimonides' *Guide to the Perplexed*. He was such a good astronomer that *Valentine's Almanack* retained him to produce the tables of nightfall throughout the country. His most typical work, however, was on the occasion of his marriage, when he dedicated to his new wife a translation of the Biblical love idyll, *The Song of Solomon*.

Adler, of course, had his critics but which Chief Rabbi hasn't? He took over as Delegate Chief Rabbi from his father at the same time as the pogroms in Eastern Europe sent millions of Jewish refugees flooding into America and Britain. The result was a growing swell of public opinion in favour of an Aliens Bill to restrict unlimited immigration. It purported to be aimed at all immigrants but it was really to stop Jewish immigration. Adler fought, like all the leaders of the community, for unlimited entry and helped to stave off the bill until 1905.

One of his tasks was to publicise the loyalty to Britain of the Jewish community. Allying the forms of synagogue procedures to those of the Church of England was part of the programme, as long as the changes didn't alter the *din*. This was where the introduction of dog collars for Jewish ministers, and the changes in nomenclature of the synagogue officers emerged. It had been part of Nathan Marcus Adler's programme as well. It was now seen as of more importance, though, when the community changed its form to one where foreign immigrants from Eastern Europe far outnumbered the native-born members of the community.

Adler wanted Jews' College to play its part in the unofficial public relations programme. Büchler had little interest in the image of the Jewish community in Britain, He did watch like a hawk, though, for deviations from the *din*. He also resented any outside involvement in the running of the College. Indeed Büchler said publicly that Adler's weekly visits to the College were more upsetting than helpful.

The problem remained the clash between the demands of synagogue office and the time available for the ministers to continue to study Torah. Even after Adler left the Chair at Jews College, a 'United Synagogue committee urged the desirability of the training of ministers in social work, disparaging somewhat the striving after outstanding scholarship'.[19]

Büchler was outraged at this and, again, said so publicly. His criticism would be remembered at the United Synagogue in 1911 when Adolph Tuck tried to get a higher contribution to the College funds. The organisation had recently received a £20,000 legacy from a member which was specified for the support of educational institutions. Tuck asked for the £200 annual contribution to be raised to £500 but the Finance Committee advised rejection.[20] Tuck said it was because of Büchler's comments. He was particularly critical of the United Synagogue's attitude because he could point out that every one of their pulpits, bar one, was occupied by a graduate of the College. The US

Council eventually approved the continuation of the £200 which had been unchanged since 1878, but wouldn't increase it.

When the dust settled and the new officers were in place, in 1910 it was finally agreed that an Executive Committee at the College would consider all matters not of an educational character, before their submission to the Council.

In the meantime the United Synagogue had issued a report stating what they considered were the correct attributes of a Jews' College graduate: that he should be able to preach efficiently and teach Hebrew and Religion; that he could read the prayers in synagogue, including the Law, and with proper intonation; that he could help the congregants with help and advice and organize the charity work of the synagogue; and that he should be able to help with the secretarial work. In addition to a knowledge of Hebrew and religion, there was wanted:

> a wide secular knowledge and considerable general culture, a knowledge of social and political conditions, acquaintance with the religious views of many different sections of the community, powers of administration and methodical habits ... academic distinction, while very desirable, is not everything, and other requirements should not be sacrificed to the attainment of profound scholarship.[21]

Büchler paid little attention to the recommendations. If he couldn't deal with non-educational matters, he could still try to build a protective wall round his educational decisions. There had also been criticism of the College in both the press and at Council meetings of the United Synagogue. When the *Jewish Chronicle* sought an interview, he was happy to give his views. He laid out his ground rules at the start: 'I am not an optimist and I am not a diplomatist'.[22] What were his problems with the College? He had many needs:

> For instance – and this is not the greatest need – the library is fifty years behind. If there was a need to teach more widely, what could be done? It was suggested I should institute some evening classes

at the College. I should like to do so, but I have not the time. My work ends at midnight and one cannot very well start evening classes then.

Asked what the functions of a United Synagogue Minister should be: 'The United Synagogue seems to know what the functions of the Minister are supposed to be – to read the prayers, to preach, and to teach as little as possible.' He felt that the Minister was not really wanted by the Middle Classes: 'The grievous mistake that is made is that the Minister is considered to be only for the poor ... the fact that there are at least 15,000 Jewish children in the Metropolis without religious instruction, is an eloquent commentary on the neglect of their prime function by the Anglo-Jewish ministry.'

And what about teaching the adults?

> Mr Jessel [The United Synagogue Vice President, often in the Chair at Council meetings] seems to think that an adequate sermon can be preached even if the minister knows nothing ... Mr. Jessel is apparently obsessed by the fear that the Jewish scholar is necessarily a dry-as-dust scholar ... The whole story of Jewish history is against this view. The Jewish sages of the past were practical men, whose scholarship did not prevent them coming to grips with the facts of life.

Jessel had also suggested that the Ministers should spend time on raising money for charity. Büchler didn't want them distracted from their educational work to do things which were quite within the scope of members of the congregation. Büchler remained negative to the end: 'I am a pessimist in regard to English Jews.'

At the College's Speech Day in 1911 Büchler went on the attack again:

> The College has been conducted as an Orthodox institution for the teaching of Orthodox Judaism for over fifty years and now it appears that certain people desired to change the character. The

means employed were not those of argument and discussion, but threats of withdrawal of financial support. The campaign had been backed up by a choice vocabulary of abuse which reminded him of the Vienna anti-Semites ... the lay leaders of the community had persuaded the exponents of rabbinic law to give a new interpretation of quite unambiguous enactments of our codes of law, thereby causing the fine old laws of family life to melt away between their fingers.[23]

Büchler was specifically referring to evidence Hermann Adler had given to the Divorce Commissioners who were considering revisions to the laws. Adler defended himself with dignity, saying that the law of the land had to be obeyed but, naturally, Büchler's speech created a furore.

The Council later in the month published an agenda for their next meeting which included a censure motion on Büchler, but it was withdrawn because it had received too much publicity and nobody wanted to wash the dirty linen in public. Its terms were, however, read out before it was withdrawn:

That the Council deprecates the inclusion in the public report made by the Principal at prize distributions of personal adverse criticism of the capacity and industry of students who have left the College. That the Council intimates to the Principal its opinion that it is undesirable, in the interests of the College, that his reports made at prize distribution shall contain criticism of outside public bodies. That the Council regards with disapproval the use made by the Principal of the occasion of the prize distribution to discuss communal controversies which are outside the purview of the management of the College and the training of the students.[24]

Withdrawn or not, the technical reason did not disguise the embarrassment of the Council. At the same time Büchler intended to defend the letter of the Talmudic law and the responsibility of the *rabbanim* to resist the lay forces demanding secular change. Nobody doubted that if he was prevented from doing so, he would walk away from the College.

Over many years there was an element in the arguments between the lay and spiritual leaders which was never discussed. It affected most Orthodox Jews and it was a problem they had to live with all their adult lives. It was the question of their level of observance.

There are many rules laid down in the religion which most Jews do not obey. To take a single example, there is the law of *shatnes* which forbids the wearing of articles of clothing containing both wool and linen. Laws of this nature can be dismissed as outdated or ignored, if only a small percentage of the community is observing them. There are a lot of laws like this, and turning a blind eye to them is the best way of avoiding feeling guilty for not carrying them out.

Ministers trained at Jews' College, however, not only knew the laws but observed them to a greater extent than most of the lay members of their congregations. There were some who would criticize the congregation from the pulpit for not observing them. As a very often unpopular consequence, these shortcomings could no longer be put out of the minds of the members.

Of course, not all the rules were kept by some of the ministers either. On a potentially rainy Sabbath day there were ministers who would carry an umbrella. Also not allowed, but if the minister did it, how could blame be placed at the door of the congregant? So the level of observance taught and practiced at the College could easily become a standing rebuke to those who did not obey the laws. It wasn't even possible to grade the laws from vital to less important because, in Judaism, all the laws have the same weight.

The lay officers would never raise the point. They could use words like 'inappropriate', 'continental' and 'non-British', but they couldn't admit that the example of the minister could show up the inadequacies of their own performance. In the years to come, the employment of ministers from even more Orthodox yeshivas would cause friction in the congregation for the same reason.

Little of this affected the students. They were more concerned with the attributes they enjoyed in their College life. In 1908 a new facility had been provided, in the shape of a Student Library, through the generosity of Claude Montefiore.

NOTES

1. JCAR.
2. Hermann Gollancz, *Personalia* (Oxford: Oxford University Press, 1928), p.47.
3. JCAR.
4. *Jewish Chronicle*, 24 August 1906, pp.10 –11.
5. Albert Hyamson, *Jews College, London, 1855–1955* (London: Jews College, 1955), p.83.
6. JCAR.
7. *Jewish Chronicle*, 13 April 1906, p.7.
8. *Jewish Chronicle*, 16 May 1906, p.18.
9. JCAR.
10. *Jewish Chronicle*, 31 January 1908, p.11.
11. JCAR.
12. JCAR.
13. Ibid., p.10.
14. JCAR.
15. *Jewish Chronicle*, 30 June 1911, p.10. He had moved on to teach Jewish history, Bible and Talmud at the Vienna Jewish Theological Seminary and was recruited for Jews' College from there. Büchler would remain Principal for the next thirty-three years.
16. JCAR.
17. Hyamson, *Jews College, London, 1855–1955*, p.83.
18. Derek Taylor, *British Chief Rabbis* (London and Portland, OR: Vallentine Mitchell, 2007), p.281.
19. Hyamson, *Jews College, London, 1855–1955*, p.85.
20. *Jewish Chronicle*, 24 March 1911, p.22.
21. JCAR.
22. *Jewish Chronicle*, 6 May 1910, p.16.
23. *Jewish Chronicle*, 2 June 1911, p.19.
24. Hyamson, *Jews College, London, 1855–1955*, p.86.

CHAPTER FIVE

The Great War

In the early winter of 1910 two major figures died to the great regret of the community and the College. The first was Michael Friedländer at the goodly age of 77. He had been much loved by his students who fondly remembered his absentmindedness and, particularly, his modesty. On the occasion of the annual prize giving he would always seat himself on the back row on the platform. He shunned the limelight, even though he had served the College for forty-two years and seen it through all its vicissitudes. He had trained a string of ministers and teachers for communities in Britain, many parts of the Empire and the United States. In his memory his students created the Friedländer Memorial Lecture.

A week before Friedländer died on 6th December, Alfred, the son of Hermann Adler, finally passed away at the very early age of 34 after a long fight against tuberculosis. He had been a student at the College and might have gone on to be a candidate to succeed his father, but it was not to be.

While it is true that there were no British rabbinic families, that was not the case with the early ranks of Chief Rabbis, even though they had been recruited from many parts of Europe. Every one of the incumbents since Aaron Hart in 1705 had been a descendent of Rabbi Zvi Ashkenazi, the Chief Rabbi of Amsterdam. The line was only broken with the death of Alfred Adler.

For the College 1910 was a typical year; the stresses and strains remained. One question still under regular public discussion was what kind of graduates should the College produce; would they be *Talmidei Chachamim*, experts on the Talmud, or would they be bureaucrats, primarily trained to run congregations. There were extensive arguments on the subject in both Ashkenazi and Sephardi circles. They both had the potential influence which came from their financial support of the institution.

In July 1907 Adolph Tuck had asked the Council of the United Synagogue to set up a Special Committee to consider the financial support the organisation was giving to Jews' College. It took the committee of laymen two and a half years to come up with a report in January 1910. This dealt at length with what the United Synagogue wanted of the graduates, but did not offer any increase in the contribution it was making to their education. Instead it made voluminous recommendations for the working of the College. Among other changes, they recommended the abolition of the Preparatory Class, more training of the students in *hazanut*, and lectures in social work.

Albert Jessel KC was in the Chair when the report was presented. The Committee was composed entirely of laymen, though the Chief Rabbi and Dr Büchler gave evidence. Jessel was a distinguished lawyer, the nephew of the first Jewish Cabinet minister, George Jessel, and a powerful advocate. He did not like the emphasis on Talmudic learning, preferring the students to gain more knowledge in such areas as how to raise money for charity. Moreover, he considered, 'it was important that the minister should possess a considerable knowledge of the New Testament'.[1] He professed himself disenchanted with the College's policy and said that, if it were his decision to make, he would: 'shut it up and start an institution of an entirely different kind'.

When it was Tuck's turn to comment, he estimated the cost to the College, over the years, of training the ministers it had provided to the United Synagogue at £18,000, compared to the US's contribution of £4,000. Everybody agreed that the wastage of students who decided not to carry on working in a ministerial career was unfortunate, though typical of theological colleges of all denominations. To the question of why they should decide to devote their careers to a position carrying a salary of about £200 a year, there was no comment.

The report compared the performance of the graduates unfavourably to those of Church of England theological colleges, but it was suggested that the status of the vicar in a parish was 'supreme' which could not be said for Jewish ministers. The Council of the College was blamed for the curriculum not being sufficiently geared to British culture, but it was pointed out that, as ten members of the Council were Oxbridge graduates, it was hardly likely to have been indifferent on the subject.

If the suggestions of the Special Committee had been adopted, there would have been less time for the teaching of Talmud and the Shulchan Aruch. The College's Annual Report reflected the opposition of Büchler to any such alterations. While it was impossible to reject the changes out of hand, the College Council stalled:

> many of the proposals had long been engaging the serious attention of the College authorities, and that given the necessary financial assistance, their efforts would be directed in the future, as they had been in the past, towards developing still further the work of the College in the desired direction.

No change there then. The differences of opinion were not, however, confined to the College and the United Synagogue. Within the College there were also different views between the Council and Büchler. These were reflected in a new section of the Annual Report: the report of the Principal. Unlike the carefully crafted and traditionally bland statements of the Council, Büchler was prepared to go on record with firm views on the problems he faced and his opinions on what needed to be done about them as soon as possible:

> The work of the staff endeavoured to follow the lines of the new scheme of studies without succeeding in its realization to a greater extent than in the previous year. In devoting time, work, and care to the first two divisions of the students [the younger ones] the claims of the postgraduates to special attention from the Staff could not sufficiently be satisfied. Those students, now free from University work and University examinations, require the assistance of the teacher ... for the examination qualifying for the

ministry, and for research work leading up to the thesis for the M.A. degree. Experience shows that, without continuous collaboration of student and teacher, no material progress towards the two ends can be achieved.

The problem the Principal delegated to the Council Treasurers was the cost of the salaries of the staff. There were sixteen students and eighteen members of the educational Preparatory Class. The employment of ten staff would seem to be ample for the purposes, but the timetable illustrated how little time they spent lecturing. Samuel Daiches taught Bible and Talmud for a total of thirty-six hours a week which was a very full schedule, but Dayan Feldman only taught Homiletics for 1¾ hours a week. Obviously the Dayan had many other responsibilities outside the College. Rev. Peckar and Rev. Roco taught *Hazanut* for a total of three hours a week; Peckar teaching the Ashkenazi form of service and Roco that of the Sephardim. Dr Hirsch, who taught Talmud, the Shulchan Aruch and the Mahzor, had a schedule of 3½ hours a week, with an additional 6½ hours in the third term and ¾ hour in the second term. A total at less than an hour a day for most of the year. Yet the cost of salaries, including pensions, was over £2,400 a year (over £210,000 in today's money). This for thirty-four students in all.

There was additional time needed for supervision on a one-to-one basis and although the staff were dedicated, the number of pupils remained inadequate to support the expenditure. Furthermore, the students were still, primarily, coming from poorer homes. So they could not afford to pay the College fees, and had to spend time earning enough to provide a reasonable standard of living. Their attention to their studies was often undermined by this necessity.

If the Jewish community at the time is compared to a manufacturing company, the core problem is easy to identify. The synagogues needed an apprenticeship scheme to provide a highly skilled work force and future executives for the community. This Jews' College had been founded to satisfy. Time and again there had followed a cascade of lip service, with reassurance that everybody wanted the College, that the community was fully behind it, and that the United Synagogue, the

Federation of Synagogues and the Sephardim all appreciated its performance.

The only ingredient missing was that nobody wanted to pay for the apprenticeships. The United Synagogue gave the College £300 a year towards a budget which, in 1910, totalled close on £4,000. In return they had representation on the Council and influence on its decision-making. Yet they considered, as a body, that where the rest of the money was to come from was none of their business. Many insisted they had more important calls on their budgets and, in fairness, there were any number of deserving charities to support.

On the Council of the United Synagogue the College's pleas were consistently resisted by Albert Jessel. His, naturally – and deservedly – effusive obituary in January 1917, was frank about his powerful views on the institution:

> It was perhaps in his attitude to Jews' College that he incurred most criticism. Essentially Occidental in his upbringing and sympathies, Mr Jessel was not in accord with the administration of Jews College in their desire to produce a high standard of rabbinic learning at the expense, as Mr Jessel thought, of English culture. He resisted any attempt to obtain an increased grant to the College from the United Synagogue and brought into the discussions a warmth and acrimony that often surprised his friends.[2]

One is reminded of the famous American Jewish comedian, Jackie Mason's comment on the opinion of his critics about his performance: 'Too Jewish!' Jessel was effective, though. No matter how hard Adolph Tuck tried in the United Synagogue Council to get more financial support on behalf of the College, the vote invariably went against him.

Tuck did have support in the press, though. The *Jewish Chronicle* considered Jessel's views and declared:

> Mr Jessel told the Council that there was a level of scholarship which for practical purposes it was unnecessary for the student at Jews' College to attain. There was a stage of rabbinical culture,

he remarked, at which it became so advanced as not to be understood by the average member of the ordinary congregation ... [The *JC*] regard Mr Jessel's contention as fallacious to a degree ... a minister of real and deep scholarship would be better able to give a simple, but at the same time effective, presentation ... than a preacher of superficial attainment.[3]

In Michael Friedländer's time, the educational policies and administration of the college were safe in the hands of Nathan Marcus Adler and Moses Montefiore, with Charles Samuel and Hermann Adler stepping into their shoes. However, it illustrates the perceived junior status of the Principal that Friedländer was not invited to meetings of the College Council where the Chief Rabbi took the Chair. In Büchler's early days, the same discourtesy applied. Büchler, however, was a more forceful character than Friedländer. In the 1912 Annual Report he complained: 'There are still no lectures in systematic Philosophy of Religion and in Theology, subjects rightly considered essential for the equipment of ministers.' He elaborated in his report for 1913: 'Though the difficulties of elaborating a system on a modern philosophical basis may prove considerable, compulsory requirement will stimulate Jewish thinkers to undertake the work that is neglected at all rabbinical colleges.'[4]

There was no progress, as no adequate lecturer could be found, even though a member of the Council offered to pay the salary. Büchler's public image, however, like that of the College, was still high in academic circles. In 1911 he was invited to Dropsie College in Philadelphia to give a series of lectures on 'The Social, Moral and Intellectual Conditions of Palestinian Jews in the 1st and 2nd Centuries of the Common Era'. In 1913 he represented the College at the International Congress of Historical Studies in London, and Dr Hyamson also went all the way to Philadelphia for the celebration of the twenty-fifth anniversary of the foundation of the Jewish Publication Society of America.

The Council appointed a committee to consider a reconstruction of the work of the College. It sat for fifteen months and came up with two reports; a majority and a minority. The majority report proposed to abandon the Preparatory Class in 1914. It had already been suspended because of the lack of pupils. The shortfall it was hoped would be replaced by pupils from secondary schools. Büchler disapproved of that decision as well:

> The Preparatory Class which has, for many years past, trained its pupils in secular work ... and has thereby supplied the College with students, has, by a resolution of the Council, been abolished ... While it is certain that students prepared for matriculation at secondary schools receive a wider education than the Preparatory Class was ever enabled to give, it is doubtful whether the number of students required will, from secondary schools, enter Jews' College, and whether the Hebrew training of such students will equal that offered by the Preparatory Class.

The spokesman for the minority also supported retention of the Preparatory Class on the grounds that the only real alternative, transforming the College into a postgraduate institution, had already been rejected. The main difference between the sides had been a part of the minority view that the College should be removed to a university town and be reconstituted there as a residential postgraduate theological seminary.

There, however, remained little support on the Council for the suggestion that the College move out of London to Oxford or Cambridge. The attractions of a closer association of the College with the two great universities was obvious, but the cost, in terms of the Jewish education of the students, was considered far too high by the more Orthodox members of the Council.

Furthermore, there was an unacceptable precedent where a few Cambridge students had entered the ministry in past years and had accepted positions in Reform communities. As an Orthodox seminary, the College was concerned that this would be likely to be an ongoing result of such a move. Furthermore, the Jewish environment at the College in London would hardly be replicated at Oxbridge.

Thus there was the majority report against the proposal, but there was also a minority report enthusiastically supporting it. One of the notable Council members in favour was Robert Sebag-Montefiore, who became a Captain in the Royal East Kents when war broke out. He had been brought up in Ramsgate in the former home of Moses Montefiore, educated at Cambridge and became a leading member of the London County Council. Unhappily, he died in Alexandria, Egypt in 1915 from wounds suffered at the Gallipoli landings. In his memory the Robert Montefiore School in Stepney was named after him and still exists.

The fact that the College Council did not propose to move produced a vitriolic press. Typical was the contribution of a writer who called himself Mentor in the *Jewish Chronicle*: 'The public is not likely to countenance for much longer support to an institution that is founded on compromises, constantly manipulated, in order to cover up the real state of affairs that subsist.'[5]

There was a great deal more in a similar vein but, of course, it is impossible to produce a defence to such generalised abuse. Its critics said the College had failed, was failing and would eventually be in danger of closing. Mentor also attacked members of the Council as the worst kind of members of the Jewish Establishment. No names were provided and, therefore, no contrary argument was easy to produce, but popular columnists in the paper did have an influence.

There continued to be an extensive love/hate relationship between the press and the College. On the one hand there were the vitriolic articles about its perceived deficiencies. On the other, there were equally passionate appeals for support for the College, which was considered indispensable in training the ministers the community needed. Between 1914 and 1918 there were well over 1,000 references to the College in the *Jewish Chronicle*. Columnists, the writers of letters on the subject to the Editor, reports and news items proliferated.

As the discussions dragged on, the opposition to moving was led by Büchler and Dayan Asher Feldman. In the end the minority report on the proposition to move was signed by three out of the ten members of the Committee; Redcliffe Salaman, Robert Waley Cohen and Robert

Sebag Montefiore. The majority report on the reconstruction of the academic work was opposed by the Chief Rabbi, Otto Schiff, one of the Treasurers, and a future Chairman of the Council, Saemy Japhet.

Arthur Franklin, the Chairman of the Special Committee, resigned seeing his minority proposal on moving the College defeated, though he withdrew his resignation three months later. There was, however, a degree of common ground. One generally agreed decision in the report was that the bond that parents had to promise to pay in case their sons decided against going into the ministry, should be abolished.

Where all were also in agreement, though some reluctantly, was that it would be sensible to stop providing bursaries for boys at secondary schools who wanted to come to the College: 'The latter system may be dismissed without argument. It has been in full force for five years without any result so far as admission to the College is concerned. Whatever it may be, it has proved itself not to be a means of obtaining recruits for the College.'[6] Büchler's forecast at the outset of the scheme had proved uncomfortably accurate.

A resolution was also approved that those students who remained determined to become ministers would in future be expected to act as an East End visitor for the United Synagogue, or as an assistant minister to an important congregation. There was never any comment in the reports on how much – or whether – the students would be paid for these services. The Jewish Religious Education Board was to be approached to see if it could arrange teaching for the students in how to handle classes, and how the students might inspect the schools to report on their effectiveness.

The United Synagogue continued to get a great deal for their £300. Furthermore, if they reduced the donation, there was no suggestion that the services of the students would be similarly reduced. It is a fair point, however, that as the United Synagogue did not operate outside London, the support of the provincial communities was even smaller.

Most were able to recruit their ministers without having spent anything at all on their education. The College continued their attempts to improve on this one-sided arrangement. In 1916 the Council would make a new arrangement with Aria House, the Jewish school in

Hampshire, for closer cooperation in producing youngsters for eventual entry into the College.

The Council appeared unconcerned by the Principal criticising its decisions in so public a manner. As his disapproving comments in the report went to press, the Council obviously continued to regard Büchler very highly. Indeed, in June 1913, they finally decided to invite him to attend Council meetings. Even so, the concept of Cabinet Responsibility, by which all members adopted the party line in public, did not seem to apply.

At the outbreak of war in 1914 the Annual Report, as usual, recorded the number of the College's graduates who had held appointments at synagogues, schools and public institutions since its foundation. These included four dayanim, forty-three ministries in London pulpits, sixty-two in the provinces and thirty-two in the Empire and the United States. Nine had become teachers at Jews' College and twenty-five occupied other academic posts. These include the founder of Polack's House at Clifton School, the Goldsmid Professor of Hebrew at University College, London, the Reader in Talmudic and Hebrew Literature at Cambridge and the Headmaster of the Von Lämmel School and Orphan Asylum in Jerusalem.

In 1914 there were twenty students at the College. It wasn't many but their contribution to international Jewry would be considerable. Looking at the future careers of just half of them, Levy Billig would be appointed a lecturer in Arabic Literature at the Hebrew University in Jerusalem. He was assassinated at the age of 36. Abraham Filer became a Hebrew teacher, and Jacob Israelstam was the minister of the Bradford Synagogue for forty-two years. Eliezer Kahan became the Harrogate minister and Jacob Mann, from Baltimore, went home to the United States and was appointed Professor of Jewish History and Literature at the Conservative Hebrew Union College. Solomon Mestel served communities in Richmond, Nottingham, Melbourne and West Ham, while Joseph Rabbinowitz occupied the pulpit at the Dalston Synagogue for thirty-three years. Max Shutske served the Wandsworth and Balham Hebrew Congregation and Louis Weiwow took office at Brighton, Torquay and Paignton, Blackpool and Nairobi. While in

Kenya he was widely appreciated for translating the Bible into Kikuyu for the Christian communities.

Honorary Officers in synagogues also had a major part to play in the development and maintenance of congregations. For example, Barnett Beckman became the Senior Warden at Dunstan Road Synagogue in Golders Green. All in all, it was a very fair return for the investment in their education.

Hermann Adler had died in 1911 and, in 1913, was succeeded by Joseph Herman Hertz. The new Chief Rabbi was born in Hungary and brought up in New York. He had spent over ten years as a minister in Johannesburg and had been deeply involved in building up the Jewish school system in that part of the Empire. As with his Adler predecessors, the College was always going to be able to count on his full support. As he soon said 'The community and Jews College stand and fall together'.

Hertz had qualities which were very necessary for the community's spiritual leader at the time. He spoke Yiddish fluently and had a great deal of experience with Eastern European immigrants in South Africa. These qualities would stand him in good stead with the immigrants in the East End. He was also well trained in how to deal with overbearing lay leaders, a number of whom could be found in Johannesburg as well.

That would come in very useful as he struggled in future with the Honorary Officers of the United Synagogue who had appointed him. He had great charm, but he was tough as nails if he had to be. Soon after his appointment, he was assessed in the press: 'Dr. Hertz bids fair to become something of an antithesis to Dr. Adler, for in the East he is becoming supreme and in the West he bids fair soon to be quite tolerable.'[7]

Over the course of his tenure he would lead the community through two world wars, play a major part in rescuing German refugees after 1933, and would become much loved throughout the community. As Chief Rabbi Lord Sacks summed him up in 2014:

> There are leaders who are peacemakers and diplomats. No one ever accused Hertz of being among their number. Combative, self-

confident, utterly unafraid to speak his mind, sturdy in appearance, trenchant in language, he was and saw himself as a defender of the faith, fighting the wars of the Lord.[8]

Hertz and Büchler were carved from the same block, but the Principal found the new chief rabbi no more acceptable than Hermann Adler as the head of the College. It was in 1913 that the dayanim of the chief rabbi's Beth Din awarded *semicha* to Louis Mendelsohn, who had been a pupil at the College. As a result Büchler publicly complained at the 1913 Speech Day that the award should have been made by the College. Hertz was, in fact, of the same opinion, but he wasn't prepared to be criticized in public when he'd hardly got his feet under the chief rabbinate table. He was as combative as Büchler and accused him of a lack of *derech eretz* (polite and proper behaviour) to which Büchler took great exception.

The Council tried to pour oil on troubled waters by saying that controversial subjects should not be aired at Speech Days, but Büchler was unimpressed and years later took the Liberal Synagogue movement to task on the same occasion. It was, therefore, difficult to understand his acceptance of an Honorary Degree of Doctor of Hebrew Law, which was given to him by the Reform Hebrew Union College in Cincinnati in 1937. On the other hand, Sir Philip Magnus, the former Upper Berkeley Street Reform minister, had been a Vice President of the College since 1915.

For the Hungarian-trained Büchler, the concept of a chief rabbi was always foreign to his upbringing. The overriding position didn't exist on the continent. For his part, it was perhaps significant that Hertz officiated at Büchler's Memorial Service thirty years later, but it was a former pupil, Dayan Gollop, who gave the address.

At the same time, both men had to try to deal with an equal level of constant criticism, which Moses Hyamson had castigated years before. As Hertz said at the end of Büchler's time in office: 'Constant repetition was most helpful in defamation.'[9]

There had been a great deal of lobbying in the election of the new chief rabbi and the choice of Hertz did not meet with universal approval. Some of the members of the Council had been against his appointment and made life as difficult as possible for him as President of the College. One particularly contentious subject was the teaching of homiletics. A Council meeting in 1914 considered the subject at such length that the agenda for the meeting was not fully covered. The argument was over the form in which homiletics should be taught. It was felt by its critics, as reported by Mentor in the *Jewish Chronicle*, that there was too much continental emphasis on Judaism and insufficient attention to 'English ideas, aspirations, methods and ideals'.[10]

The Chief Rabbi was pragmatic, and was actually attacked for supporting this view. He wasn't a British citizen himself at the time. He needed defending in the *Jewish Chronicle*, where the Chairman of the Council, Joshua Levy, pointed out that Hertz, as the President of the College, had the absolute right to set down whatever conditions he considered appropriate. Levy praised him as filling an office where he was: 'no roi fainéant' [a do-nothing king]. The newspaper's readership's knowledge of French terminology, seems quite admirable – if somewhat questionable. Certainly, on this subject, Hertz and Büchler were not in accord. A compromise was reached with Rev. A. A. Green recruited as honorary teacher of the technique of sermon making, but with Dr Daiches remaining as the teacher of Homiletics.

Although the right to grant *semicha* had been confined to the chief rabbi in the time of the Adlers, Hertz was anxious to improve the image of the College and here he and Büchler saw very much eye to eye. In December 1913, Hertz had written to the Council about the granting of *semicha*:

> Under the rules of the College ... the examination for that highest degree is confined to a most searching test of the candidate's knowledge of Talmud and Shulchan Aruch. In all other matters appertaining to Jewish learning, such as the Philosophy of Religion, Theology of Judaism, or the Liturgy, nothing more is required of the candidate than that he shall have passed the Third Theological Examination ... In order, however, that the English

degree of Rabbi be on a par with that of the best institutions elsewhere, a much wider and riper acquaintance with the whole range of 'Science of Judaism' should be required ... Again, there is today no possibility of external students receiving their Rabbinic Diploma at Jews' College. By thus compelling external students to appeal to the Chief Rabbinate for the conferment of such degree, Jews' College needlessly weakens itself. The Rabbinate ... is most anxious that ... Jews' College become the seat of degree-giving power.[11]

Hertz only retained the right to judge in exceptional cases. He now proposed a fourth Theological Examination to deal with the additional aspects of Jewish learning he had identified, and advocated the right of Jews' College to grant external students *semicha*. Both of which recommendations were exactly what Büchler had been trying to achieve for years.

When war broke out, the community faced a major task in reiterating its loyalty to Britain. Around the country there were large numbers of German and Austrian Jewish refugees, not to mention those from the Russian Empire, who had no desire to fight alongside their former persecutors. Jews' College was not excluded from this effort. Many of the best teachers had been educated in Germany and Austria, including the principal. Their adherence to the strictly Orthodox approach was associated by their critics with European practices, including those in enemy countries.

It was the same thing with Yiddish, a partially German language, which leaders like Lord Rothschild, President of the United Synagogue for thirty-six years, found particularly offensive. The suggestion of a less Orthodox approach and a move to Oxbridge could now be advocated as a form of patriotism. It was a distortion of the arguments, but it was put forward anyway.

Even Hertz had difficulties, because he was known to be an enthusiastic Zionist. He had represented the South African Zionists at the 1900 Zionist Conference in London. The problem with Zionism in 1914 was that it was headquartered in Berlin, with senior German

Honorary Officers and an Austrian founder in Theodor Herzl. It also had the support of the Kaiser who hoped it would stir up anti-British feeling in the Middle East. Many in the British Foreign Office suspected that Zionism was part of the German Foreign Office.

As a Zionist, Hertz was very much in a minority in the community. The general view of the lay leaders was that support for Zionism threw doubt on the community's loyalty to the land of their birth and they had a great deal of support for that view. The government, however, hoped that the promise of a National Home would win the support of American Jewry to come into the war on the allied side. In fact, their influence on American foreign policy was minute, but it was perceived to be much greater than it was. Hertz, as a Zionist Chief Rabbi raised and educated in America, would have naturally endorsed the suspect view.

During most of the years immediately before the war, the College finances had been sustained by the £1,000 donation from the Sephardim, as well as various other donations and dividends on investments. Each year there were dire warnings of financial disaster. The results for 1911 were predicated to show a loss of £600 which improved to an actual loss of £137. The United Synagogue contribution had risen to £300 in 1912 but then the Sephardim donation dropped temporarily to £750. And so it went on.

What was not anticipated was an economic situation which hadn't arisen for forty years. What would happen to the value of the College investments if there was inflation? Where inflation is a commonplace today, it wasn't in late Victorian times. If the Retail Price Index was 100 when Victoria came to the throne in 1837, it was down to 74 in 1900. The reason was the effect on prices of cheap American food imports.

It was difficult for the treasurers in 1912 to conceive of the possibility that by the time Canadian Northern Ontario Railways 3½ per cent matured in 1938, the pound would be worth a great deal less than in pre-war days, and, therefore, the value of the asset would have declined in real terms. The fact that you could buy £100 of the stock for £90 in 1912 would only give the College an extra 10 per cent profit on maturity.

If there was no inflation in the next twenty-six years, the 10 per cent was admittedly a bonus. Inflation, however, over those years, would be far more than 10 per cent. What would the £30 a year, provided by the Lord Mayor's Commemoration Scholarship in 1856, buy in 1938? All the scholarships for Jews' College would be adversely affected in the same way.

The really difficult times started with the outbreak of war. To begin with, the £1,000 from the Sephardim stopped. The income they were receiving from their investments was severely diminished by the war. The money for Jews' College actually came from their earnings from the Imperial Continental Gas Company. This was the creation of Sir Moses Montefiore and specialised in installing street lighting in European cities. Now their plant had been destroyed by the Germans and they, temporarily, found it necessary to take stock of their financial position. It would not be until 1921 that the subvention would be reintroduced, and even then it would drop to £500.

As a result of their enforced lack of financial support, their representation on the Council was lowered in number. Admittedly, one of the conditions for the annual donation had been that representation, but the quid pro quo suggests that there was a view that it was their only justification for membership, which surely could not be maintained.

The only solution to the financial problems, according to Büchler, was 'relentless economies'. He pointed out that the only refurbishment that had been possible to the College was the whitewashing of the walls. There was the option of starting a fund-raising effort, but all of the Jewish charities had agreed not to do so while there was a need to sell War Bonds. The United Synagogue voted not to replace the contribution of the Sephardim or to raise their own donation from the then diminished £100 to £500. Their chairman recommended instead that the staff at the College be reduced. Adolph Tuck, on behalf of the College, was furious. As he said:

> That the Spanish and Portuguese body are satisfied that their annual outlay of £1,000 is a good investment for the Jewish

community as a whole, is well evidenced by the fact that one of their leading Elders, as Chairman of Jews College, as well as various other gentlemen from that body, on the Council of the College, have had every opportunity of thoroughly acquainting themselves with the work of the College at first hand. The Executive of the United Synagogue, unless they wilfully shut their eyes, possess the same knowledge and assurance.[12]

The subvention did return to £300 in 1916 but it was a miserly figure under the circumstances.

When war broke out, the Senior Jewish Chaplain to the Forces was a former student at the College, Rev. Michael Adler. It was only in 1892 that it had been accepted that Jewish members of the armed forces should have a chaplain and Frances Cohen was then appointed. Adler succeeded him in 1904 and was given a Territorial commission. There was a national appeal for more chaplains in 1914 but when Solomon Lipson, who had been at the College in 1893, volunteered, the War Office rejected him on the grounds that Jewish troops were too widely dispersed on the ground to benefit.

This was true of the chaplain's physical presence, but there was a lot more that needed to be done besides holding services. Provisions for Passover, the distribution of prayer books and of Hertz's iconic *Book of Jewish Thoughts* were just three tasks that needed attention. In fact, Jews, as a proportion of the population, served in greater numbers than other denominations, and this was soon recognized.

Lipson complained in the press and was accepted as a chaplain soon after. Adler served in France from 1915 till the end of the war and was awarded the Distinguished Service Order (DSO). Lipson was Mentioned in Dispatches. The opportunity to attend services before going into battle was obviously some comfort to the troops and Adler travelled all over the front. It was the first time that Jewish chaplains had been appointed to an expeditionary force on active service.

Other chaplains were eventually appointed, including Rev. John Geffen who was the *hazan* at the New West End synagogue. When

General Allenby conquered Jerusalem, however, there was no Jewish chaplain serving in the area. Eventually all five army areas in France had Jewish chaplains and there were three at the headquarters' bases. Michael Adler told Adolph Tuck how well the Chaplains had performed and Tuck was able to tell the Jewish press triumphantly that most of them were Jews' College graduates.

The Annual General Meeting in 1915 saw the strongest criticism of the Jewish community in Britain for many years. Rabbi Professor Hermann Gollancz went on the warpath:

> There is scarcely a kind word for the labour and efforts so sedulously put forth by managers, teachers and students. As a whole the community is as ungrateful as it is ungenerous in its relation to Jews' College. It never responds to its claims and then finds fault with its limited results. And what should we say of those atrabilious [melancholy, ill-tempered] critics who are so obsessed with their own preconceived judgement as regards Jews' College that facts and arguments are wholly lost on them?[13]

The audience may well have felt self-righteous as they listened to the harangue, but if you're raising money for charity, it usually isn't wise to criticise those you want to support you. The College needed good fund raisers rather than aggressive critics, no matter how justified the criticism was. They didn't have them. The success of the 1908 dinner should have led to it becoming an annual event, but that opportunity was ignored for very many years to come.

The position deteriorated by 1915 to a state where the College couldn't find the money to buy books for the students. The *Jewish Chronicle* had to appeal for some donations and £84 was raised (about £6,000 today). Nobody thought to congratulate the College on educating dedicated chaplains.

The attacks on the College continued, but one of the lecturers, Dr Samuel Daiches, wrote a spirited defence. He quoted the comments of Rabbi Dr Chaim Tschernowitz who had visited the College for some days to study its work. Rabbi Tschernowitz was the head of the Odessa

Rabbinical School and he reported: 'I have visited nearly all the Rabbinical Seminaries in Europe and I may tell you that in no other seminary is the work done so well and so thoroughly as at Jews' College. The value of Jews' College is not sufficiently known yet. It is supreme.'[14]

That, of course, was the view of a traditional head of a Yeshivah rather than those who felt that the methods of the Church of England were a better guide to the best way of teaching Jewish ministers. What it illustrated was that Büchler was maintaining the standards which had been followed by the *rabbanim* over the centuries, in the process of teaching students to gain *semicha*.

Solomon Schechter died in 1915. He had taught at the College and had gone on to become the head of the Jewish Theological Seminary in New York. His view of the attitude of the Jewish community in Britain to the importance of Talmud teaching was not positive.

As the war dragged on, the financial situation got even worse and the annual deficit was heading towards £1,000. In extremis, however, it was always possible for the College to fall back on the generosity of its friends. It wasn't just that Adolph Tuck was the Treasurer and had a major business. It was also observable when gifts arrived, like book cases from Mrs Harris Lebus. The furniture company, Harris Lebus, was by far the largest in the country and a major government supplier. It was no surprise that when the deficit reached £1,200 in 1917, 'Since the close of the year under review, a generous friend, who has asked that his name shall not be disclosed, had presented the College with the sum of £1,200 to cover the deficiency'.[15] Admittedly, it only solved the problem for one year, but at today's equivalent of £58,000, it was a very substantial lifeboat. Happily, more help was on the way when the war ended.

The United Synagogue was trying to Anglicize the education of the students even further. It was now suggested that students should be encouraged to take degrees at University College in other subjects than Semitics, and so two students were permitted to read Classics instead. The results for the students did not please Adolph Büchler. Although the annual report was massively reduced in size to save money, there was still room for the principal to report:

> Though only one year of this experiment could as yet be observed, its disadvantages have already become evident. University College has prescribed for our students a course of lectures extending over three years, instead of two, and as a consequence these two students have had their attendance at Jews' College curtailed, and have been prevented from joining in its work. The successes won at University College – in this case – in no way further the progress, nor compensate for the neglect, of the special work of our Institution.[16]

Büchler's view was that Jews' College had been set up to educate Jewish ministers and teachers, not classical scholars.

As the war dragged on, the stringent economies, perforce, continued. The Prize Giving, the high point of the year for the College, was cancelled in 1916 and 1917 and the annual report remained a shadow of its former self. Students were called up when conscription was introduced, and others were poached by congregations whose ministers were serving abroad as chaplains. Büchler was very annoyed; he felt that while senior students were ready for their pulpits:

> It is deeply to be regretted that some congregations, without enquiring of the College about the qualifications of candidates, who had not passed even the preliminary stages of their preparations for the Ministry, are, thereby, without necessity, weakening the efforts of past years of the Staff to raise that standard of the qualifications of the Ministry. Strong blame attaches to such unqualified students whose unwarranted action is sure to react on the qualifications of some of the future ministers.[17]

At the end of the war Joshua Levy, the Chairman of the Council, resigned through ill health and died in 1922. A pillar of the Sephardi community, he had been a member of the College Council since 1879 and acted as Honorary Secretary and Chairman from 1908. Levy was one of those dedicated leaders of the community to whom so much was owed and who asked for little in return except to serve.

He had been the President of the Board of Shechita and Treasurer of the Board of Deputies. A faithful colleague, out of loyalty to the Board, he had resigned with the other officers when the Deputies had voted against their President over his letter to *The Times* in 1917, denouncing the idea of the Balfour Declaration. Ironically, the rejection wasn't because the Deputies were Zionist. It was because the large number of provincial deputies hadn't been consulted beforehand and were gefruntzled.[18] Samuel Emanuel KC, the Recorder of Winchester, was appointed in his place at the College.

The demand for ministers continued to be difficult to satisfy and one member of the Council complained in 1917 that it had not been possible to find a suitable candidate for a synagogue in Sydney, Australia. The Chief Rabbi, who was presiding at the meeting, suggested that the salary was too low to attract applicants.

He made the point that if he had been married when he was recruited for the pulpit he occupied for many years in Johannesburg, he would have thought long and hard before leaving America to take up the post. As usual, the Empire congregations wanted to have the chance to get Jews' College graduates without giving any thought to making a donation to the College finances.

NOTES

1. JCAR.
2. *Jewish Chronicle*, 15 January 1917. p.14.
3. *Jewish Chronicle*, 4 February 1910. p.7.
4. JCAR.
5. *Jewish Chronicle*, 23 October 1914, p.9.
6. JCAR.
7. *Jewish Chronicle*, 18 January 1946, Editorial.
8. Chief Rabbi Lord Sacks, Foreword, in Derek Taylor, *Chief Rabbi Hertz, The Wars of the Lord* (London and Portland, OR: Vallentine Mitchell, 2014), p.xv.
9. JCAR.
10. *Jewish Chronicle*, 3 July 1914, p.12.
11. JCAR.
12. JCAR.
13. JCAR.
14. *Jewish Chronicle*, 26 November 1915, p.12.

15. JCAR.
16. JCAR.
17. JCAR.
18. Gefruntzled – felt overlooked and unimportant, patronized, neglected and treated as second-class citizens

CHAPTER SIX

Defending the Fort

At the end of the war there was a very welcome new source of funds. This came from a new charity, the Jewish War Memorial. Even before it was formally organized, it gave the College £1,000 and this was one reason why the College suddenly had a surplus for 1921/22 of £1,320.

The Jewish War Memorial was the brainchild of Sir Robert Waley Cohen (1877–1952), who was appointed Treasurer of the United Synagogue in 1913 and Vice President from 1918. He was first elected to the Council of Jews' College in 1901. The rationale for Waley Cohen's election had nothing to do with theology. The Council needed the support of the rich families within Anglo-Jewry, later known as The Cousinhood, to which Waley Cohen belonged, and also of representatives from the younger generation. In 1901 Waley Cohen was 24 and a Cambridge man with a degree in Natural Sciences. He had been educated at the Jewish boarding house at Clifton and his family had loyally served the community in many different ways.

In addition he was related to Marcus Samuel, the founder of Shell Petroleum, and would become a very powerful industrialist within the company. So he had just the wealthy, young and respectable image that the College wanted to present to the community. The only problem with Waley Cohen, which was discreetly overlooked, was that he was non-observant himself and his mother taught the children's classes at the Reform synagogue in Upper Berkeley Street.

Waley Cohen had sat on the Council of Jews' College for nearly twenty years when he had the idea for the Jewish War Memorial to commemorate the fallen in the war. It was a noble objective but there was a hidden agenda; it was designed to be the instrument by which

Waley Cohen would achieve three objectives. First, he wanted to upgrade the image of Jewish education represented by Jews' College. He had watched it struggle year after year from the vantage point of the Council, and it had little of the esteem of an institution like his Cambridge college. So he set out to transfer it to one of the university towns.

Hertz had no problem with this. In South Africa he had been appointed Professor of Philosophy at Transvaal University College as long ago as 1907. He was comfortable in academic circles. He, too, would have recognized the boost to the image of the College if it was considered good enough to became part of an ancient university. But its main task, the rock-solid foundation which he had been appointed to defend, had to be the teaching of the Talmud and the observance of the *din*. An association with Oxbridge could diminish both.

Waley Cohen's second objective was to reunite the United Synagogue and the Reform movement by compromising over their differences. These were not necessarily insurmountable, as the real moves away from Orthodoxy for the Reform would not come until the 1930s. Neither was he alone on the Council in this objective. After the war there were Council members who worshipped at Upper Berkeley Street and others whose views were more secular than *frum* [observant Orthodox]. He might expect resistance from the chief rabbi and the College principal, but the financial support of the United Synagogue was likely to be a powerful weapon in helping him get his own way. That would be the chosen weapon, even if the vast majority of the members stuck resolutely to their Orthodox credo, as Waley Cohen also professed to do.

The third objective was the one which would lead to the worst relations ever between the Chief Rabbi and the head of the United Synagogue, the organization which appointed him and paid his salary. Waley Cohen wanted to make the chief rabbinate subservient to his leadership of the United Synagogue.

From their foundations, organizations like the Board of Deputies of British Jews, Jews' College and the United Synagogue had specifically ruled that the ultimate religious authority in Britain would be the Chief

Rabbi. Waley Cohen, throughout Hertz's ministry, would try to get round these agreements and replace them with the lay power which controlled so many synagogues. By 1919 he was accustomed to rule at Shell without meaningful opposition. He was never too concerned about those who disagreed with him anyway, although his arrogance would eventually destroy his business career.

In 1919 though, he had all the advantages of wealth and rank– he was knighted for his services to the war effort – and, by contrast, the new chief rabbi was an American from a poor family, who was very likely to be out of his depth in the higher echelons of British Jewish society.

It was true that the Chief Rabbi would have no quarrel with an ambition to improve the status of Jewish education. Beyond that, though, Waley Cohen would discover that there was no way he was going to compromise on the *din* in order to meet the theological position of the Reform movement halfway. Hertz, moreover, would fight tooth and nail to maintain the spiritual authority and hegemony of his office.

Waley Cohen set about raising £1 million (at least £40 million in today's money) for his educational dream and, naturally, Hertz did all he could to help him. In August 1920, when the Chief Rabbi made the first pastoral tour of the Empire ever undertaken by the holder of his office, raising money for the War Memorial was one of his objectives. The tour was a great success and he raised £50,000 (at least £2 million today). That was the good news. When, however, he got back to London in 1921, he found that Waley Cohen had been negotiating behind his back with the Liberal's Claude Montefiore, and that the Orthodox form of Jews' College was in real danger of being undermined.

The eventually insuperable problem for the Jewish War Memorial was that the early reaction to the Council's efforts had soon shown that £1 million was not going to come, in toto, from the Orthodox section of the community. One possible additional source was indeed the members of the Reform movement, but Waley Cohen knew they would need to be offered a benefit in return. So he came up with the idea of an entirely new organization which could help him achieve all his objectives.

He conceived of an Academy, part of which would be Jews' College, while the other part would be devoted to providing diploma courses for other religious denominations within the community. The two bodies were predicated to have a common home and a common council. There is no doubt that Waley Cohen would have made sure that he was invited to take the chair. The Chief Rabbi's Jews' College would then have become subordinate to the Academy. So without telling Hertz, Waley Cohen had opened discussions with Montefiore about an Academy to recruit both more pupils and additional funds. The solution they agreed was to introduce a course for Progressive students for the rabbinate, in the new organization.

From Waley Cohen's public point of view, it would help the finances of Jews' College and achieve his objective of bringing the opposing movements within the religion closer together. Shell would have admired the commercial logic, but it was astonishing that Waley Cohen could ever imagine that he could undermine the Chief Rabbi's position as the head of Jews' College, by presenting him with a fait accompli of this kind.

The ex-minister of Upper Berkeley Street, Sir Philip Magnus, had been elected a Vice-President of Jews' College in 1915 and was much in favour of the discussions. Magnus was both influential and popular. He would die holding the Jews' College office in 1933, but the gap between Orthodoxy and Reform would still be there and, in fact, would grow. Claude Montefiore, of course, wanted to achieve an improved status for his new denomination, which would have emerged from religious cooperation with the Orthodox United Synagogue.

To Montefiore's disappointment, his Liberal movement had not acquired adherents in anything like the numbers for which he had hoped. If Montefiore's religious beliefs were even further distant from the Orthodox than those of Waley Cohen, both men were at least from very much the same social background. Their future cooperation was feasible and, depending on the viewpoint, the gap between the Orthodox and the Progressives would thereby narrow, or the wedge become thicker.

When Hertz found out what was happening, he went to work to have the idea of the Academy rejected. He knew that Jews' College would have become a laughingstock in Orthodox circles around the world if it became part of an organization which also trained Progressive students. When he returned to London, however, negotiations were already at an advanced stage.

Hertz's first line of defence had to be to ensure that, if there were to be two organizations, then they would be separate and distinct. Waley Cohen, the man whose word was law in Shell, now found himself with a fight on his hands. For his part, Hertz also found himself under attack from the Right Wing, for having anything to do with the Academy idea at all.

Waley Cohen pleaded for the Academy. He promised Hertz that considerable segments of the United Synagogue congregations had contacted him to register their approval, and that the Right Wing had also given him their support. He argued that if the Jewish War Memorial didn't achieve its objectives, Hertz would always rue the day he had opposed the establishment of the Academy. He insisted that it would be enough to trust to the loyalty and wisdom of the Anglo-Jewish community to protect the future religious direction of the College.

None of these arguments carried much weight with Hertz because their credibility was questionable, particularly the claim of the support of the Right Wing. What they did do was undermine what was left of Waley Cohen's relationship with the Chief Rabbi. In future years this would eventually sink to a quite disastrous level where the two leaders could only communicate through intermediaries.

Even as early as 1923 Sir Robert presided at a meeting of the Memorial Council and lost his temper with Hertz: 'Sir Robert's exhibition of petulant ill temper against the spiritual head of the community was particularly absurd ... to insult the Chief Rabbi is surely a strange piece of inconsistency'.[1]

There was, of course, the plus side to closer contacts with the Progressive movement. As the future of Jews' College had been threatened by underfunding almost from its inception, so the possibility of continued financial aid from another wealthy section of the Jewish community was very attractive; ample support from the whole Jewish community at home and within the Empire was the unfulfilled ambition of the College authorities over the previous sixty years. Moreover, Claude Montefiore had been, personally, very generous to the College and was, in fact, on friendly personal terms with Hertz.

In 1923 Isidore Harris was appointed to the Council. He had been a student at the College but had become a Reform minister fifty years before. With Sir Philip Magnus, he increased the representation of the Progressive movement, but their wealthier members still constituted only a very small percentage of the Jewish community, and the organization's actual financial support had been restricted to the £50 which had occasionally come from the Upper Berkeley Street congregation. It was widely recognized that Waley Cohen's Academy concept was attempting to make the tail wag the dog. Long acrimonious discussions ensued within the Jews' College Council.

The situation was becoming dire because the College could no longer even afford the pre-war bursaries it had provided for penurious students. There had also been an ever decreasing number of students for the past ten years and, in 1921, there were only ten at the College and two of those left shortly after the report was written. The available posts for graduating students were also getting more difficult to find. The solution sometimes had to be an overseas posting. Jacob Mann may not have achieved *semicha*, but he was a good enough brain to be appointed Professor of Jewish History and Literature at the Hebrew University College in Cincinnati.

For his part, Hertz could see that the two proposed Academy divisions, with opposing theologies, would be at each other's throats from the start. He also found any willingness to compromise opposed by a new body formed to defend the status quo. The Organisation of Observant Traditional Jews of Great Britain soon had a membership which included five *dayanim* and the Chief Rabbi of Ireland, Isaac Herzog.

When it convened, Hertz wasn't there, but he recognized the strength of feeling among Orthodox *rabbanim* and saw that any compromise was impossible, as he had suspected from the outset. He did point out that, when he returned from the Pastoral Tour, he had been faced with a plan for an Academy which would be one joint organisation. He had argued successfully for it to be split into two totally separate bodies, which had been progress for his viewpoint, but he now set his face totally against that idea as well.

In January 1922 the College Council reached agreement. In view of the fact that the fund raising had fallen well short of the target, the move to either Oxford or Cambridge would have to be abandoned. The other proposals were adopted, usually by a majority of one out of twenty votes.

It was reconfirmed that Jews' College would continue to teach Traditional Judaism by teachers who accepted those principles. Students would be admitted without a religious test but, if they joined the College, they would need to comply with the approved level of Jewish Orthodox religious conduct. 'The Council did accept the Academy concept but only as separate from the College: All presentations of the Jewish Religion as taught in the synagogues represented on the Council of the Jewish War Memorial may be freely expounded.'[2] This decision was bitterly contested, but Hertz voted for it as the best way to split the Academy from the College, and it was passed by 10-7.

> The students admitted to the College were expected to have a university degree, and some postgraduate scholarships were approved, tenable at Oxbridge. There was also to be a department of Jewish Pedagogy. £2,000 a year would be given to the College for increased maintenance (£1,000) [for] the new department [and] £600 [for] additional scholarships and a lectureship in the Academy. It was also agreed that a hostel was desirable.[3]

The decisions became dead letters. In the event, the scholarships were reserved for students who intended to become rabbis, ministers, *hazanim* or teachers. Otherwise, although anybody could become a student at the College on the payment of the fees, the Academy concept was never launched. Only the College had a workable infrastructure.

Hertz won this first battle with Waley Cohen, and the College would, effectively, carry on as before.

It remains difficult to understand Waley Cohen's belief that he could take over the Chief Rabbi's religious authority in the area of education. If Jews' College wasn't Hertz's responsibility, then the United Synagogue Act, which gave total spiritual authority to the Chief Rabbi, was abrogated. It should also have been obvious that, if he didn't have Hertz on his side initially, his objective was going to be that much more difficult to attain. In the oil business at the time, however, a great many agreements were valid only as long as it wasn't advantageous to break them. That was the world in which Waley Cohen laboured for many years, and obstructive juniors could usually be brushed aside.

Waley Cohen could never accept that Hertz was, in no way, his junior. The fact was, however, that in working with the Chief Rabbi, it was at best a meeting of near-equals. If it came to the crunch, Waley Cohen was going to finish up the junior partner because Hertz always retained his ultimate weapon: his possible threat of resignation on religious grounds. The risk to the United Synagogue Honorary Officers that he might do this simply wasn't worth taking. At the same time, Waley Cohen had on his side the effective control over the funds the United Synagogue would provide for the College.

To his credit, Waley Cohen went to a great deal of trouble to personally identify suitable candidates for training for the ministry and was highly regarded by those young men he took under his wing. He might have lost the battle for the overriding Academy, but he now intended to attack the Chief Rabbi's authority on another front. The renamed War Memorial Council passed a resolution that: 'As a result of its enquiry into methods of improving the status of the Jewish Ministry will, in consultation with the ecclesiastical authorities, weigh the various needs throughout the Empire and give the advice accordingly to ministers and to those who are making appointments in the Jewish Ministry.'[4]

That was also, of course, an outrageous suggestion. Pausing only to offer the sop of 'consultation with the ecclesiastical authorities', the aim was clearly to seize powers for which the War Memorial Council had no authority or mandate, and thereby to undermine the status of the Chief Rabbi. Hertz was furious at the use of the plural in 'authorities'. He insisted, correctly, that he was the only authority, according to the United Synagogue's constitution, and that he intended to remain the sole holder of that responsibility.

This had been the case since at least the beginning of Nathan Marcus Adler's ministry. When the present Chief Rabbi, Joseph Hertz, had been appointed to the pulpit of his Johannesburg synagogue in 1898, he had received a warm letter of congratulations from Hermann Adler, whose approval had been initially sought, as it always was. Adler's approval might have been to ask for a rubber stamp but, in extremis, the Chief Rabbi's veto did exist.

The Council's statement was dismissed in the *Jewish Chronicle* as another example of: 'a growing disposition in the Chairman, Waley Cohen, to indulge in a high handed and imperious manner in the position he takes in public affairs'.[5] There was certainly always a need to recruit able ministers, but the College believed their main qualification should be their *halachic* expertise. Jews' College now had a very good record in producing men suitably qualified in the Talmud.

How Waley Cohen or his Council were to become the final arbiters on the subject of a minister's suitability was unclear. They had no theological qualifications which would be acceptable internationally. The proposal was obviously a political manoeuvre. Eventually, this idea also came to nothing, but Jews' College's position at the hub of Jewish education was still under threat.

The long discussions between representatives of the War Memorial Council and the College descended into bitter vituperation on the question of where to house the Academy. The WMC wanted both the Academy and the College to be in the same building. The Chief Rabbi wouldn't hear of it and the Beth Din rejected the idea out of hand. Everybody knew the Academy curriculum would be designed to teach Reform Judaism. The War Memorial Council planned to discuss the subject at a meeting in March 1924 and beforehand Hertz wrote to the Chairman, Lionel de Rothschild: 'I look to you to secure for me a fair hearing free from unmannered interruptions and hysterical abuse.'[6]

Rothschild provided no such guarantee and the meeting was turbulent and confrontational. Hertz pointed out that he had been instrumental in raising much of the WMC money on his pastoral tour in 1920 and that, therefore, Jews' College had a claim to it. The bargain of financial support in return for joint premises was, therefore, totally unreasonable. The fact that, eventually, there wasn't enough money for a separate Academy was another reason why the idea died.

Nevertheless, in July 1924 the joint committee of the College and the WMC were able to come up with an agreed revision of the College constitution. It covered three main areas; the representation on the Council needed changing because of the money it was confirmed the WMC were going to give the College; the admission policy of the College also needed clarifying; and there might be ways of improving the efficiency of the College.

The WMC said it couldn't afford more than £2,000 a year. It also said it wanted a member of staff who had been to an English university, plus a professor of Jewish Religious Education, higher salaries for the staff, new courses in Pastoral Theology and Social Services, and also in English Language and Literature.

Where was the money to come from? It was agreed that a shortfall of £1,785 would need to be covered every year, without the costs of the new academics and the new courses. These would, therefore, happen, it was agreed, 'as opportunity offers' and, in addition, there should be an appeal to the community, even if that solution had proved ineffective on so many previous occasions.

It was also agreed that if anybody gave £300 a year, they could have a seat on the Council, and multiple seats for multiple £300s. There was, however, an implied threat that if the university trained staff member wasn't appointed within two years, the £2,000 a year could be reduced to £1,500. In fact it took until 1928 to find Dr Isidore Epstein, but it would prove to be worth the wait.

As far as admissions were concerned, anybody could attend lectures – Jews or non-Jews – if they paid the fees, but bursaries and scholarships would be confined to students who intended to become synagogue ministers or Hebrew teachers. The Orthodoxy of the institution continued to be fully protected.

Another problem was that Samuel Emanuel was now both the Chair of the Jews' College Council and of the WMC. At the next meeting of the College Council he resigned because he was, himself, in favour of the two bodies being under the same roof. There were immediate pleas for him to stay, but he was adamant. Unhappily, he died a year later.

It was in 1923 that another Jews' College shibboleth finally ended with the appointment to the Council of Nathan Laski, who was the head of Manchester's Orthodox community. It had always been held before his election that members of the Council had to have a home in London. Laski broke the mould and his son, Neville Laski, went further and became the first Jew from the provinces to become President of the Board of Deputies.

Laski had been invited to preside at the prize giving in 1920 and, on that occasion, he had spelt out some of the problems:

> It was sad there were few in the Provinces who realised the contribution Jews' College made ... to a large extent the lay authorities of the College had themselves to blame. The College had been too much considered an institution of London alone.
>
> There was too great a tendency in the community to regard the Minister as the servant of his congregation. In some of the smaller congregations there was too great a tendency to regard him as the maid of all work. They must realise that in the spiritual sphere the Minister was not the servant of the officers of the synagogue, but the servant of his G-d. He felt certain that it was the subservience which was forced upon so many ministers by the autocracy of the synagogal executive which had deterred many of the sons of more comfortably placed Jews from entering the ministry.[7]

Another opportunity for Waley Cohen to undermine the Chief Rabbi came up in December 1925 when the War Memorial Council decided to convene a conference on Jewish Education. It was noticeable that Hertz did not attend and the community wondered whether he had decided not to do so, or hadn't been invited. All was made clear in the *Jewish Chronicle*:

> The War Memorial Council insist that any speech, address or sermon in connection with the Memorial delivered by the Chief Rabbi shall, before it is published, be submitted to the censorship of the Council. That body claims the right to omit anything Dr. Hertz may have said and to send it out to the public in the form of which they approve.[8]

Hertz paid no attention to the resolution and refused to attend or speak at the conference. The *Jewish Chronicle* denounced the Council's diktat as outrageous and blamed Waley Cohen for it: 'Does Sir Robert realise the enormity of the position he has assumed? ... It surprises me that you should associate yourself with anything so mean and unworthy as the vendetta you are carrying on against Dr. Hertz.'[9]

In fairness, Waley Cohen was the Chair of the War Memorial Council, which Hertz supported, but had not created. Because the subject was religious education, any comments Hertz made could be automatically assumed to have the approval of the War Memorial Council, but this was, by no means, always the case. Hence Waley Cohen's attempt to muzzle the Chief Rabbi. He was not going to have anybody else assumed to be speaking in his name. As neither man had any intention of giving way, the likelihood was that the situation would later deteriorate even further. This danger had no effect on Waley Cohen or, indeed, on the Chief Rabbi.

It was obvious that Waley Cohen's concept of the ideal United Synagogue minister was some considerable distance from a Jews' College trained Talmudic scholar. The old arguments were paraded afresh in all their class and religious formats. The Jews' College curriculum for *semicha* hadn't changed, though. Hertz, of course, also wanted more candidates for the ministry and he had worked hard to collect donations for the War Memorial Fund, as he had proved on his overseas tour: 'From our first landing ... I made the vital necessity of providing efficient teachers and interpreters of Judaism for the congregations of the Empire, the burden of practically every sermon, address, or public appeal I delivered.'[10]

The Academy question hung over the College in the immediate future, but its normal life continued. There was the usual problem with the balance sheet. There had been a degree of relief when the eminent personage invited to preside over the prize giving in 1921, Samuel Samuel, MP gave £250 to wipe out the year's deficit. In 1922 it cost Sir Edward Stern £300 but when Flora Sassoon only gave £50 in 1923, this promising source of funds was no longer the solution. Mrs Sassoon had created a precedent, though, by being the first women ever to hand out the awards at the prize giving.

The staff salaries had already been reported to be totally inadequate and the College was fortunate to have the free services of two doctors, a solicitor, an architect and an auditor. In 1924 the bedrock of the College income was £1,500 from the War Memorial Council, £500 from the Sephardim, £300 from the United Synagogue and a new contribution from their Benjamin Levi Educational Trust of £325. The Rothschilds were still sending their very welcome £200 cheque, unchanged since 1855; a total of nearly seventy years.

There was, surprisingly, an additional very substantial contribution in 1924 of £750, and a further £1,400 in 1925, from the Distribution Committee of the Shechita Board. In 1923 they had found themselves with no less than £80,000 in their coffers (about £4 million today). This was the accumulated profit from the charges for licensing kosher meat over the years, and to a community constantly complaining about the cost of eating kosher, it was very difficult to explain away.

As the Board of Shechita was considered a charity, a large-scale programme of distributing the money had to be instituted. In addition the charge for killing a cow was reduced from £1 to 62½p, resulting in the Board of Shechita making a loss in a couple of years of £12,000. The process doesn't seem to have been costed very accurately. Another welcome gift in 1926 was the establishment of a scholarship, donated by the South African community, which was tenable at the College and at either Kings College or UCL.

Some educational difficulties only emerged very slowly until they intruded upon the day-to-day work of the College, for example, the reduction all over the country in the teaching of Latin and Greek. While the universities continued to demand the ability to pass examinations in the classical languages, students coming into the College seldom had been taught the subjects. There was now, therefore, a necessity to teach Latin and Greek to the Matriculation class at the College, and this could add on a year to the student's period of study.

The annual reports, as regularly as clockwork, contained Büchler's lament that there was still no systematic Jewish Theology or Philosophy of Jewish Religion being taught. Although Büchler and the Chief Rabbi had their differences, they were totally united in their view on the importance of that aspect of the College's forward thinking. As Hertz said when installing Solomon Mestel as a rabbi in 1926:

> In some quarters at home, every now and then, laments were heard that there was too much scholarship at Jews' College, that the professors were too learned, and the students knew too much. Hebrew and rabbinical studies alone could bring the Jewish minister closer and closer to his fellow Jews. Rabbi Meir had said ... he is called friend, beloved, a lover of God, a lover of mankind. It clothes him in meekness and reverence; it fits him to become just, pious, upright and faithful ... through him the world enjoys counsel and sound knowledge, understanding and strength.[11]

By 1926 the row caused by the Academy concept was being papered over. Sir Robert Waley Cohen was presiding at the College Speech Day and the new Chair of the Council, Saemy Japhet, was celebrating the seventieth anniversary of the first AGM. He had, himself, been on the Council for over twenty-five years and ruefully reminisced that: 'Throughout the whole of those years they had never been free from criticism. I have yet to experience the pleasure of endeavouring to render public service to the community without that stimulating condiment.'[12] Japhet was not discouraged. One of his first acts was to convince eight of his friends that they ought to commit £500 each to

Defending the Fort

the Bursaries Fund. As a result the College finances moved onto a sounder footing than for many years past.

The Council had its differences too but, at least, it had always been in full agreement that it did not welcome competition for the College. Yeshiva Etz Chaim was acceptable because it simply sought to enable its students to study Torah. A new potential competitor, however, now emerged.

In 1926 a few pioneers in Gateshead started a yeshiva and invited Rabbi Abraham Sacharov to come to England and accept the post of Rosh Yeshiva. They did not consult with the rest of the Gateshead community who already had a synagogue rabbi. A letter to the *Jewish Chronicle* from a Gateshead member even suggested that starting a yeshiva was a 'harebrained idea'.

From Hertz's point of view, having struggled for years alongside the Council to raise sufficient money to keep Jews' College going, the last thing he wanted was a competitor for seminary benefactions. Furthermore, it was perfectly possible that Gateshead would prove more fertile ground for such a foundation than London. The Gateshead community had always been devoted to Talmudic study.

One of Hertz's first engagements as Chief Rabbi had been to consecrate Etz Chaim's new building in 1913. He would do the same when it moved to larger premises in 1937. Hertz had good relations with the London yeshiva, but the one in Gateshead was very likely to be less prepared to be influenced by his views.

Etz Chaim had been underpinned financially in its early days by the Federation of Synagogues who acknowledged the Chief Rabbi's authority. This was very unlikely to be true of Gateshead, whose original founders were a breakaway congregation from Newcastle, formed because they did not consider the level of Orthodoxy in that city to be acceptable by their standards. It was financially underpinned by members of a very Orthodox congregation in Sunderland, whose roots were originally in Lithuania.

With unemployment high, work permits for foreigners were hard to come by, and when the Home Office investigated the application for an entry permit for Rabbi Sacharov, Hertz persuaded the Home

Secretary, the anti-Semitic William Joynson-Hicks, not to grant him a permit. When news of this came to light, Hertz explained his behaviour by saying that there were already plenty of equally qualified *rabbanim* in Britain who could fill the post and who needed the job. In view of the difficulty he found in recruiting Talmudic experts for his own needs, this argument was somewhat questionable. When a question was asked in the House of Commons in February 1926, Joynson-Hicks replied:

> The application for the admission of this Polish Rabbi has not been supported by any argument beyond the fact that the Gateshead congregation have elected him, and though I have made enquiries, I have been unable to ascertain any special grounds for acceding to the application.[13]

Although Rabbi Sacharov's application was refused, the Gateshead pioneers were not discouraged. In 1929 the 27-year-old Rabbi Nachman Landynski was chosen and this time a visa was granted. Nonetheless, for some further years, Hertz decreed that if they didn't acknowledge his authority, he wouldn't agree that the congregation was authentically Jewish. Without that approval they couldn't have a marriage secretary. Weddings would have to be held in a Registry Office before a synagogue ceremony for the marriage to be legal. As there was really absolutely no question of the Orthodoxy of the Gateshead community, this was a petty gesture on the Chief Rabbi's part.

Eventually the Gateshead Yeshiva settled down with the continued financial support from Sunderland , and Hertz gave his permission for them to have a Marriage Secretary. The physical conditions under which the students laboured were extremely primitive, but the dedication they gave to their work certainly could not be faulted. The community still doesn't recognise the Chief Rabbi's authority today, but the Gateshead Yeshiva is famous throughout the Jewish world, and its authority in religious decisions is highly regarded.

Back in 1926 the United Synagogue was expanding rapidly as more and more emigrant families moved to the wealthier London suburbs and joined the more upmarket congregations. The US recognized that this would lead to them needing even more ministers and, for the first time, they took the problem of financing the College seriously. They decided to apply a 25p minimum levy on their seat-holders and this enabled the salaries of the College staff finally to be increased.

In addition Rose Hertz, the Chief Rabbi's wife, agreed to take a hand and formed a Ladies Auxiliary Committee for the College. Jewish mothers moved in to see that the public rooms were cleaned and redecorated, that there was a proper dining room and kitchen, and that hot lunches and teas were available for the students.

It is easy to have 20:20 hindsight, but the way in which the College's funds were invested at the time was still destined to lead to disaster. They had a nominal £60,000 of fixed interest stock, normally at 3 per cent a year interest. These included, for example, £2,000 of Newport, Monmouthshire, 3 per cent 1915/1955 and £1,800 of Hastings Corporation 3 per cent 1915/1954. The long-term problem remained that inflation was likely to play havoc with the value of all such stock long before they matured.

These were the funds, however, on which all the bursaries, scholarships and prizes were based. They helped to finance the five new entrance scholarships which were very welcome. They were underpinned by a guaranteed £800 a year for five years by new donors recruited by Saemy Japhet. The value of money, however, would halve during the forthcoming Second World War, due, additionally, to the drop in the value of the pound as the country tried to pay for the conflict.

Unlike, say, the Hedge Funds of today, charitable organizations couldn't take risks with their capital assets and had to invest a great deal of it in some sort of gilt edged security. In addition, looking into the financial future accurately was an impossible responsibility; practically nobody foresaw the Slump.

A number of long-term supporters of the College died in 1926: Adolph Tuck, Delissa Joseph, the Hon. Architect, Lord Bearsted and Bertha Friedländer, the former principal's wife. It would also be a great loss when Rose Hertz died at a very young age in early 1930.

The College administration settled down under Saemy Japhet who had been on the Council since 1902. Japhet was a successful banker and, to mark his 70th birthday, in 1928, he gave £5,000 to the College. Interviewed on his plans for the future of the institution, he said how important he felt it was to produce ministers of British birth and real English education. He said he wanted to turn the College into a purely English institution, teaching the students how to relate to the communities among whom they would have to live.

The problem with these ambitions remained that they did not necessarily fit in with the Talmudic abilities, outlooks and commitments which were essentials in the CVs of the College staff. The President, Joseph Hertz, was Hungarian, brought up in New York. The Principal, Adolph Büchler, was also a Hungarian, trained in Vienna, and Arthur Marmorstein, who had taught Talmud, Codes and the Bible since 1912, was another Hungarian. Japhet himself was born in Frankfurt and only came to England at the age of 37. The strategy read well in the papers, but even the new English, university-trained lecturer, Isidore Epstein, had been born in Lithuania.

The predominance of Hungarians could have side effects. As a people in the old Austro-Hungarian empire. they were treated as second-class citizens and they were keenly conscious of this. Although this treatment didn't specifically apply to the Jews, the effect of the culture could sink deep roots. Hungarians particularly sought equality, and looked to see if those appointed above them deserved the positions they occupied.

Epstein wasn't the first choice, as the position had been offered to, and accepted by, a former student, Rabbi Israel Brodie. He was, at the time, the minister in Melbourne, Australia, and his community eventually persuaded him to remain in office. Epstein, as the replacement choice, was the rabbi in Middlesborough. He had a BA, a PhD and a D.Litt. He had received very favourable media coverage for his paper at the 1927 Jewish Preachers Conference, and for his defence of the *siddur* [prayer book]. The suggestion that the Singer prayer book should be dropped and that all *siddurim* should be combined into one for the entire Jewish community, was regarded again as the thin end of the Progressive wedge.

Epstein was brilliant in many academic fields. He was highly competent to teach Semitic languages, the Bible, Aramaic, comprehensive Hebrew grammar and composition, Syriac, North Semitic Epigraphy (the study of inscriptions), Philosophy and Arabic. He was certainly a better academic than Brodie, but he didn't have Brodie's very English background.

Even with their expert academics, the College could still only grant *semicha* to its own students. Those who applied from outside the College had to be approved by the Chief Rabbi. This became an issue in 1929 when the qualifications of the minister in Durban, South Africa, Rabbi Levy, were queried.

If *semicha* is granted by rabbis in one country and then the recipient applies for a position in another country, the local Beth Din are often asked to confirm the certification. That is why the question of Rabbi Levy's qualifications were eventually referred back to London. The matter was settled by the Chief Rabbi stating that the rabbis who had approved Levy's *semicha* had provided the necessary documentation, which the London Beth Din had approved, and had then been properly presented by Rabbi Levy when applying for the Durban post. At the same time Hertz was anxious for a separate official body to be set up in London to deal with the bureaucracy in future. He therefore created a Rabbinic Examining Board for candidates who could not be dealt with by the College.

In 1928 there was a large meeting at the Great Synagogue to review the progress of the War Memorial Council. From its inception in 1919, the Council had increased its annual contribution to the College to the present handsome level of £2,000 but, compared to its ambitious initial programme, its progress had been a disappointment. Where £1 million had been the original target, only £150,000 had been raised in the end, of which Hertz had raised more than £50,000. Admittedly, it had been possible to start a pension scheme for the Jews' College staff but, at this point, its funds only amounted to £25,000 where it had hoped for £50,000. For all the initial disagreements, in the years to come it would be the financial contribution of the WMC which helped to keep the College afloat.

The WMC had also supported the Etz Chaim Yeshiva and Aria College, but its main educational achievement had been the introduction of a stiff teacher's examination at Jews' College. In the past three years sixty-six examinees had passed and, of those, forty were now at work. With Büchler as the Chairman of the Central Committee for Jewish Education, the high standards were well maintained.

There were continued attempts to identify the reason for the lack of sufficient numbers of students. One sore point was the question of their authority when they became ministers. Their status in their communities still always seemed to be compared to a Church of England vicar, to the detriment of the Jewish minister. The idea was floated again of creating District Rabbis, so that not everything had to be decided by the Chief Rabbi. The idea got no further than on previous occasions.

In fact, the whole question of the treatment of religious scholars was sadly neglected. At least the graduate students, when they got a congregation, would have a salary, plus income from teaching and officiating at funerals, *brissim*, bar mitzvahs or weddings. For the part-time lecturers at the College, the same could well apply. The lecturers who really had to make substantial sacrifices were the permanent ones. They might write books to augment their incomes, but authors are poorly remunerated unless they appeal to the general public. Otherwise they had to survive on their College salaries which made life very hard.

When asked why they settled for positions which put pressure not only on themselves, but on their families, the answer was their devotion to the cause. They regretted the effect on their loved ones, but they had the support of their wives and they believed 100 per cent in the importance of what they were doing. For the most part, the community took their commitment for granted. In times of difficulty the United Synagogue would recommend reducing their paltry salaries even further. The lecturers were also aggrieved as they felt that their students were treated like servants when they became ministers. They remained, however, totally committed.

That relationship of synagogue and employee still went particularly against the grain of the principals who had come from the Continent. In very Orthodox communities there, most of the rabbis were revered and their word was law. They were spiritual leaders in the true meaning of the words. It wasn't true in a British congregation unless the minister was exceptional. There would be praise for his services, accolades for his knowledge, but it was so obviously shallow when they were eventually left to a penurious old age.

It would have helped if the College could have paid higher salaries and given a good example to the lay leaders, but instead the end of the decade saw the start of the Slump and a disastrous move to a new building.

NOTES

1. *Jewish Chronicle*, 16 February 1923, p.5.
2. Albert Hyamson, *Jews' College 1855–1955* (London: Jews College, 1955), p.100.
3. JCAR.
4. *Jewish Chronicle*, 27 January 1922, p.20.
5. Ibid.
6. *Jewish Chronicle*, 21 March 1924, p.14.
7. *Jewish Chronicle*, 22 October 1920, p.14.
8. *Jewish Chronicle*, 11 December 1925, p.9.
9. Ibid.
10. Opening address by Hertz in 1923 at the Conference of Anglo-Jewish preachers. *Jewish Chronicle*, 20 July 1923, p.18.
11. *Jewish Chronicle*, 11 June 1926, p.16. Rabbi Meir was a second-century sage and the third most mentioned in the Mishnah.
12. JCAR.
13. *Jewish Chronicle*, 11 June 1926, p.15.

CHAPTER SEVEN

Woburn House and the Second World War

Adolph Büchler's lengthy campaign to get a lecturer on Jewish Religious Philosophy and Jewish Theology moved a step nearer in 1929. He got agreement for a research student to go to Germany to study the subjects and £250 to pay for his expenses. The intellectual level of tuition was also improved with the continuation of the Friedländer Memorial Lectures, with papers on Mystic Elements in the Book of Psalms and, in 1931, on Ideals of Education in Rabbinic Simile.

Büchler was still struggling, however, with the accepted qualifications for a minister. There were many congregations in the major cities which had been started as the immigrant Jews succeeded in business and moved to the pleasanter suburbs. These communities needed ministers, and candidates from Jews' College were very acceptable. If they were prepared to accept relatively low salaries, so much the better, and those who had minimum qualifications would come into that category. Büchler didn't want anyone appointed until they had passed the Third Jews' College Examination:

> It is a Jewish Minister's privilege and duty to be armed with the requisite knowledge of Jewish Theology and Rabbinics, in addition to a University Degree, and the essential test of such knowledge is the training imparted at the College as proved by the Qualifying Examination.[1]

The seventy-fifth anniversary of the founding of the College came in 1930 and it was celebrated with a synagogue service and a festival dinner, in conjunction with the United Synagogue who were celebrating their Diamond Jubilee. The Grand Rabbin of France and the Secretary of State for the Dominions were guests, along with the Principal of the University of London and the Provost of University College. Jews' College was now held in high esteem, and fraternal greetings came from as far away as the Jewish Theological Seminary in New York, the Juedisch-Theologisches Seminary in Breslau and the Collegio Rabbinico Italiano in Florence.

The Council, however, never seemed to learn from past mistakes. Just as the stock market crashed and the Slump began, it was agreed with the United Synagogue that the College would move to a new home. It would become the main part of a block of buildings to be built in Tavistock Square, opposite the headquarters of the British Medical Association.

> In addition to ample accommodation for teaching and studying purposes, including the necessary Common Rooms and Refectory, the new Jews' College will have the use on one floor of a large hall, which will also be available for Communal use. This hall will have a seating capacity of 400 persons ... another floor will be devoted to the College Library, with facilities for quiet study and research ... there will also be a small Hall adjoining the Library. The Council feels that it can rely confidently upon the entire Community, both at Home and Overseas, to give it the necessary practical support to bring the scheme to a successful conclusion, so that [it] can start upon its fresh career ... unhampered by financial anxiety.[2]

The grounds for this confidence are difficult to identify. The College had struggled for the past seventy-five years to keep its head above water and it was now proposing to undertake two thirds of the cost of maintaining this large new building. If it was to have a hall capable of seating 400, the rent for the space, once built, would be substantial but the College had no need for it. It would be another ten years before it was regularly used, when the Central Synagogue was bombed during the war and the congregation set up home in the new Adolph Tuck Hall until the synagogue could be rebuilt many years later.

Before that the only item which came under the heading of income from hiring out the hall, was for £54 in the first year, but only £26 had actually been paid a year later. What was extremely helpful was a contribution arranged with the United Synagogue of £1,000 a year for the training of ministers. If the reaction within the Council was 'not before time', it would have been a reasonable comment. Unfortunately, the money would be needed to pay the additional rent which the United Synagogue had managed to persuade the College to underwrite for the new building.

In 1931 there were thirty-seven students and fourteen in the Matriculation class. The country was still in the depths of the Slump but, on the other hand, the number of students was increasing. For this welcome expansion to continue, however, the needs of the students would have to receive more attention.

One long-standing problem that had concerned the Council was the housing of the students. It was now decided to buy a house in Brondesbury, a pleasant part of North London, and use it as a student hostel. It was well run and had a great deal of support, both financially and motherly, from the College's Ladies Auxiliary committee. The problem, which was only recognized too late, was that Brondesbury is a long way from Tavistock Square and a lot of the students found more convenient lodgings nearer at hand.

Between 1931 and 1936, the hostel lost a total of £2,000 (over £100,000 in today's money) and was closed in May 1936 'the Council, however, feel that the experiment was well worth trying.' The students to whom the College couldn't afford to give bursaries would have felt the £2,000 could have been better spent.

The press were becoming critical again: 'It is a regrettable fact that a spirit of unrest and dissatisfaction prevails within the College. It shows itself in the general relationship between the members of the staff and in the demeanour of the students.'[3]

Many of the students did not even choose to attend the official opening of the new College building. There were a number of suggested reasons. That the atmosphere was cramping and the students, often from Oxford and Cambridge, couldn't adapt themselves to the new and strange conditions. That the curriculum might be too ambitious, the hours of study too exacting, the standards of exams too high, and the number of lectures they were expected to attend too great. Those considerations were meant to explain why so many didn't finish the course and decided not to go into the ministry after all.

What were these strange conditions? What was not discussed was the fact that obtaining a degree at Oxbridge at the time was, indeed, far easier than passing Jews' College exams. It was not compulsory to attend lectures at Oxbridge unless you were studying a subject like medicine or law. Arts undergraduates could enjoy an extensive social life and get a degree with a relatively small amount of work.

A great deal of time at Oxbridge could be spent on the sports field, taking part in dramatic productions, or playing a part in one of the numerous university clubs. It was certainly difficult to get into Oxbridge, but once there, it was only necessary to pass exams at the end of each year, and 95 per cent managed to gain some kind of degree. One essay a week, read to a tutor, was often the sum total of the work prescribed. The contrast with the necessary discipline involved in obtaining *semicha* was quite likely to be a shock to all but committed students at Jews' College. Only nobody was going to be so academically off-message as to come out and criticize the standards of Oxbridge.

The concentration on the study of the Talmud at Jews' College left precious little time for anything else. It was expected that students would want to devote their time to study, as rabbinical students had done for centuries past. The lecturers would have expected a level of application to their studies that many students from a gentler academic regime would have found too demanding. The lecturers – led by Adolph Büchler – would have expected and settled for nothing less. They would not have let their standards drop and, after all, probably for the same reasons, there was a considerable dropout rate at Christian theological colleges as well.

It was also a major factor that the Jews' College students effectively were taking two degrees; one on Jewish subjects: Talmud, Shulchan

Aruch, the Bible, Homiletics, Elocution and Hazanut; the other on secular studies, like Latin and Greek, where exams had to be taken, even though few of the students had been introduced to either language at their former schools. Even with that level of work, Büchler had looked for years for a teacher on Jewish Theology and Ethics.

So in 1932, the College moved from Queens Square House to the new building in Woburn Square. It would house not only the College, but also the Jewish Board of Deputies, the War Memorial Council, the United Synagogue and the Jewish Museum. The Museum had a wonderful collection of antique silver, but it would be found to bring its own problems.

Woburn House was planned as a Jewish Communal Centre. It was an idea which had been floated some years before, and now, 'revived in the fertile brain of Sir Robert Waley Cohen, who was still on the Council of the College and, effectively, the Acting President of the United Synagogue'.[4]

The College became part of a new company called Concordia Estates, in which it had two thirds of the shares and was responsible for two thirds of the cost of running the building. Its share of the cost of erecting what became known as Woburn House was £20,000, of which the family of Adolph Tuck provided £5,000 and Saemy Japhet another £5,000. The remaining £10,000 (about half a million pounds in today's money), hung round the College treasurers' necks for many years.

To mark his 60th birthday in 1932 the Chief Rabbi appealed for more annual subscriptions from the community:

> Today the situation has become so critical that the Council is faced with the grave necessity of reducing the stipends of the Professors, besides curtailing the number of the students. Such drastic measures can only be avoided if a considerable number of annual subscriptions – any sum from five shillings [25p] to five guineas [£5.25p] is secured.[5]

Where previous chief rabbis had usually relied on the Council members to solicit additional funds, Hertz remained very much hands-on. His appeal raised £250 in new annual subscriptions, and he also collected £555 in donations. This, as he said, was essential as the Treasurers had to insist that Bursaries be reduced by £500 from an unsustainable £1,800 a year. It was fortunate that the War Memorial Council was still able to provide the College with its annual £2,000.

The College now had its new home and Adolph Büchler gave his views on it in the Principal's Report for 1933. He was, in turn, bitingly sarcastic and hilariously witty. He had the script of a stand-up comedian:

> The hopes, raised in the Council and the lecturing Staff by those responsible for the ambitious and comprehensive change ... and to the promotion of the special work of the lecturers and students in a new atmosphere of an academic character, have not been realised. The general aspect of the section of the imposing building assigned to the College has from the outset stirred, and to this day kept alive, in the lecturers and the students, the desire to return to the old premises in Queens Square House. The magnificent hall assigned to the Library offers the great advantage of uniting in one room the several sections of the Library ... but the presence of the Jewish Museum, placed incongruously in the centre of the same hall, and open to visitors ... impairs the security of the books ... and exposes the Library to unforeseen risks.
>
> The five lecture rooms of the College have ... proved too small for the ordinary needs of the regular instruction, and are acoustically unsuitable for their purpose, not soundproof and exposed to the great noise of the traffic ... the obvious solution to all the difficulties [would be] the removal of the College to a building of its own, as was originally planned.[6]

As still happened periodically over the years, there appeared to be nothing incongruous about the Principal criticizing the decisions and optimistic views of his own Council; if there were ever attempts to get the Principal to tone down his remarks, they either weren't successful, or his original views were even less flattering.

Büchler had done his best, in the most public way, to get the right academic atmosphere and facilities, but the die was definitely cast and the College had to operate in an unsuitable setting at far greater cost than before for many years to come. In the accounts for 1931 the cost of the rent for Queens Square House was £347. In 1937 the Woburn House rent had increased by over 400 per cent to £1,568.

The College was paying the bill for Waley Cohen's Jewish Community Centre, which was a watered down version of his idea ten years before for an Academy. If it had been possible to rent all the available surplus space to other Jewish organisations, as well as the shops on the ground floor, all might have been well. It should have been recognized, however, that the building wasn't in a natural shopping area – it still isn't – even if the Slump couldn't have been foreseen when the original plans were approved.

Waley Cohen was still not able to influence the curriculum at the College, but when it ran into serious financial difficulties trying to pay for the maintenance of his fertile brain's new building, the opportunity would exist to make recommendations to economize on expenditure by cutting down on the academic side. As the financial situation continued to worsen, the College did set up an Economy Committee in 1933 when, 'the annual expenditure of the College has grown considerably, whilst the annual income has remained totally inadequate for its vital needs'.[7]

Sir Robert was also on the Economy Committee. Their solutions were considered by the Council but, led by Büchler, they decided not to reduce the hours of the staff; they agreed that the recommendation to rearrange the curriculum would reduce the efficiency of the teaching and supervision, and that security of tenure for the staff was essential to maintain the academic reputation of the College. It was further decided that salaries would not be reduced; they were low enough in all conscience. In 1931 six lecturers, including Büchler, and two librarians shared just under £4,000. Sir Robert had hit a brick wall again when it came to undermining the College's approach to educating its students. Economies would have to come from elsewhere.

Adolph Büchler, in his Principal's report, spelt out the problems of the less than dedicated student:

> It is to be recorded that some students on account of the difficulty of providing for themselves without receiving any support from the College, others by discovering only some time after entering Jews' College their unsuitability for the Jewish ministry, others again by being drawn away from Jewish studies and attracted to the Bar, left the College in unusually large numbers ... it is to be regretted that the College should have lost students who could no longer continue the struggle against material worries, but whose qualifications justified the hope of the Staff that they would once serve the Community as Jewish ministers.[8]

Another result, which Büchler continued to criticize, was the instances when students were hired for congregations before they had completed their courses. Büchler was insistent that a university degree was not a sufficient qualification for a minister.

Two long-serving members of the staff resigned in 1932: Samuel Daiches and George Washington Kilner. Dr Daiches had taught Bible, Talmud and Homiletics in a career at the College which spanned more than twenty-five years. When he died in 1949, the tributes came flooding in from past students who remembered the affection he had shown for them and the help he was always ready to give when they had problems. His legacy, though, was summed up by a former student in South Africa: 'From Cape Town to Salisbury [Zimbabwe], from Sea Point [South Africa] to Nairobi, Dr. Daiches' disciples are spreading Jewish learning far and wide.'[9]

This was the challenge: to spread Jewish learning. This was the result and the reward Daiches would have wanted above all. For those who remained committed to a career in the ministry, the College discipline, which had been questioned at the time of the move to Woburn House, was the price they were happy to pay to achieve the objective. For those men, it was well worth the effort.

Academically, Daiches' ability would be summed up by Chief Rabbi Israel Brodie, who had been one of his pupils at the College:

> anyone who has read the biblical studies of Dr. Daiches would recall that not only was he equipped with the modern apparatus necessary for the work, but he had the most extraordinary intuition when approaching the Bible. There was love and sympathy, and those two qualities of his approach seemed to evoke a meaning from obscure words which gave sense to the passage and certainly removed all necessity for ill-informed emendations and tinkering with the sacred text, which was so casually produced by some non-Jewish scholars and weak Jewish imitators.[10]

George Washington Kilner had taught at the College for an immense fifty-three years. His responsibility was the teaching of Classics to enable the younger students to get the qualifications they needed in Greek and Latin for University College matriculation. Again, he was both admired and liked for his dedication to the College.

In 1933 Hartwig Hirschfield died. He had taught at the College for thirty-one years until his retirement in 1926. He had first come to the College when the Sephardim closed the seminary in Ramsgate, where he had also looked after the Montefiore Library.

> After a brilliant career in Germany, Hirschfield had been appointed lecturer in Biblical Exegesis [explaining the text] and Oriental Languages ... Having married a daughter of Louis Loewe, the first Principal of the College, also made him in a sense at home there.[11]

Unhappily, the domestic concerns of the College and its students were about to be overshadowed by events abroad. The anti-Semitic legislation of Hitler in Germany led to new entrants for the College. As Büchler reported in 1934, 'In consequence of the almost total exclusion of Jews in Germany from the professions, four lawyers, on passing the prescribed entrance Examination, were admitted into the College proper.'[12]

Another German lawyer also came to the College and, together with his wife, they made great contributions to the community. Isidor Grunfeld was made a Dayan by the Chief Rabbi from 1939–1956, and his wife, Judith, was at the right hand of Rabbi Dr Solomon Schonfeld, one of the pioneers of the modern Jewish faith schools and Hertz's son-in-law.

One post-war innovation which continued to prove very useful was the setting up of the Teachers Examination Committee. While the College had been established to produce ministers, the need for it to produce teachers was considered equally important by the founders. The holiest Jewish prayer, the Shema, instructs parents to teach their children thoroughly, but the personal responsibility they were supposed to shoulder was often delegated, primarily, to Sunday school teachers. If their ability was below par, the children could well be alienated by inadequate teaching. After all, the youngsters went to school every day, they might well go to synagogue on the Sabbath, and then they had further lessons on the Sunday when they would have preferred a day off. *Cheder*, as it was called, could be seen as an intrusion unless the teachers were good – and often, while they were always well meaning, they may have had little previous training in the art.

The core difficulty was that they were not just teaching an academic subject. If you were unsuccessful in teaching chemistry, the student just gave up chemistry; which was no big deal. If you were unsuccessful in teaching Judaism, the students might be tempted to give up their religion when they grew up, which would have rightly been considered disastrous by the parents.

So the need for qualified Hebrew Teachers for the children was always a problem for synagogues, and it was welcome news that a new syllabus had now been introduced at the College with a school-leaving certificate in Hebrew and Religion for successful candidates. In 1935, when it was fully grown, there were over 100 candidates in all and fifty-two passed.

Speech Day in 1936 introduced to the College supporters a Glasgow businessman called Isaac Wolfson. It was Wolfson who built Great Universal Stores and would become the first President of the United Synagogue who had not come from the families of the Cousinhood. Indeed Wolfson came from a very impoverished upbringing, but he financed the creation of both Wolfson College, Oxford and Wolfson College, Cambridge. His contribution to the Jews' College finances in 1936 was a princely £200 (over £10,000 today). It helped, but Jacob Wassermann, the Joint Treasurer, had had enough:

> As for myself, I have, unfortunately, not a single subscriber to my credit. That may be due to my lack of eloquence, but I think it is to be ascribed chiefly to the indifference of my friends to religious matters. There are precious few among them whose children have ever made the acquaintance of a Jewish teacher, let alone a Minister, but Jewish feeling must be engrained in the young.[13]

Wassermann was replaced by Alan Mocatta, a Sephardi representative on the Council, and a distinguished barrister who became a High Court Judge. He would serve the College enthusiastically for the next twenty-five years. Even this was short-term by comparison with Dr Cohen, the Honorary Medical Officer, who died in 1936 after fifty years in office.

A large number of people still thought they could run the College better than the incumbents. A typical exchange of views came in 1937 when the Synagogue Guild for Social Services held a meeting to discuss the future of the College. Ewen Montagu, who would be the last of the Cousinhood Presidents of the United Synagogue, presided.

There was the usual claim that the College hadn't forged a 'keen and ardent sympathy with the rising generation' and should move to the more congenial atmosphere of Oxbridge. This at a time when the Oxford Union voted that it wouldn't fight for King and Country. The Jews' College students were accused of only wanting to make a livelihood and the combination of preacher and *hazan* was regretted, as it was considered that few men could excel at both.

One speaker went so far as to record a report a year or so before, produced by a Special Jews' College committee: 'the report produced as the result of that enquiry was a condemnation of training at the College, yet that report never saw the light of day.' This criticism was balanced out by Ephy Levine, on behalf of the College supporters, telling the speaker that as he wasn't a theologian, he wasn't competent to judge. Ephraim Levine was the son of the minister at Garnethill in Glasgow and won a scholarship at the College which took him to Cambridge in 1903 where he got a first. In 1916 he became the minister at the prestigious New West End Synagogue in London. He stayed in office for thirty-eight years, taught homiletics at the College and became its Hon. Secretary.

Ephy Levine was an inspiring speaker and a great friend of Chief Rabbi Hertz. The saying that Hertz always sought the peaceful solution to a problem when all else had failed, was put down to Levine, though he insisted Hertz had said it first. Ephy Levine anecdotes were numerous. He was, for example, a keen racegoer. At a meeting of the Jewish Historical Society of England, a speaker said that new blood was needed on their council. They should get rid of old wood, like Ephy Levine. One of his friends said that it was unfair to call him old wood; Goodwood, yes! When he died in 1966 at the age of 81, the College lost a firm and constant supporter, and the community lost an inspiration.

There was no one, typical reaction to a student's move from Oxbridge to the College. There was the experience of Eric Lipson, who came from a very religious family in Cheltenham, where a relative of his was Mayor and later MP. Lipson was young, very intelligent and destined to play a large part in the Sheffield Community. 'I came down from Cambridge full of enthusiasm. The conditions at Jews' College were such that I felt my enthusiasm ebb away. If I had any spirituality it seemed to be deadened.'[14]

There was another student, however, who made a point of writing to thank the Council for all the help he had received. This was an Egyptian non-Jew who had asked to attend lectures at the college to enable him to get a BA in Semitic languages. He said that he had been treated like any other student and wrote that he hoped his government would send more students to the College.

Always short of money, run with Spartan-like economy, Jews' College couldn't compete with the immensely rich Oxbridge colleges. The grass in Woburn Square couldn't be as green as the upmarket lawn at the back of Kings College, Cambridge. It was worse than that though. By 1938 it was again found necessary to reduce the amount committed each year in the accounts for bursaries. As Büchler furiously, but accurately, commented:

> The inability of the College to grant bursaries to students has forced several of them to devote the greater part of their free time, which should be given to University and Jews' College work, to travelling and private lessons in order to earn a living. One group of students could not bear the hard and often fruitless struggle of earning a scanty living by private lessons and left the College.[15]

The curriculum was put under scrutiny again, and it was decided to allow three years for the BA Honours degree in Semitics at the University of London, instead of two. It was also agreed to substitute Mediaeval Hebrew texts for Syriac. The resulting changes would take time to implement and were unlikely to be introduced before 1940.

Abraham Cohen (1887–1959) taught homiletics from 1936–38 and on his retirement Israel Brodie took over. This was thanks to the generosity of Israel Sieff of Marks and Spencer, who had undertaken to pay his salary for five years. Meanwhile the number of students was thirty-three, including the Egyptian Moslem.

The graduates were still obtaining ministerial appointments from Becontree to Manchester and with the war looming ever closer, and the need for Chaplains to the Forces on the horizon, there was not likely to be a lack of employment in the next few years. The Teachers' Examinations were still well supported and of the 132 candidates, sixty-nine passed.

The effect of the anti-Semitic legislation on the Continent had undermined the work of the yeshivas, and the Chief Rabbi and the

Principal could see Jews' College becoming the last European theological seminary. Six Austrian and German lawyers, versed in Bible and Rabbinics, had now been accepted into the College to train for the ministry.

Büchler was getting old, and he took the opportunity in his Principal's report of 1938 to record in writing his core beliefs in the mission of the College:

> It would be not only a grave mistake to discourage him [the student] from the necessary study of Talmud and the Codes, but it would, at the same time, lower the esteem in the sight of the students of the Rabbinical Degree and Rabbinical learning, with ultimate consequences harmful to the foundations of Judaism itself. The future of Jewish religious observance depends on the Minister's deeper knowledge of the materials upon which the practice of Jewry throughout the 2,000 years of its European existence has been founded and, unless the teachers and Ministers are trained to become the trusted interpreters of Jewish law, Jewish psychology, Jewish tradition, and the Jewish positive and conservative mind, Judaism in Britain will not remain faithful to its past.[16]

Büchler died within twelve months of this declaration and the Chief Rabbi pointed out that he was more than just a great scholar. He praised 'his iron strength of character, his Spartan sense of duty, his Jewish exaltation of study. Dr. Büchler's strikingly original monographs on the history and theology of first-century Palestine are not easy reading, and are not intended to be; he is the scholar's scholar'.[17] The press were also anxious to emphasize the difficulties he had to overcome in his early days as Principal, to gain recognition of the Rabbinic Diploma as the ultimate goal of the course. He had fought his corner for over thirty years.

Since foreseeing the future at that time was near-impossible, it was decided not to appoint another Principal, and the Chief Rabbi took on the post temporarily. He wasn't well either and made it clear that he hoped he would only need to hold down the post for a short while. Hertz, however, had led the community from the front since 1913 and he never dodged a challenge. He celebrated his Silver Jubilee as Chief Rabbi in 1938 and was given a Special Address by the Council.

For most of its existence the critics of the curriculum at Jews' College had complained of it being too concentrated on Talmud, at the expense of studies in the social sciences. The concern was always whether the graduates would be able to operate in the world outside the academic calm of the seminary.

In 1939, with the outbreak of war, there came the acid test. What could the graduates do for the war effort? Over 60,000 Jews served in the armed forces and more than half the British Jewish Chaplains to the Forces, over forty of them, had been at Jews' College. The Senior Chaplain was Dayan Mark Gollop who had received his *semicha* at the College in 1923. When his health broke down under the strain, he was succeeded by Rabbi Israel Brodie, also a 1923 graduate and a Chaplain in both world wars.

Brodie's elevation was against the wishes of Waley Cohen who worked to have the only Liberal Synagogue chaplain succeed Dayan Gollop. Hertz, pointing out the predominance of Orthodox Jews in the services and the overwhelming proportion of Orthodox chaplains, overruled the committee which nominally had the responsibility for the appointment.

Among the other chaplains was South African, Israel Levinson, who had been at the College when Adolph Büchler first arrived in 1906, and also served in both world wars, as did Arthur Barnett, the long-serving minister at the Western Synagogue, who was there at the same time, and Isaac Livingstone, nicknamed the Vicar of Golders Green due to his elegant clerical appearance.

The Chaplains came from communities all over the country, with the oldest being Benjamin Michaelson, who had got his *semicha* at the College in 1899. Other rabbis from the College included Sheffield Minister, Barnett Cohen (1908), Liverpool Minister, Simon Lehrman (1933) and the future Chief Rabbi of South Africa, Bernard Casper who had been at the College in 1934.

Wolf Morein died soon after he became a Chaplain, as did Emanuel Berry. Harry Bornstein died in 1943 in the Middle East. He had been one of the brightest graduates and an extremely popular student. His loss was very keenly felt. Before the war he had been the first minister at the new Hampstead Garden Suburb Synagogue. On the occasion of the opening of the new annex at the local Henrietta Barnett School, he had been left off the invitation list by Mrs Barnett. The new head teacher said that if he wasn't invited, the head teacher would be missing as well. The invitation was duly sent.

In the heart of London's garment district was the West End Great Synagogue and its minister was Maurice Lew. This was until the war, when he found himself the senior Jewish Chaplain for the India Command at the age of 33. As was pointed out at the time, he had to cover the area from Bombay to Calcutta and from the Himalayas down to Ceylon. Meanwhile, one of his colleagues, Maurice Jaffe, 'has for his parish the whole of the fighting front in Burma'. Jaffe was 27 and made *aliyah* to Israel in 1948. He would be the driving force behind the building of the Great Synagogue in Jerusalem and became the President of the Union of Israel Synagogues.

Maurice Unterman, who was the Minister at the Marble Arch synagogue for many years, was another Chaplain, as was Louis Sanker from Bristol, Arthur Super from Leeds, and Joseph Weintrobe, who later became the Religious Director of the Jewish Concord Hotel in the Catskills in New York State.

It wasn't easy being a Chaplain. Apart from the dangers of war, Simeon Isaacs remembered the difficulty of becoming a vegetarian for the whole six years. The problem paled into insignificance, however, when compared to the experiences of the future College Librarian, Michael Elton. He was attached to the British forces which liberated the Belsen concentration camp. His task was to be in charge of the mass burials of those who had died but remained disinterred. After the war Elton went on to serve the Reform community in Southend.

Most of the Chaplains saw six years of their lives dissipated fighting the enemy, and were desperate to get back to careers as ministers of congregations. When, after the war, the College developed its

Rabbinical Studies programme, the ex-chaplains had the opportunity to add *semicha* to their qualifications and many took it. They worked hard to make up for the years that had passed.

Living through the Blitz, with the possibility of death or injury always present, it is not surprising that people assess their past lives to see whether they did a reasonable job. Saemy Japhet, the Chairman of the College, presided at the 1942 Speech Day and looked back over the forty years he had spent helping the institution. At the turn of the century, he reminisced, 'the College and the community faced each other ... like inhabitants of different spheres'.[18] He felt the old-timers on the Council didn't realize that things had changed. They didn't understand the immigrants who had flooded in from Eastern Europe. Those same immigrants who attacked the College, through the United Synagogue, for not setting high enough standards from their point of view. 'The United Synagogue in those days hated controversial problems. They were annoyed by such attacks and, while resenting them, they turned at the same time against the College, in which they saw the source of the problem.'

Japhet had memories which ignored the imperative need of the impoverished newcomers to find some way of proving their superiority to the Jewish establishment and thereby retaining some self-confidence. He also ignored the desire of the lay leaders for unfettered authority in their congregations. He was on firmer ground when he recalled the reaction of the College Principals: 'Much as they deplored the unwise behaviour of the United Synagogue, they took no notice of it. Jews' College had become a seat of learning, and unmoved by outward influences, they toiled on and worked with a serene demeanour.' Japhet also commented on the occasions when the financial position eased: 'They were, so to speak, nouveau riche, and rather extravagant with their money.'

War did have the effect of eliminating every vestige of unemployment in the ranks of the College graduates. Where they weren't able to join up, they were needed to replace those who had been recruited. They were also needed in areas to which people had fled for safety outside the major cities; there were many communities which suddenly emerged in towns which had never seen Jews in any number before, and they needed spiritual leaders as well. In 1941 graduates were to be found in such unlikely locations as Berkhampstead and Torquay.

The students also acted as liaison officers between the Jewish evacuees and their non-Jewish hosts. One of the effects of the war was that Jewish children in Christian homes, and without Jewish contacts, could well finish up lost to the faith. The College supported the Central Jewish Committee for Problems of Evacuation by paying some of the bills for the students; they were not going to economise on looking after Jewish children.

The effects of the war were many and varied. The first question was whether to stay in London or not? The Council decided to stay put, but to move some of their most valuable books to the country where they would be safe. There was also the question of bomb damage. Being so close to railway stations such as Euston, Kings Cross and St Pancras, the Woburn House area was a prime target for the bombers. As Dr Epstein said years later, in reflecting on his twenty-five years at the College, his record, 'covers also the hard and bitter years when the College seemed to dissolve before our eyes'.[19]

Although large areas of London were devastated, the bigger the building, the less likely it was to be destroyed. The power of incendiary bombs was not great, though land mines could be devastating. Woburn House had its windows blown out on occasions, but the structure of the building withstood the blast of the raids during the Blitz: 'The actual college rooms shared the damage done to Woburn House by air raids, but with remarkable promptitude they were adapted again for academic and social use, so that the state of the walls and some of the windows is the only evidence of disturbance.'[20]

The Central Synagogue was not so fortunate and was totally destroyed. The congregation moved into the Adolph Tuck Hall for the next fifteen years, and their rent reduced that element of the cost of the upkeep of Woburn House.

Many of the students spent time in civil defence, acting as air raid wardens and fire watchers. Those teachers who had moved to the suburbs to avoid the Blitz had additional support for their extra travel costs. Academically, quite naturally, the war concentrated the minds of both students and graduates, and the application of the students to their studies became exemplary. This was particularly praiseworthy as many of the students still had to earn a crust by teaching privately and in synagogue classes.

Financially, the war years meant that private subscriptions were ever more difficult to provide. The income tax rate became astronomic as the government attempted to pay for the war, and charities inevitably suffered. The annual £200 which had been coming from the Rothschilds like clockwork, almost since the College opened its doors, dropped to £150 in 1940, and fell back to its original 1855 figure of £100 in 1941. There was no subscription at all in 1942 but £25 arrived in 1944 and that figure would continue to be provided for the next twenty years. The Memorial Council and the United Synagogue continued to be the College's main support.

As the dreadful news of the Holocaust became more widely known, the College Council and staff realised that they would be the only Jewish seminary left active in Europe. The great yeshiva names of the past, from whom they had gathered so many of their staff, and to whom they looked for great Talmudic scholars, were no more. Jews' College remained alone and the responsibility bore heavily upon their minds. They also mourned the deaths of George Washington Kilner and Pinkus Harris, who had been teaching elocution at the college since 1927.

At the outbreak of the war the students had stopped working on their secular studies and the curriculum had been concentrated into four days a week rather than five. There were many other demands on the students' time in those early years but, in 1943, when things had settled down again, the college reverted to a five-day programme of lectures, and secular studies were restarted.

Indeed it was decided to add another layer to the lectures, and special courses were finally started on Jewish Philosophy, Theology and Ethics under the direction of Dr Epstein. In addition, Dr Ivy Pinchbeck gave lectures on Social Administration and Professor Ginsberg on Social

Psychology. Both the recommended programmes of Adolph Büchler and the United Synagogue Council were finally being satisfied.

What remained a problem was the absence in many of the synagogues of ministers who were now on active service. The students were needed as teachers as well as to replace the ministers. As a consequence the College had perforce to grant leave from their studies to students thus engaged. What concerned the staff was the possibility of students being appointed to permanent roles in the synagogues before they were fully trained, which had happened on occasions before the war as well.

The Chief Rabbi, as temporary principal of the College, arranged a rota by which a different lecturer acted as principal for one term a year. The Council meetings were replaced by joint meetings of the Executive and the Education and Finance Committees. Ephy Levine replaced Dayan Feldman as the Hon. Secretary and also took over Israel Brodie's lectures in Homiletics. Two of his witticisms about sermons have stayed with his pupils over the years: 'If you can't put any fire into your sermons, put your sermons in the fire', and 'If after 10 minutes you haven't struck oil, stop boring.'

Hertz was under great pressure throughout the war. His hearing was adversely affected when he was injured by a bomb falling nearby when in Yorkshire. He had several tempestuous arguments with Waley Cohen on subjects as varied as matzas for evacuated children over Passover, and the replacement for Dayan Gollop as Senior Chaplain when he fell ill. He was also suffering from heart trouble and died very soon after the war ended.

A good case could be made for Joseph Herman Hertz being one of best Chief Rabbis the British community ever had. He wrote more than any of his predecessors, including editing his world-famous *Chumash* and *The Book of Jewish Thoughts*, which comforted servicemen in two world wars and printed half a million copies. He had been instrumental in the decision to produce the Balfour Declaration and his support for the College had never wavered.

He was the first Jew to receive the Order of Merit and, with his son-in-law, Solomon Schonfeld, his Chief Rabbi's Religious Emergency

Council performed particularly well in organising the Kindertransport, and taking care of Jews interned on the Isle of Man.

In 1945 the chairman chosen for the Annual Speech Day was Councillor Abraham Moss from Manchester, who would be elected Lord Mayor in 1953. This was an overdue move in the right direction, to get the provincial leaders to take an interest in the College. The Councillor duly promised to make it his business to further the cause of the College outside London and, in the future, there would be some movement towards that objective.

When Samuel Daiches retired after thirty-seven years' teaching at the College he was awarded the title of Emeritus Professor. Two members of the Council died: Augustus Kahn and the eminent historian, Charles Duschinsky, as well as one prominent benefactor, David Sandelson. Daiches would die only a few years later in 1949.

The number of students at the College averaged about twenty during the war, but there would be a surge in the number of new entrants seeking *semicha* in the years to follow.

The end of the war gave the College an eminence it was heartbreaking to accept. It was now the oldest Jewish Theological College in the world. The mantle was a tragic inheritance from the Holocaust, but its adoption only ensured that the College became more determined than ever to keep the flame of Talmudic teaching burning brightly.

In the years to come, there would be every kind of financial difficulty, but the College was not a business; it was a continuing part of the millennial-old struggle to keep the faith alive and there would always be sufficient support to ensure that it could continue to play its part.

It was also confidently believed that, if all else failed, G-d would provide. There was now work to be done to get back to peacetime conditions. There would be a new principal and a new chief rabbi, as president of the College. Many of the former students would be seeking *semicha* and many of the demobilised members of the armed forces would take up religious careers.

NOTES

1. JCAR.
2. JCAR.
3. *Jewish Chronicle*, 4 March 1932, p.7.
4. Albert Hyamson, *Jews College, London, 1855–1955* (London: Jews College, 1955), p.107.
5. JCAR.
6. JCAR.
7. JCAR.
8. JCAR.
9. JCAR.
10. JCAR.
11. Ibid., p.67.
12. JCAR.
13. JCAR.
14. JCAR.
15. JCAR.
16. JCAR.
17. JCAR.
18. JCAR.
19. JCAR.
20. JCAR.

CHAPTER EIGHT

The Golden Age of Kopul Kahana

The search for a replacement principal outside the College did not produce an acceptable candidate. So the Council took the wise decision to appoint Isidore Epstein as Director of Studies in 1945. When he took over, though, there were only five students on the register. When he was appointed Principal in 1948 the number had swelled to over fifty.

In 1946, after thirty-eight years in the post, Arthur Marmorstein died in harness. Born in Hungary in 1882, he had taught the codes since Adolph Büchler had recruited him before the First World War in 1912. A self-effacing academic, he had studied at the famous yeshiva at Hildesheimer and was a well-liked teacher. When he died he was the senior member of staff and noted for his prodigious memory and indefatigable industry. As Epstein wrote: 'There is scarcely a scientific journal in the world devoted to Jewish or allied studies to which he was not a frequent contributor.'[1]

The Hungarian triumvirate of Hertz, Büchler and Marmorstein now gave way to a more international grouping of British, Lithuanian and Polish scholars. The immediate post-war students were often very different from the youngsters who had come to the College before 1939. When they were demobilised, they were in a hurry to make up for the years they had lost fighting the enemy. They were much more mature and many had experiences they would rather forget, helping to liberate concentration camps, comforting the badly injured and the dying. They attacked their studies with great energy and were the example that lecturers would point to in future years as the ideal intake.

Isidore Epstein was anxious to extend the opportunities for Jewish education to the general Jewish public and, in 1947, in cooperation with the University of London, a series of university extension courses was started. These were aimed at lay people, and took place in the evenings. In the first year as many as 120 signed up and, in the opinion of the University Registrar, it was the most successful course in which he had been involved.

The training of the students followed the usual line. They were accepted in the first place if they had matriculated and then passed the College entrance exam. At the end of their first year they were expected to pass the Intermediate Arts Exam, and at the end of their third year the University of London Arts Examination. At the end of year five they were ready to obtain the Minister's Diploma and if they worked on for another two years they would be equipped to obtain *semicha*.

Epstein's reputation was such now that he was invited to take part in the University's Academic Procession on the occasion when degree certificates were handed to successful candidates. The courses continued to be organised until he retired from the College.

In February 1946 Epstein had also introduced a Rabbinical Diploma Course which he announced as the first major effort to train rabbis since the Resettlement in England. Fifteen students, mostly former graduates of the College, had taken the opportunity now offered.

Also, in 1947, the College introduced a special course for the training of *hazanim*. Many of the *hazanim* in British synagogues had been trained in Europe and that source of supply was, alas, no longer available. The Rev. S. Pincasovitch was recruited for the purpose and the United Synagogue financed the development as they finally recognized the obvious fact that they would be the main beneficiaries.

The curriculum for *hazanut* was extensive and the course took three years of study. In general the students needed to learn pitch and sight singing, voice culture, the rudiments of musical theory, and modulations – intervals, tetra chords, keys and modes. The specifically *hazanut* subjects included Hebrew music and its origins, the reading of the law and *seder ha-Tefillah* (the order of prayer). In 1951 there would be a diploma for passing a *hazanut* examination. Unhappily, Rev.

Pensacovitch died in 1952 which was a severe loss as: 'his rare musical gifts, as well as his unequalled power in the interpretation of Synagogal music and song, have proved an inestimable asset to the College in its efforts to provide for the training of *Hazanim* for Anglo-Jewish congregations'.[2]

Some of the students had come to Britain as refugees after the war. One who made a great impact was Simon Hass who had endured dreadful experiences in Eastern Europe before joining the College in the *hazanut* class. Hass had a most beautiful voice and was soon snapped up by the Central Synagogue as their *hazan*. For many years it was Hass who was asked to sing at important community services, and the sufferings he had seen were only recalled on Yom Kippur when, during the memorial service, with his voice breaking, he would name the concentration camps where so many had died.

In 1948 a lectureship in Modern Hebrew was established in the name of Rev. J.K. Goldbloom, one of the veteran leaders of the Hebrew Cultural Movement in Britain. It was sponsored by the Education Department of the Zionist Federation and the lectures were to be delivered in Hebrew. The restoration of Hebrew as a modern language with modern literature was a priority with the establishment of the State of Israel. Over the centuries Hebrew had never become a dead language, but before 1948 it was used as a lingua franca by very few people: 'The purpose of the lectures is to emphasise the spiritual value of Hebrew Literature, from Moses Chayyim Luzzatto to the present day, which have contributed so greatly to the revival of Hebrew literature in its modern form.'[3]

By 1949, Epstein had recruited Kopul Kahana (1895–1978) to replace Arthur Marmorstein and had twenty-two students studying for *semicha*, apart from those studying *hazanut* and for diplomas. The question arose at the Council of whether the College should teach *shechita* (the slaughter of animals for food by the most humane method) as many ministers did not have sufficient understanding of the topic. Kahana explained the subject in his lectures, but the detailed teaching of *shechita* was best undertaken by Yeshiva Etz Chaim and it was agreed that, as they taught it thoroughly, it was not necessary for the College to do so as well. At the College Abraham Cohen returned to teach homiletics in 1950 until his death in 1957.

In 1949 Dayan Moses Hyamson died in New York at the age of 86. He had been in charge of the *semicha* examinations at Jews' College for some time at the turn of the century, but had taken the very Orthodox pulpit of Orach Chaim in New York, when Chief Rabbi Hertz relinquished the position on taking up his office in London.

Hyamson had found no conflict of interests in accepting the role of Rabbinic Vice President of the Union of Orthodox Jewish Congregations of America and, at the same time, a Professorship at the Jewish Theological Seminary in New York from 1915 to 1940. It would only be after his death that the Seminary moved towards the Progressive theology it holds today.

From now on, it is possible to add to the records of Jews' College the personal reminiscences of more of the students. Happily, there are still alumni of Jews' College who were studying there fifty years ago, and remain alive and well. It is, therefore, possible to get first hand accounts of what the College was like in those far-off days.

Among the overseas students who came to Jews' College at the time was Raymond Apple, who would become the minister of the Bayswater and then Hampstead Synagogue, before he went back to his native Australia and served as the minister of the Sydney Great Synagogue, becoming the *Ab Beth Din*. Looking back in retirement in Jerusalem in 2015, he recalls being at the College from 1958:

> I grew up in an Australia that still called Britain 'home'. It was more or less natural that when I wanted Judaica training I should go to London (these days the options are quite different and it would have been Israel). I went by sea and spent much of the voyage reading the Hertz *Chumash*. I arrived at the College on a Sunday afternoon and was daunted when I met Dr Epstein in his top hat – he had just been to the opening of the new Central Synagogue. Fortunately I settled down well and made friends. As I got up early in the morning, they got me to walk up and down with the bell to wake people for *davening*. Dr Epstein said we

were one of the best generations of College students and indeed almost all of us remained in the ministry; the few who dropped out were exceptions to the rule. I had the largest bedroom because I had come the furthest with a cabin trunk of books.

The first few days were spent seeing London, including Buckingham Palace, and being entranced by the Jewish bookshops. It was revolutionary when they started the Teachers' Institute with women students; the first marriage was that of Marian and myself in 1960. Since I spent so much time on my typewriter (these days it would have been a computer) my fellow-students were amazed that I had any time for other things like girls. I got involved in the extracurricular activities of the College, e.g. the intercollegiate debating competition, IUJF [Inter-University Jewish Federation] and the College Union Society, of which I was secretary and then president.

I was a bit older than many of the other students because I had been to university first, and indeed I tried to replicate university life in the College microcosm. Until now I had lived at home and it took time to get used to a residential college with Mr Poulson, the caretaker, complaining that we left the bathrooms dirty, the warden and matron, Harold and Hannah Levy, not entirely succeeding as in loco parentis, and the cook, Miss Arons, not completely happy with us (one day she and I had a shouting match but we ended up the best of friends).

I learnt a few things about diplomacy from the Secretary, Mr Stephany. I enjoyed most of the lectures, but had never studied Talmud, so it was a triumph when Dr Zimmels (who taught us the difficult tractate of *Hullin*) told his wife, 'If Mr Apple says he understands the Gemara, he understands it!'

The only College teacher of my generation with any feeling for the ministerial career was Epstein (behind his back we called him Eppie), and Marian and I had great affection for him and his wife Gertrude, who were *Unterfuhrers* when we got married.

Gertie discovered that Moshe Golomb was a good mimic and she urged him to mimic her husband for her entertainment;

fortunately Moshe had more sense. But if Moshe got back to College at night after the front door was locked I would hear (from my 3rd floor bedroom) a squeaky Epstein-like voice calling 'Apple! Apple!' from the street and I had to throw down the key.

Naphtali Wieder [who taught Liturgy, Midrash and Talmud] was not a personal but a scholastic inspiration. Eli Cashdan [who taught Bible] was warm and loving and probably the best teacher of the lot. Zimmels was a great savant but not much of a personality. Kahana was the only one who gave us a feeling for rabbinic learning and he tried to be a father to his students and encouraged them to cry on his shoulder. He was small in size but a giant in learning. He picked up English by listening to the BBC in Manchester during the war.

When the College offered a hundred pound prize (big money in those days) for a research essay, he told me to enter because no-one else wanted to and I would win unopposed. I had to bring my draft to him at home and all he did was to tell me how to phrase certain points in better English (he made no comment on the content). He possibly had a wife in pre-war Poland but, if so, what happened to her we never knew. His wife Ada disappeared from the scene, possibly because she got fed up with him. He had terrible eyesight but his photographic memory meant that he knew what was in every book. When we were learning the laws of Shechitah and I asked why I had to know this, since even then I did not want to eat meat, he said, 'You learn it for the *lomdus* [deeper understanding]!'

He enjoyed conspiratorial anti-Jacobs [Rabbi Dr Louis Jacobs] talks in the corridor with his colleagues. Before leaving the lecture room he told us to work out a *Tosafot* [mediaeval commentary on the Talmud]; when he came back he quizzed us and gave us barely a pass mark. We said, 'Rabbi Kahana, you explain it then!' He did so brilliantly and said he gave himself 95 per cent. We said, 'Why not 100 per cent?' and he answered, 'Because only God gets 100 per cent!' Aged about 75 he went to a secretary somewhere to teach him how to type (he wrote or intended to write a whole sheaf of books) and asked her whether he would be able to type by the time he was 70. She replied, 'It won't take you 15 years!' So however lonely he was at home, his life and his fun were his classroom.[4]

After the war Jews' College remained the only theological seminary in the British Commonwealth but it was now far more than that; it was the only seminary left flying the flag for European Jewry. Part of its raison d'être, in the eyes of the surviving Jews, was to prove that the Nazis hadn't won, and never would as long as institutions like the College survived.

The Chief Rabbi, after Hertz died in 1946, was Israel Brodie who, as the Senior Jewish Chaplain to the Forces during the conflict, had seen at first hand the horrors of the Nazi concentration camps and the total destruction of the intellectual and Talmudic life of the Jews on the Continent. In a sermon, he recalled watching the surviving remnants of one camp gathered round a blackboard, learning Hebrew. On the blackboard was written: 'I am going to Israel, You are going to Israel, We are going to Israel.' Brodie was deeply affected and the audiences listening to him were equally moved.

The Holocaust had done its worst and, effectively, all that remained in good order in Western Europe was the United Kingdom Jewish community and Jews' College. Brodie realized that this would have to be the lighthouse for the renewal of European Jewry. In Isidore Epstein he had a first class lighthouse keeper.

In Kopul Kahana, Epstein had, in his turn, brought in a teacher who could attract and inspire the students to achieve higher degrees. *Semicha* was finally more than a distant possibility and at last the community was coming round to the idea that it was an advantage to have clergy with traditional rabbinical learning. When Cyril Shine was appointed as minister at the prestigious Central Synagogue in London, it was on condition that he gained *semicha*, which he did at the College.

Kopul Kahana was a Lithuanian authority on Jewish, Roman and English Law. He was short, nondescript, and had thick pebble glasses. He had emigrated from Poland to Cambridge before the war, learned

English almost from scratch, and produced a doctoral thesis in a few months instead of the prescribed few years. Cambridge gave him an M.Litt., as the thesis was good enough for a doctorate but they couldn't deal with the speed of its production.

Epstein knew Kahana was a Talmudic giant, and recruited him to teach Talmud and Codes at the College. When the new Rabbinical Diploma Course was started, in his first year eighteen students applied to join it. Fifteen of them were already ministers, but without *semicha*. By 1947 he had thirty *semicha* students and during his time at the College over fifty were granted the diploma.

Kahana was said to be able to quote the exact words on any page of the Babylonian Talmud. When he died in 1978, he was recorded as having said: 'There are only three outstanding Jewish scholars in this country; Dayan Abramsky, Rabbi Rabinow and myself – and not necessarily in that order.'[5]

Meanwhile the Sephardim had their own challenges. In 1949 they had appointed their first Haham since 1917. Solomon Gaon had been brought over from Bosnia before the war as a *hazan* and had been enrolled at Jews' College to study for his *semicha*. This he was awarded in 1948 and the next year he was elevated to Haham. Solomon Gaon would remain Haham for twenty-eight years and during that time he would also serve as the Deputy President of the College.

The relations between the Hahamim and the lay leaders of the Sephardi community had often been difficult in the past. Indeed, when the incumbent died or retired, it was often many years before the Elders of the community took the plunge again by appointing a successor. In the years between the appointment of the first Haham, Jacob Sasportas in 1664 and the present day, there have been 187 years when there was a Haham in office and 165 when there wasn't.

The other, and more serious, difficulty the Sephardim faced, after the establishment of the State of Israel in 1948, was that their communities in North Africa were soon under attack and disintegrating. The religious life of the congregations lacked leadership and so the British community set about solving the problem. They recreated the Judith, Lady Montefiore, College in Ramsgate and offered scholarships to men from North Africa who would come to be trained as ministers and teachers.

The only condition was that, on qualification, they would return to their homes in North Africa and teach for three years. The College reopened in 1953 and a steady flow of students helped a great deal. In 1961 it would remove to London, because the lack of a community in Ramsgate, itself, divorced the students from a wide Jewish environment. The College would continue its work until 1985 when the supply of applicants from North Africa dried up.

In 1955 the College was 100 years old and the Chief Rabbi took the opportunity to reminisce on his own experiences as a minister in Melbourne thirty years before. It illustrated the challenges for which the College had prepared them:

> We were of those alumni of the College who were encouraged, persuaded and recommended by the Chief Rabbi of our time to leave our homes and associates to carry the sustaining message of our ancient faith to congregations in distant parts of the Empire, as also to communities in the United States of America ... we had been stimulated by the inspiration, instruction and personal interest of beloved teachers, known for their scholarship, their understanding and piety ... Loneliness of the spirit can be the despairing experience of those whose cherished ideals and outlook are out of harmony with the prevailing excitement and eager concentration in material speculation characteristic of pioneering and developing virgin countries ... They [the rabbis] demonstrated that the Jewish contribution to the welfare of their country could be expressed in the arts and sciences as well as industry and trade, with which latter it is more usually identified.[6]

The year 1956 saw the arrival at the College of one of those men who was more than happy to devote his life to studying and teaching Judaism. Irving Jacobs would be a student until 1962, when he went on to serve as the Sutton Synagogue minister for the next three years. He went back to the College in 1965 to teach Bible, Liturgy, Rashi and

Hebrew and obtained his doctorate from the University of London in 1970.

He was made Senior Lecturer in 1976 and Dean of the College in 1984. In 1991 he was appointed Principal and retired through ill health in 1993. Dr Jacobs, apart from those three years at Sutton, spent thirty-seven years at the College. In 2015 he looked back over his lifetime:

> I was dyslexic when nobody knew much about it. So I failed my 11 plus exam but our rabbi told my father I shouldn't be written off and he taught me for years until I went to the College. The College was a revelation and I immediately fell in love with the vibrant Jewish atmosphere I found there. You couldn't find that in an average Jewish community in London like West Ham.
>
> The College wasn't a yeshiva. A yeshiva is a monolithic institution with no interest in academia. The College was a rabbinical seminary, which meant that it believed that Jewish scholarship should be a matter of scientific study in a historical context.
>
> The Principal, Dr Epstein, was regarded with much affection. Kahana with adoration. Education was taken seriously, though. If you didn't turn up for a lecture you were hauled over the coals. With Rabbi Wieder, if you had turned up without a jacket, he wouldn't have let you into the room. Wieder was the strong influence. He was a mixture of Berlin academia and Hungarian Chassidism.
>
> As a full-time lecturer, you didn't have the income of those ministers who came part-time. It was tough. I couldn't afford a car and I didn't have a new suit for ten years. Even in 1977 when I was appointed the first Sir Israel Brodie Chair in Biblical Studies, there was no increase in my salary. There had been a lot of money raised for the Chair but the financial situation of the College was so dire that it had to be used to reduce the overdraft.
>
> That kind of commitment is hard on the family as well, but my wife and I agreed that the College was worth it.[7]

That depth of commitment is still not recognized by the community as a whole, but the survival of Judaism in Britain depends on there being enough men and women who are prepared to make great sacrifices for the common good. Irving Jacobs was a great advertisement for the College's ability to train students to the highest level. Jacobs was a Londoner without the scholastic background of the great Continental yeshivot. He still became an internationally recognized lecturer, speaking, for example on 'The Selection of Proemial' [introductory discourse] and 'Proof-Texts in Aggadic Midrashim', in Boston to the American Association for Jewish Studies in 1990. He spoke in Israel and, in 1992, he was back in America, chairing a session of the Centre for Medical Ethics programme. He also spoke to organizations all over Britain. When London University created an MA in Jewish Studies, he was the first Chairman of the Board of Examiners. The reputation of the College outside the British community was enhanced by his efforts and those of his colleagues.

Adolph Büchler's initial criticisms of Woburn House as a centre for Jews' College as far back as 1933 had not been able to be corrected: 'The Council are conscious that there is considerable dissatisfaction with the present inadequate accommodation. Apart from the inadequacy of the facilities now available in its home, the College has a right to resemble a College in the generally accepted view of what such an institution should be.'[8]

From the time of his installation, the Chief Rabbi had wanted a building for the College which would be more than a Woburn Square office block. So he set out to raise the necessary capital by launching the Jews' College Centenary Building and Endowment Fund in 1954. It would be a monument to the fallen yeshivot, which was a defiant gesture, when the sorrow of the survivors of the Holocaust was still overwhelming. The target was set at £250,000 (over £5 million in today's money). Unfortunately, to slightly paraphrase, the road to disaster was once again paved with good intentions.

It was one thing to raise money for a building, but the elephant in the forward planning room was that it would have to be maintained. That had been the problem for the College since its inception 100 years before. The optimists, once again, decided to rely on the generosity of the community for both the structure and the ongoing expense.

That was the unfulfilled hope which had sustained all the Chief Rabbis and their supporters from Nathan Marcus Adler onwards. The maintenance of Jews' College had, however, never depended in extremis on the charity of the community; it had depended on the generosity of individual members, and if there ever came a time when a white knight did not come galloping to the rescue of the annual deficit, any major financial burden could well drag the college down.

A suitable site was found in Montagu Place, but planning permission was needed for the building. Although ten years had passed since the end of the war, much of London was still in ruins and permits to buy scarce building materials were still difficult to obtain. The Minister of Town & Country Planning eventually gave his permission in July 1954 and the aim was to have the building opened in time for the centenary of the College.

Alan Mocatta, the Chairman of the Council, set out with the Chief Rabbi to raise the money, and if the opening had to be delayed, at least the foundation stone was laid in November 1955, exactly 100 years after the opening of the original building in Finsbury Square.

Both President and Chairman worked extremely hard and the first £125,000 had been raised by January 1955. As was pointed out by the Chief Rabbi, three quarters of the money had come from a few individuals, but fund raising dinners were held all over the country, with Brodie and Mocatta speaking in support of the venture. Leeds produced £6,400, Manchester £5,000. Cricklewood in London £2,500.

There were valuable contributions from other communities, large and small. A reader's desk for the College synagogue was donated by the Wanstead and Woodford Synagogue Ladies Guild, together with a fine *sefer torah* mantle. An antique *yad* [pointer] came from Mrs Ephraim Levine and there was a silver *kiddush* cup donated as well. A fine display cabinet for the library's treasures came from the Dollis Hill Synagogue Ladies Guild.

The fact remained, however, that in December 1956 the fund had reached £200,000, but the cost of the building was now estimated to involve a great deal more expense. So the Chief Rabbi called together the representatives of twenty-three London synagogues to get them to make an even bigger effort. In addition, Fanny Brodie, his wife, organized the Ladies Guilds of the synagogues and this produced £4,000 to pay for the kitchen equipment.

In February 1957 Montagu Place was finally opened, but Alan Mocatta sounded a grim warning: 'the amount so far raised for the Centenary Building and Endowment Fund will not nearly suffice to meet the additional expenditure which will be incurred in the new premises.[9]

By 1958 he predicated a loss of £15,000 a year and pointed out that there had been a deficit every year since 1947. The £1,000 given by the South African Board of Deputies in 1955 had helped, but it was too little, if not yet too late. The total loss for those ten years had been over £27,000 (£500,000 in today's money). In fairness, the building itself, into which the College moved from Woburn House, was certainly worth the wait.

The loss for 1958 was, in fact, £13,000 even though the College had been launched with a dinner which 800 guests attended at the very five star Grosvenor House Hotel. Where the opening ceremonies were in the books as costing £1,300, there is no indication that the inaugural dinner produced a commensurate profit. If the tickets for the dinner had been increased in price by £10, which would have been unlikely to have aroused many objections, the deficit could have been substantially reduced. Another Treasurer, David Franklin, resigned at this point after ten years service.

Whilst the new synagogue at Marble Arch was being erected, the members used the synagogue at the College for their services. At no time over the next few years were they charged as much as £10 a week rent. The alternative was to hire a cheap hall somewhere, but the new synagogue at the College was beautiful and the Marble Arch members were well-to-do.

On the last Speech Day, when the College was still in Woburn House, Dr Epstein summed up what had been achieved since they first moved there in 1932:

> According to my computation, based on our Annual Reports, eighty-seven ministers, thirty-three of whom have also qualified as rabbis, have during these twenty-five years proceeded from these walls. These include the Haham, two members of the Beth Din, the Senior Chaplain of HM Forces, and many other distinguished rabbis and ministers in leading positions, both at home and in communities overseas. We have also trained fourteen *hazanim*, of whom not a few hold today important positions in London and the provinces, and also thirteen educationalists, two of whom have recently been appointed to Chairs of Semitics at American Universities. In the strictly academic sphere eighty-four students have obtained through the College the BA Hons Degree of the University of London, twelve the MA Degree and twelve had conferred on them the Doctorate of the University.[10]

Since the period covered the war years, the record was even more commendable.

The Chief Rabbi was a good fund raiser, but he had sewn the seeds for the College to sink even further into debt. There remained practically no income from the students in fees, the adverse effects of inflation were now well known, and if the banks were prepared to give the college credit – at considerable rates of interest – there would inevitably come a time when they would want their money back. Optimistic as he was, the Chief Rabbi admitted publicly to 'a degree of trepidation'.

Another of the students at the time had come from Gateshead Yeshiva. Rabbi Jeffrey Cohen, who built the Stanmore community over many years into a pillar of the United Synagogue, had gone to Gateshead immediately after he had done his School Certificate – today's GCSEs:

> My father was a successful optician in Manchester and was very happy that I wanted to be a rabbi. The great yeshivas in Israel at the time would never have considered an applicant with as little

knowledge as I had, even though I had attended every evening and on Sunday morning the Manchester Yeshivah *cheder* for five years. Gateshead, however, had no entrance exam and were happy to take those who had a vocation but no record of full-time study.

I stayed at Gateshead for three and a half years. It was a very spartan regime with only one bath per twenty students, so we went to Newcastle on Fridays to the public baths. The standard of Talmudic learning was high and it was totally dedicated to producing worthy graduates. There was also a *Mashgiach* [moral tutor] to monitor the behaviour of the boys and the faculty considered themselves in loco parentis for them.

At 19 I went on to Jews' College. When I told my tutor at Gateshead, he said 'And you want my blessing for that!' Gateshead did not consider Jews' College sufficiently Orthodox and it was implacably opposed to studying religious texts from a critical historical perspective. At the time the College had recently moved into Montagu Place which was absolutely palatial compared to Gateshead. There were over twenty bedrooms for the students and I remember on my first day being invited to the room of one student who offered me a drink from a cocktail cabinet! There was even a stag party for Cyril Harris [later Chief Rabbi of South Africa] who was getting married. It was a totally different atmosphere from Gateshead, with no attempt to dictate any particular religious standard.

Basically, Jews' College was run like a university college. There was a separate Institute of Jewish Education in the building and they got me through my A Levels which I needed to go on to get a degree. There was a very effective non-Jewish woman teacher, Dr Williams, who enabled us to pass our English Literature exam within one academic year – eight months.

The Principal, Isidore Epstein, had recruited a good faculty of teachers and under the tutelage of Kopul Kahana it was possible to study part-time and get *semicha* at the College. Kahana was certainly a Talmudic genius but he could be cutting in dealing with comments from the class. I think he was a lonely and introverted man.

> There were two inspiring teachers; Eli Cashdan and Naphtali Wieder. They were very different but equally effective. Eli Cashdan taught Bible and his lessons were always great fun. He was a father figure and much loved. Naphtali Wieder moulded us all. He was a brilliant lecturer and a great scholar. His lessons were full of dramatic impressions, as he walked up and down, and he demanded total concentration from the class. If you dropped a pencil, you wouldn't pick it up for fear of stopping the flow.
>
> What he told us he wanted was rabbis who were also scholars. His view on marriage was that you should study for twenty years and then think about it. He, himself, got married very late in life.
>
> Of course, I was there in Louis Jacobs' time as well. He was a great friend and the idea was that he would take over when Isidore Epstein retired. Only the Principal didn't want to retire and I think he was, therefore, implacably opposed to Louis Jacobs, particularly as he was the blue-eyed boy. I don't think it was an accident that he was allocated the section of the syllabus dealing with Biblical Criticism issues because his views were always controversial. He seems to have been given sufficient rope to hang himself.
>
> With Louis Jacobs there was an aura of spirituality and he was a very impressive human being. He was deeply interested in the welfare of the students and he had a passion for intellectual honesty. I'm sure he wouldn't have approved of the present-day philosophy of the movement he started, because he would have thought it a distortion of his views.[11]

One of the graduates was to be connected with the College for the next sixty years. Abraham Levy came from a Gibraltar Sephardi family of rabbis who could trace their lineage back to at least the seventeenth century. The Levy family's attitude towards the role of a rabbi was the one based on ancient tradition; that rabbis shouldn't earn anything from carrying out their sacred tasks. Instead they should have occupations and, as a result, the Levy family were comfortably off.

Abraham Levy was sent to the Jewish Boarding School, Carmel College, and went from there to Jews' College at 17 as soon as he had completed his O Levels, as GCSEs were known then. He had always wanted to be a rabbi. When his headmaster, Rabbi Kopul Rosen, had asked the class who did, he was the only boy to put up his hand.

At Jews' College he passed his A Levels and joined the new Rabbinic Diploma Class of Kopul Kahana:

> Kopul Kahana taught Codes, the anglicised term for the Shulchan Aruch. His field was Jewish Law and he had been taught by the greatest expert on the subject in Eastern Europe – the Chofetz Chaim, Rabbi Yisrael Meir Kagan. He was so knowledgeable that he even had a dispute with Blackwell, the great British jurist. When Isidore Epstein started a Rabbinic Diploma Class, it made all the difference.[12]

The status and validity of any *semicha*, though, depended internationally on the standing of the rabbis who awarded it. Kahana had the necessary reputation.

Abraham Levy obtained the Ministerial diploma, got his *semicha* in 1968 and went on to gain a doctorate for a thesis on 'The Court Jews in 14th and 15th century Castile'. Abraham Levy has fond memories of his early days at Jews College aged seventeen. He was interviewed by Isidore Epstein, Abraham Cohen and Sir Alan Mocatta, the chair of the council. He learned many lessons at the college; for example, he often points out to young rabbis the importance of punctuality by telling them that he had been told to meet Eli Cashdan at nine am on the first day of term. The day before he caught a bus to see how long the journey would take, to make sure he wouldn't be late for his appointment.

After Rabbi Levy left the college he remained the Chair of the Union Society, so his connection with the college wasn't broken. When he was doing his rabbinical diploma from 1962-1967, he had lectures on Monday, Tuesday and Wednesday. By then he was a Sephardi minister in London and Kopul Kahana would tell the students to make sure that none of their congregants died on those days! Eventually when Haham Gaon retired Rabbi Levy replaced him as Deputy President, representing The Spanish and Portuguese Community.

In the 1970's Nahum Rabinovitch was Principal. He was a brilliant mathematician and a brilliant halachist[13] but Rabbi Levy thinks he felt that Anglo Jewry was too immersed in its own religious politics and not enough in serious Jewish scholarship. He believes Rabinovitch never really felt at home in this country.

On 20 February 1957 the 100th Annual Report was produced for the Annual General Meeting. In it was a list of the synagogues which had made official contributions of £10 or more to the College funds, as against bursaries and scholarships, over the 100 years. There were just thirteen of them; five in London, six in the provinces and two in Rhodesia (Zimbabwe).

The largest single contribution from a synagogue over the years was £100 from St Johns Wood in London. By contrast, the Centenary fund produced over fifty contributions from synagogues, but the largest cheque for £5,000 came from the property developer Harold Samuel, and was greater than the donations of all the synagogues put together. Lord Bearsted (Marcus Samuel [1853–1927] the founder of Shell) gave £2,000, and The Hon Mrs Nellie Ionides, his daughter, £600. Such limited support was the norm with the community. It was no wonder that Jews' College was still being referred to as the Cinderella of Jewish Charities.

The student intake at the college was improving. In 1957 there were twenty-eight students, plus fourteen studying for *semicha* and eight for *hazanut*, a total of fifty, in addition to which another eight were doing research for PhDs. In 1959 there were seventy students in all.

Jewish schools were slowly growing in popularity and more Jewish teachers were needed. It had been a problem for a long time. One of the few Jewish boarding houses in the country, Hillel House at the Perse School in Cambridge, had to be shut because, in 1948, no suitable Jewish housemaster could be found to take on the responsibility. There was also a need to improve the standard of teachers at cheder – Sunday morning Hebrew classes in the synagogues.

The United Synagogue organization dealing with the problem was the London Board of Jewish Religious Education (LBJRE) and, in 1949, they had agreed with the College to set up a Faculty for the Training of Teachers. By 1956, however, it had to be admitted that this initiative had failed to attract many students, and discussions were opened to see what changes might be beneficial.

It was the view of the College and of the Chief Rabbi that producing a course which would culminate in a London University degree would be the answer, but the LBJRE rejected the solution. Their objection was attributed to the cost involved, though there were funds available from German reparations. The more likely suggestion was that a degree course could only be undertaken by the College and this would reduce the LBJRE to a subsidiary position.

The Chief Rabbi asked the LBJRE to accede to the idea but his appeal was turned down. The other possibility was for the College to go it alone, even with the additional costs involved. This was the solution adopted, and in July 1957 a BA course for intending teachers was inaugurated. The LBJRE said they would support it but take no responsibility for it. An Institution of Teacher Training (ITT) was, therefore, set up and by 1958 had twenty students, including four women. The problem of a lack of teachers was being addressed, but the deficit increased as a result.

The ITT had its own Board and Executive with thirty members. They included the Chief Rabbi and the Haham, the Principal of the College, the headmaster of the highly successful Hasmonean School for Boys, two treasurers, Dr Snowman, the Medical Officer, four members of the clergy, three lawyers, and many distinguished laymen. What it lacked was the financial support which might have come from the membership of the chairmen of major Jewish companies.

In 1959, the College Union Society celebrated its Diamond Jubilee. Throughout its sixty years it had welcomed many distinguished speakers and kept going through two world wars. During the College's centenary year in 1955, 'A long awaited lecture was given by General

Yigal Yadin on "The Use of T'nach [the Bible] during the Israeli War of Independence".'

There was also a contribution from Rabbi Dr Louis Jacobs on 'The Use of Chassidic Material in Sermons', and the Presidential Address was delivered by the eminent Jewish Historian, Cecil Roth, on 'The Science of Judaism in England'. Dr Epstein also spoke at the Jubilee lunch and was able to compare the present facilities very favourably with the 'poor and limited' ones the initial meetings had taken place in.

In 1960 the centenary of the College Library was celebrated and Isidore Epstein reviewed the scope of the British contribution to Jewish scholarship. Before the library grew to its present size of 60,000 volumes, the largest collection in the country had, in fact, been at the Bodleian Library in Oxford, which had spent over £2,000 in 1829 on the collection of Rabbi David Oppenheim of Prague. His 7,000 books and 1,000 manuscripts had been researched and catalogued by Adolph Neuberger, who had introduced his one-time assistant, Adolf Büchler to Britain.

Epstein rightly felt that the publications of Jews' College lecturers were often overlooked by the Jewish community in Britain. Their contribution had, however, been very considerable and Epstein particularly emphasized the work of Samuel Hirsch who had taught at the College from 1875–1912 and whose *Cabbalist and other Essays* had aroused widespread interest.

There was also Dr Hartwig Hirschfield (1854–1934) who became a great authority on Jewish/Arabic History and edited the Arabic text of Judah Halevi's *Kuzari*. His most important work was *New Research into the Composition and Exegesis of the Koran*, published in 1926. Arthur Marmorstein (1882–1946), whose Masoretic Midrash *Haseroth we-Yeseroth* showed it to have originally been a polemical tract against the Karaite schematics, was another internationally renowned scholar.

The influence of Jews' College academics was also to be found in works with which they were hardly recognized. as Epstein said: 'The publication in this country of the monumental Soncino editions of the Talmud, Midrash, Zohar and Bible which have been described as "the envy of the five million strong American Jewry" have, in the main, been made possible through the scholarly collaboration of members of the staff and alumni of the College.'[14]

It was a powerful endorsement of the extra-curricula work of the faculty.

NOTES

1. JCAR.
2. JCAR.
3. JCAR.
4. From personal email.
5. Robert Henriques, *Sir Robert Waley-Cohen, 1877–1952* (London: Secker & Warburg, 1966), p.348.
6. *Jewish Chronicle*, 8 October 1954, p.1.
7. Interview with Dr Jacobs.
8. JCAR.
9. *Jewish Chronicle*, 15 February 1957, p.14
10. JCAR.
11. Interview with Rabbi Cohen.
12. Interview with Abraham Levy.
13. Ibid.
14. JCAR.

CHAPTER NINE

The Isidore Epstein and Hirsch Zimmels Years

The question of who would succeed Dr Epstein had to be resolved as the Principal approached his retirement age. The first idea was to promote a very bright 40-year-old rabbi called Louis Jacobs. He was appointed a Tutor and Lecturer at Jews' College and was even tipped to succeed the Chief Rabbi in due course. After which everything went pear-shaped.

On 18 December 1961 there was a meeting of the Council of Jews' College with the Chief Rabbi, Israel Brodie, in the chair. At that meeting there was a proposal to decide on the appointment of Rabbi Louis Jacobs as the successor to Dr Epstein. The Chief Rabbi asked for the discussion to be deferred until he had returned from a visit to Australia in April.

The Chairman of the College, Sir Alan Mocatta, who had served in that role for the past fifteen years, did not want the decision delayed. When an amendment to approve the deferment was passed by fourteen votes to six with four abstentions, Mocatta announced his intention to resign his office, and one of the Joint Treasurers, Lawrence Jacobs, said he would resign as well.

Mocatta was not particularly concerned with the minutiae of religious observance. He practiced very little himself, but he had been a power in the Sephardi land for many years and his resignation would reverberate through the community. Mocatta's view was that such a deferment would lead to the loss of Rabbi Jacobs' services to the College and the Rabbi did indeed resign. The Chief Rabbi, at the meeting, had said that he would not agree to the appointment of Rabbi

Jacobs as Principal, though he might reconsider the question when he came back from Australia. In the meantime, as Dr Epstein had already resigned in July, he would himself serve as the Acting Principal with Dr Zimmels as Director of Studies.

This was the crucial point in what became known as the Jacobs Affair. It led to a giant row within the community and, even after fifty years, any account of the arguments leading up to Brodie's decision is likely to be seen as highly contentious. A great deal was written at the time and even more as the years have gone by. Accusations and counteraccusations have been advanced by the supporters of the Chief Rabbi and Rabbi Jacobs.

Of course, conclusions can only be reached on a historical event when all the facts are in the public domain. This only happens after the dust has long settled. The eventual historical verdict can then take into account the long-term results of the decisions made at the time.

For example, in writing in support of Rabbi Jacobs' candidacy in July 1961, the *Jewish Chronicle* journalist said: 'the intake of new ministerial students to the College has dwindled almost to vanishing point'.[1] This wasn't true. By October 1962 the Council was able to announce that twenty-one new students had been accepted for the College, with a further seventeen under consideration. It is now possible to record that sixteen students achieved *semicha* during the 1960s, including Hans Grunewald, later Dayan of the Munich community, Bent Melchior, later Chief Rabbi of Denmark, Cyril Harris, later Chief Rabbi of South Africa, and Abraham Levy, later to be the senior rabbi of the Sephardim in Britain. The whole truth usually emerges only after many years have passed.

What are the undisputed facts? Reviewing the personalities involved, the Chief Rabbi, Israel Brodie, had been a very popular appointment when he succeeded Chief Rabbi Hertz in 1948.

> The Grand Dukes were content to have a real Englishman as Chief Rabbi [he was one of only three chief rabbis to have been born in England]. The communal power-wielders were relieved to have a Chief who was a gentleman and diplomat. The Zionists felt

Isidore Epstein, Principal during the Golden Age. Reproduced with permission from Hyamson, *Jews College, London, 1855–1955*.

assured by his love for Zion. The ex-service people remembered how well he had cared for his troops [he became the Chief Chaplain to the Jewish forces during the Second World War]. The ministers had a warm feeling for a good colleague who had always been a good friend, the mighty Dayan Abramsky and Sir Robert Waley Cohen, miles apart in religious standards, were united in their respect and support for the Chief.[2]

The other main character in the saga was, of course, Rabbi Louis Jacobs. He was born into a poor family in Manchester and always kept his Manchester accent. After attending Manchester Yeshivah and gaining *semicha*, he had been appointed Assistant Rabbi at the Golders Green Beth Hamedrash in the time of Rabbi Eli Munk. Rabbi Munk was well to the right of the United Synagogue, revered by his community – the synagogue is still referred to as Munks – and impeccably Orthodox. It is irrefutable that Rabbi Jacobs would never have been accepted as a minister by Munk if there had been the slightest doubt about his Orthodoxy.

Rabbi Jacobs went on to be the minister at the Manchester Central Synagogue and moved from there to the New West End Synagogue in Bayswater. He worked for a degree at University College, London but there he had:

> become acquainted with the critical study of the Scriptures, leaving him with increasing doubts as to the validity of the traditional doctrine of *Torah Min HaShamayim*, the Divine origin of the Torah ... his first major book, *We Have Reason To Believe*, published in 1957 ... was not entirely Orthodox, but until someone (maybe Dr. Epstein, maybe Dayan Dr. Isidor Grunfeld of the London Beth Din, maybe both) brought it to Brodie's attention, it caused Jacobs no great harm.[3]

At the time, the Chief Rabbi regarded Rabbi Jacobs highly. He even considered him for tenure on the London Beth Din. A student, then at the College, recalled: 'I have to say that, as one of Jacobs' students, I was impressed with his capacity for rapport, but things he said in class worried us ... the College staff had their reservations about Jacobs and made this clear to the students.[4]

There is no doubt that Dr Epstein did not want to retire from Jews' College. As Rabbi Jacobs was his expected successor, the relations between the two men were influenced by that fact. It was definitely suggested to the Chief Rabbi that Rabbi Jacobs' views would be inappropriate in the role of Principal of the Orthodox College, and arguments for and against his likely appointment began to be widely voiced.

After Brodie had considered the arguments carefully, he reached a decision not to appoint Rabbi Jacobs, and when pressured to do so at the Council meeting in December 1961, that was his ruling. As it was part of the constitution of Jews' College that the Chief Rabbi had the final say on the appointment, that would be the outcome.

The press had a field day. Everybody had a view and in putting forward their opinions, the language was often intemperate. The story was news in the national press and on the two television channels. The upshot was that Rabbi Jacobs resigned from the College and eventually became the minister of a new synagogue community in St Johns Wood in London. He went on to found the Masorti movement in Britain which is now associated with the Conservative movement in America.

Within the United Synagogue, the President, Ewen Montagu, resigned, but his successor, Isaac Wolfson, a powerful businessman and highly Orthodox, supported the Chief Rabbi. At Jews' College, Hersch Zimmels was appointed Principal, Isaac Levy, the lecturer in homiletics, resigned and the College tried to get back to normal. Epstein died in 1962, the year after he retired from his office.

In the general community the arguments continued to rage for months and even, in some cases, for years. The *Jewish Chronicle* supported Rabbi Jacobs, though it printed contributions from both sides. The Chief Rabbi told one of his nephews that he came to dread Friday mornings when the paper came out. Rabbi Jacobs was made a CBE in 1990 and died at the age of 85 in 2006.

In early 1962 the IUJF student conference considered a proposal by the Jews' College Union to invite Rabbi Jacobs to be Hon. President of the Federation for 1962, and this was enthusiastically passed. A very senior rabbi, Harris Swift, formerly of St Johns Wood Synagogue, said he would have made Rabbi Jacobs the Principal of the College. On the other hand, Orthodox rabbis like Immanuel Jakobovits, the future Chief Rabbi, came out strongly for the position of the Chief Rabbi. Elkan Levy, later President of the United Synagogue, was a student at the time and remembers how divided the students were, for and against.

At the United Synagogue, the then President Ewen Montagu appealed to the Chief Rabbi not to use his veto to bar Rabbi Jacobs. There was then a movement to pass a vote of No Confidence in Montagu and when this was dropped, a large number of members of the Council still recorded their support for Brodie.

The stumbling block to appointing Rabbi Jacobs was his views on the Torah coming from heaven. He had stated: 'There are many things recorded in the Torah which G-d did not say ... there is a human as well as a divine factor in revelation, G-d revealing His Will not alone to men but through men'.[5]

Although he had a lot of support, for some reason Rabbi Jacobs then burnt his boats. In his letter of resignation, he said that 'no reputable scholar in the world has an approach that is basically different from mine', implying that anyone who disagreed with him could not be a reputable scholar, a view which is surely not sustainable, and was absolutely guaranteed to alienate all those scholars who felt they did not need anybody to tell them whether they were reputable or not. Which would have included nearly all of them. Like almost everybody else, academics are sensitive to criticism.

Looking back there are a number of obvious points. Most important, a great many of the people who voiced their opinions had no in-depth knowledge of the arguments. Higher Biblical Criticism, as the field is called, is as expert a study as any science.

There were also many hidden agendas. There was the ambition of the younger generation to take over the reins from the old-timers. There was the reaction of the Progressive movement, seeing an Orthodox rabbi endorsing at least one of their contentious views. There was the rallying round of a charismatic advocate, who could easily be portrayed as a victim of bureaucratic authority. There were those who resented the sole authority of the Chief Rabbi in spiritual matters anyway. There were even those who wanted to keep the discussion going in order to sell more newspapers.

Fifty years later, there is still no single view on the rights and wrongs of the Jacobs Affair. Rabbi Raymond Apple, who apart from being an eyewitness, is a highly respected Anglo-Jewish historian, sums up the Jacobs Affair as follows:

The Jacobs episode was a tangled skein. Jacobs was an attractive personality and a dynamic teacher. Many in the community felt that with him at the helm of the College, and in due course as Chief Rabbi, the future of Judaism in Britain would flourish. But Jacobs' theological stance gave Rabbi Brodie and the Beth Din no choice: with all their liking for Jacobs, they feared that he would lead Anglo-Jewry away from traditional orthodoxy.

The fact that most people, with the probable exception of Dayan Grunfeld, did not completely understand the problem or indeed the risk associated with Jacobs, veered the controversy into technical questions such as the Chief Rabbi's constitutional rights. Others raised quite irrelevant issues, such as a lady member of my Bayswater congregation, who wrote to the *Jewish Chronicle* backing Rabbi Brodie because he spoke such beautiful English. Chaim Bermant [a very influential *Jewish Chronicle* journalist] made the valid point that Jacobs wanted the community to think, but it was not (and had no interest in becoming) a thinking community. At the College there were personal as well as theological issues, and the veteran lecturers used to conspire in the corridors about how to put the interloper in his place. We students liked Jacobs immensely but were a bit shocked by his ideological latitudinarianism.

Jacobs cooked his own goose when he made the inappropriate comment that no reputable scholar had an attitude different from his – not only over-egotistical but an open insult to reputable scholars like the College faculty. It was not very smart to make this assertion; he could have made his point much more diplomatically. But very few people were very diplomatic at the height of the episode, e.g. Alfred Silverman, the Secretary of the US, who told the media to go and talk to the gardener at Willesden Cemetery.[6]

At the end of the day the Chief Rabbi made his decision and Jews' College moved on. The Annual Report for 1961/62 listed Rabbi Jacobs on the teaching staff and for 1962/63 it didn't. There was no reference to his departure, and none of the usual thanks for his contribution. The only reference in the Council's report came at the end: 'In a period of difficulties and transition, the College has endeavoured with no little success, to preserve all that is best in its long tradition, while at the same time striving to meet the challenge with which it is faced.'[7]

Many years later when Louis Jacobs died, the Chief Rabbi and the Senior Sephardi Rabbi attended the funeral, but the breach was never repaired. The Council confined itself to wishing the new Principal, Dr Zimmels, bon voyage: 'In tendering congratulations to Dr Zimmels on his appointment, the Council expresses the hope that his tenure of high office may afford him a period of academic satisfaction and tranquillity and the College an opportunity for consolidation.'[8]

Hirsch Zimmels certainly had the academic qualifications. His book on the Ashkenazim and Sephardim had won wide acclaim and remains a classic text. It reflected his wide range of knowledge that his first book in 1932 was on *The Marranos in Rabbinic Literature*, his second, in 1952, was entitled *Magicians, Theologians and Doctors,* and he also wrote *Contributions to the History of the Jews in Germany in the 13th Century.* He was also a noted Talmudist and had received his *semicha* and doctorate in Vienna before the war. Polish by birth, he had taught Jewish History and Rabbinics in Breslau until 1933, when he had to flee. He became the Communal Rabbi in Vienna from 1934–39 and then managed to escape to London just before the war started.

As an alien he was interned and sent to Australia for two years. When he came back to London he succeeded Samuel Daiches as the teacher of Talmud at the College in 1944 and at the end of 1961, he was appointed Director of Studies. He was appointed Principal just before he was due to retire in October 1964. The College Council extended his term of office for a further four years and he ran it well. He was also made one of the Editors of the *Jewish Encyclopaedia*. He would finally retire in 1970. Zimmels was just one of the thousands of refugees who made a substantial contribution to the culture, well-being and economy of Britain during his lifetime.

The more historic problems now returned to the forefront of the Council's mind in October 1964: the finances were looking even worse than usual. At a meeting in Brodie's home it was agreed to create a

National Co-ordinating Council of the Friends of Jews' College. The idea was that groups of Friends would be formed around the country and within the Commonwealth to raise funds for the institution. This was the route which should have been followed 100 years before.

In addition it was agreed to try to improve the relationship between careers masters at schools with a number of Jewish masters, to encourage more of the boys to come to the College. A newsletter was produced to communicate the activities of the College to a wider audience. If this was an improvement in public relations, behind the scenes Naphtali Wieder was helping with the new edition of the Singer Prayer Book, as Michael Friedländer had contributed to the first version.

The College badly needed to settle down. The Jacobs affair hadn't ended outside its walls. Most of Jacobs' former congregants set up a new community. Agreement was reached with the Chief Rabbi to honour weddings conducted by Rabbi Jacobs but that was about as far as it went. Within the College, the certificate awarding *semicha* was altered to insist that the recipient would adhere to the tenets of Orthodox law and tradition, as well as the fundamental Orthodox beliefs. Failure to do so could result in the certificate being withdrawn. This was considered a reaction to the right wing sensitivities in the community. At the College, on reflection, the Council broadly supported the Chief Rabbi.

There was only one change in personnel after 1962 and four at the end of 1963. There was no comment in the Annual Report on why the Council members concerned had decided to withdraw. The student body had also been divided over the issue, creating a tension between them and members of the faculty. The 1963 Annual Report took the opportunity of recording that the Purim party and Israel Independence Day breakfast had been attended by both students and faculty.

The main task for the Council was to get over the bad publicity which the Jacobs Affair had produced. In 1962 Bruno Marmorstein took over as Chair of the Council. His father, Rabbi Arthur Marmorstein, had come from Austro-Hungary and was appointed to teach Bible and Talmud at the College in 1912. He was still in post when he died in 1946. His son, a lawyer, was equally anxious to support the College and followed in his father's footsteps. He would lead the Council until 1972 and died at the age of 79 in 1990, still usefully involved in Jewish communal affairs.

The new Chair found a dispirited organisation. He set out to counteract the pessimistic mood and was able to report in 1963, 'If we have done nothing more in the past few months, we have at least obliterated for ever the image of the College that has been projected on the communal screen, that we are some kind of obscurantist stronghold. Nothing could be further from the truth.'[9]

It made a good press release and there was much truth to it. The College in 1963 had eighty-seven students in all and the accommodation at Montagu Place was 100 per cent full. This contrasted favourably with the previous year when some London University students were able to occupy empty rooms. Particularly popular were Rabbi Kahana's lectures on Jewish legal subjects which drew considerable audiences from outside the College. Nevertheless, 'for ever' would prove an underestimate of the staying power of the College's critics.

One future problem would be the result of the appointment of a Deputy Principal; Rabbi Dr Jacob Joshua Ross, who had degrees from the University of the Witwatersrand and Cape Town in South Africa, a PhD in Philosophy from Cambridge, and was only 34 years old. He had come from Bar Ilan University in Israel where he headed the Department of Philosophy after a stint as Visiting Assistant Professor of Philosophy at Brown University in Rhode Island. Fitting in to the College ambiance did not, however, depend entirely on academic brilliance.

Eli Cashdan had achieved recognition by London University as a teacher and Naphtali Wieder was setting up a Post-Graduate department to enable more advanced research to be carried out. Rabbi Jacob's work had been divided up between the Chief Rabbi and other members of the staff and if permanent replacements were not easy to identify, the gaps were well covered by members of the community.

In the absence of one teacher, Miss J. Kitto came in from the Hasmonean School for Girls to teach Latin. It was also in 1963 that the College appointed Jeffrey Cohen, one of its graduates, to lecture on Bible and Commentaries immediately after he had obtained a first class degree.

The number of students was growing but the College was still in serious financial straits, though the Federation of Synagogues had now agreed to contribute £600 a year and were granted two seats on the Council as a result. One traditional problem which could now be alleviated was the maintenance of the students, seventeen of whom had Major County Awards in 1966.

It emphasised the size of the problem, though, that in 1963 the expenditure was £37,000 and the income from student fees and the sale of books was £378. One of the largest sums in the income column was the £3,750, out of a total of £12,000 from communal organizations, which came from the Conference on Jewish Material Claims against Germany.

The Treasurer announced that the College needed a regular annual income of £15,000 and suggested that an Endowment Fund of £300,000 should be raised. Within a year it had reached £5,000, of which Mrs James de Rothschild had provided £2,000. The bank overdraft, though, had reached £10,000 and there was a shortfall in the pension fund as well.

The accounts included a comparison between the sources of funds in 1926, when the Jewish Memorial Council contribution started, and 1963. This showed that income from Communal Organizations had slipped from 51 per cent to 32 per cent. Subscription income had gone up from 9 per cent to 40 per cent, and the income from investments had declined from 40 per cent to 14 per cent. The College could now invest in equities but the risks involved were a heavy responsibility. Better to denounce the lack of support from the community than explain why the shares you fancied in International Tadpoles had dropped in value.

In a *Jewish Chronicle* supplement Dayan Maurice Lew, a former student at the College, tackled the question of the relationship between

Jewish studies and scientific developments. Still unlike the attitude of the principals of many yeshivot, he wrote: 'A university education and uncontracted views are best fitted to teach and mediate Judaism.'[10] The Dayan quoted Maimonides, the Vilna Gaon and the sixteenth-century scholar, Moses Isserles, as former Talmudic leaders who had taken the same view.

The College was 110 years old in 1966 and this coincided with the 70th birthday of Chief Rabbi Brodie and the appointment of the new Chief Rabbi, Immanuel Jakobovits, as President of the College. It was an excellent opportunity for the College to parade in all its academic finery and a splendid dinner was held for 400 guests in December. The speakers included Lord Kahn, Solomon Teff, the President of the Board of Deputies and a former pupil of the College, and the Master of Balliol, Chief Rabbi Brodie's old Oxford college. Also present were Cardinal Heenan, the Lord Mayor of Westminster, the President of the Anglo-Jewish Association and the future Lord Chancellor, Quintin Hogg, Lord Hailsham. It was Hailsham, as Lord Chancellor, who spoke in a debate on *shechita* some years later. He pointed out that the laws of *shechita* could only be changed if you could convert all the Orthodox Jews, which he said Christians had been trying to do for 2,000 years 'with only limited success'!

To celebrate Chief Rabbi Brodie's 70th birthday, Dr Zimmels presented him with two testimonial books of lectures, written by forty of the greatest Jewish scholars in the world. It was also announced that the second floor wing at the College and a lecture room would be dedicated to Jack Green, who had built a major company called Evans Outsize, and given £5,000 to the appeal.

There was no question that the College was deeply respected in the community; this was well illustrated by the eminent list of lecturers who were prepared to participate in its 1966 series of public lectures on various aspects of English and Jewish Law. Among others, David Weitzman, QC, MP, spoke on the English Law of Evidence, Rabbi Plitnick on the Right to Privacy in Jewish Law, Judge Bernard Gillis on the problems of abortion, and Rabbi Feuchtwanger on the problem of Acceptance of Interest by a Jewish Corporation.

Ephy Levine died in 1966. Apart from being a great character in the community and a fine minister, he had taught Homiletics at the College, served as its Honorary Secretary and sat on the Council. When he was too old to attend the Council, he was made an Honorary Member. Two years later, in 1968, Myer Stephany died at the age of 81. He was one of the unsung heroes of the College, having served as its Secretary from 1921 to 1962. An accountant by profession, it fell to Stephany to deal with the day-to-day administrative problems, and he tackled them with quiet efficiency for all the years he served.

The effect of a college on a student depends both on the student and the approach of the college. One student, Elkan Levy, decided he wanted to attend the Jewish Theological Seminary in New York and Naphtali Wieder encouraged him to do so. This was somewhat strange as the college was the fountainhead for American Conservative Judaism. It was, therefore, accused by the Orthodox of setting lower standards than one of their institutions, on the question of obeying the *mitzvot*.

Few students were in a position to compare the two, but Levy was. His father was the *hazan* at the New West End Synagogue where Ephraim Levine was the minister, and Elkan Levy would remain a pillar of the Orthodox British community all his life, as a future president of the United Synagogue and for many years the Director of the Office for Small Communities. As he remembers:

> We were fond of Eppy as we called him. I think Dr Zimmels was more of a Talmudist than a Principal. It wasn't a very strenuous curriculum at Jews' College when I was there. There was no homework, except for Naphtali Wieder who wanted a Classical Hebrew translation every Monday morning. All the useful courses at the College were, of course, mandatory, like *hazanut*, elocution and homiletics. We had little to do with the IUJF [The International Union of Jewish Students], and I think I drifted at the College. I really only worked at the finish.
>
> JTSA was a revelation. Within a short time I had to go to the doctor who said I was suffering from overwork. Really! As far as the *mitzvot* at JTSA were concerned, keeping *kashrut* was

> mandatory and so was keeping two days for Yom Tov. We laid *tephillin* every morning and in many ways JTSA was *frummer* than the College.
>
> There were no female rabbis, of course, and some of the graduates even went on to take Orthodox pulpits. One of the things that irritated me at the College was that we sat at desks, just like school, with old-style inkwells in place into which you could put your pen. When I went to JTSA and found the armchairs with enlarged sides, that they had in America, I really felt like a student and not a schoolboy.[11]

The College had extended its coverage of academic work. Those who wanted to study specific areas of Hebrew or Judaica, in order to gain higher degrees at London University, could now take post graduate courses. Additionally, there was now a Goldbloom Lectureship in Jewish Philosophy, conducted in Hebrew, and taught by Dr E. Weisenberg, who was seconded from University College, London. There was also a teacher from Israel to conduct Hebrew studies on a three or four year secondment.

In spite of all this, the Haham, Solomon Gaon, could still lament that, 'The significance of Jews' College for Anglo-Jewry has never been properly appreciated or fully understood'.[12] Gaon was particularly concerned at the fact that the College was still not recognized as a school of London University. This had been the wish of the Council for many years, but negotiations with the university had never come to a successful conclusion. The best that had been achieved was that the academics at the College could be recognized as university teachers.

From the point of view of the university there were two problems. First, that it was a fundamental that all their schools should have academic self-government; the admission of students, the appointment of lecturers, the syllabuses and the exam requirements had to be under the control of the academics. At Jews' College the official controlling body was the lay Council, headed by the Chief Rabbi.

The second problem was that the University of London was against any form of religious test for the admission of students. It had actually been founded to be open to students of all religions, contrary to the restrictions which applied at Oxford and Cambridge. The College, on the other hand, could not compromise on the demands of Orthodoxy, those being the core of the institution.

With some reluctance it had been agreed to teach Higher Biblical Criticism, even knowing that this was severely frowned upon by the ultra-Orthodox yeshivot. The College had to teach Higher Biblical Criticism because it was part of the university syllabus for the Classical and Mediaeval Hebrew and Aramaic course. This was really a language degree with a viva examination as well. All the rabbinical material, such as Talmud and Codes, Jewish History, *hazanut*, elocution and homiletics, were part of the internal *semicha* course.

It had also been agreed that the College would accept students of other faiths and occasionally this had happened in the past. That was, however, as far as the College had moved. Gaon came up with a plan to meet the objections of the university, and a committee of Jewish academics had been created to see if it could be implemented. There was, however, little interest in progressing the ideas and the committee disbanded.

The combination of youth and experience, with Zimmels and Ross, should have been a strong one, but Ross became steadily more aggravated by what he saw as unreasonable interference by the Council in the academic affairs of the College. As, however, the Chief Rabbi was the President of the Council, he obviously had a watertight mandate to be the final judge of the actions of the academics who also did not have his stature.

In 1968 Ross resigned and went back to Israel. His parting remarks were not complimentary. He said the staff were disgruntled, there was no esprit de corps and the students were mostly second rate. As Cyril Harris, the future Chief Rabbi of South Africa, and Abraham Levy, the future senior Sephardi rabbi, were among them, there were obviously many exceptions he couldn't foresee.

He could have appreciated, however, that the involvement of the Council was always going to be greater than usual, simply to see that any suggestion of another Jacobs Affair was dealt with much more effectively at the outset. Rabbi Dr Irving Jacobs, who was a young lecturer at the college at the time, does not recall the kind of atmosphere the Deputy Principal described.

Ross also dismissed Zimmels as a figurehead and didn't make any allowances for the Council's concern with the College's reputation. Rabbi Dr Irving Jacobs laid into them: 'One even gets the impression that the Council Room is the main room at the College and that all other activities in the building are merely a pretext to allow communal politics to take place.' The Council contribution to the discussion was to warmly thank Ross in the Annual Report for all his hard work as Deputy Principal and to wish him well in his future career. Organisations like Jews' College seldom change from the outside, and Ross was not going to be a factor in the future.

The argument over who was responsible for the lack of ministerial candidates split even the religious leaders. In 1968 Zimmels had said: 'The blame must be laid on the attitude of some lay leaders towards their ministers and on the generally low status of the ministry.'[13] At the Speech day in 1969 Dayan Lew, the Guest of Honour, agreed: 'If you knew how some ministers are treated, simply because they are unworldly, pious and studious, and because they are neither organization-men nor publicity-men, you would say that no self-respecting young man would tolerate such treatment.'[14] The Haham, however, disagreed, contending that the ministers were not pro-active enough: 'When it comes to important issues and problems, do we make our voices heard in the country?'[15]

A great deal depended on the characters of the individuals. In Zimmels's defence, back in September 1966, the College had enjoyed a supplement in the *Jewish Chronicle*, though the paper was careful to point out that all the editorial content had come from the College. The opportunity was taken to review the progress the College had made over the years.

It could certainly boast of distinguished alumni. Zimmels also pointed out the gap that Jews' College helped to fill after the destruction of the European yeshivot during the war. He called it the Beth Hamedrash of the Commonwealth and pointed to the students who had come to the College over the past few years from France, Germany, Scandinavia, Israel, North and South Africa, Australia and Aden.

From 1883–1967 ninety-one students had qualified as ministers with university degrees. In 1967 there were seventy-six students in all at the College and since 1948 no less than forty-seven men had been given *semicha*. The College now offered a post-graduate department for students studying for higher degrees, a *hazanut* department, a Reader Teacher course for those who were going to serve smaller communities, and an Institute for training teachers to BA level. Nor were the laymen neglected as there was a weekly shiur for the public by Dayan Grossnass.

The press faithfully reported Ross' remarks, but the President of the Jews' College Union Society waded into the usual critics to the manner born. Leonard Tann held that:

> University education is what the student makes of it. Jews' College should be judged on the achievements of its students, their preaching, *hazanut* or teaching, not on the political or educational disputes that occur in every academic institution, nor on the 'brilliant' ideas or misguided concepts that people have about Jews College.[16]

Tann insisted that to increase the number of students by not insisting on a proper level of Orthodoxy, would make the graduates suspect when applying for positions in Orthodox communities. He also denied that the students were somehow locked away in an academic backwater. As far as he was concerned, there was nothing to stop the students mixing in the wider life of London University.

He was, himself, the Deputy Chair of the Student Council of the London Union which meant that he represented 37,000 students. Indeed he had discussed religion with a number of students at other theological colleges. He eventually became Chair of the Students' Representative Council.

He said he learned Biblical Criticism from Eli Cashdan and he could read whatever he liked: 'I was not chained up or declared a heretic!' In

Tann's opinion, teachers of Hebrew or *Hazanut* could not be chosen solely on academic ability, and the appointment of the lecturers had to be a matter for the College.

After he left Tann completed his *semicha* and, in 1986, became the minister at Singers Hill, the largest Orthodox synagogue in Birmingham. He never ceased to be passionate about inter-faith relations. After 9/11 he very deliberately went to the Central Mosque for prayers after it had been daubed and subject to much abuse. When a new rabbi was appointed at the Reform synagogue, she always remembered that he had phoned her to wish her well over the High Holydays. As a result he was much loved and respected among all denominations. He died at 62 in 2007.

Another graduate of the College who played an important part in public life was Cyril Harris, who was at the forefront of the move towards the reconciliation of the races after the end of apartheid in South Africa. Nelson Mandela was full of praise for his contribution. It was also overlooked how the graduates had proved their competence during the war in the demanding role of Chaplains to the Forces.

The appointment of a new Principal when Zimmels retired was, obviously, going to be an important decision for the Chief Rabbi. Zimmel's appointment had been extended when Epstein retired and was extended for one further year in 1968. Student numbers were steady at approximately eighty, but it could not be expected that Zimmels would hurry to seek out new initiatives at his age. To make matters worse, the most senior lecturers were of a similar age to Zimmels. Cashdan and Wieder were within a couple of years of retirement and Kahana retired at the end of 1968. Only Irving Jacobs, at 29, had youth on his side. As Bruno Marmorstein recorded:

> Scholars of the calibre essential to Jews' College to maintain its high academic standard are not easily found and a world-wide search is proceeding in order to appoint men well equipped to meet the religious and intellectual challenges of our age. The limitations of a tight budget make the task of reconstruction all the more difficult.[17]

What Marmorstein was saying was that it would be difficult to replace such luminaries as Kahana, Wieder and Cashdan for the kind of salaries the College could afford. Yet the figures for 1966 showed a £5,000 bill for the redecoration of Montagu Place, which was one of the terms of the lease. It was no wonder that the deficit continued to grow – £5,000 in 1966 is conservatively over £80,000 today.

There was a published list of contributions from communal organisations in the Annual Report for 1966. The total was £9,000, and two thirds of this came from the Jewish Memorial Council, the United Synagogue and the Memorial Foundation for Jewish Culture. The Memorial Foundation had been created by the Conference on Jewish Material Claims against Germany after the war, and it distributed funds to survivors and Jewish religious institutions all over the world. By 1974 the College would have received £10,000 but Gateshead was given £23,000 over the same period. The reason for the difference was never explained, but it certainly looks like better negotiating skills in the North East.

Analysing the remaining third of the contributions, the South African Jewish Board of Deputies had given £1,000, the Federation £300 and the Sephardim £200. None of the other forty-eight organizations had given as much as £100. The average was £15.

One very worthwhile addition to the College's activities in 1969 was a series of lectures organized by the Jewish-Christian Group. In these, subjects were discussed by two speakers, one from each faith. Thus the Venerable C. Witton Davies and Rabbi Morris Nemeth talked on the Shechinah [the presence of the Almighty in everyday life].

The College now had to adjust to another Principal.

NOTES

1. *Jewish Chronicle*, 21 July 1961, p.18.
2. Rabbi Raymond Apple, Kovno and Oxford: Israel Brodie and his Rabbinical Career', www.oztorah.com/2008/o2/kovno-oxford-Israel-Brodie-his-rabbinical-career/
3. Ibid.

4. Ibid.
5. Rabbi Louis Jacobs, *We have Reason to Believe* (London: Vallentine Mitchell, 1965).
6. Rabbi Raymond Apple in correspondence with the author.
7. JCAR.
8. JCAR.
9. JCAR.
10. *Jewish Chronicle*, 2 September 1966, Supplement, p.ii.
11. Interview with Elkan Levy.
12. JCAR.
13. JCAR.
14. JCAR.
15. JCAR.
16. *Jewish Chronicle*, 15 August 1969, p.8.
17. JCAR.

CHAPTER TEN

The Nahum Rabinovitch Years

At the beginning of the decade the Chief Rabbi had taken on the role of Acting Principal on the retirement of Dr Zimmels. He, personally, took charge of finding a suitable successor and managed to persuade 41-year-old Nahum Rabinovitch to take up the post in March 1971.

Rabinovitch came from Canada and he was not only a synagogue minister in Toronto but also lectured in maths at Toronto University. He had been given his *semicha* in Baltimore when he was only 20, a PhD in Philosophy at the University of Toronto and he was an expert on Maimonides, on whose work he had written voluminously. He was a seriously brilliant academic and one point of contact between Jakobovits and Rabinovitch was that they had a mutual interest in the work of the Association of Jewish Scientists.

Rabinovitch had six children and, consequently, the benefit package had to be substantial to attract him across the Atlantic. He eventually accepted a £5,000 a year salary plus a free home. This was £2,000 more than Zimmels had received. It was not, therefore, surprising that the permanent staff at the College complained, because senior lecturers were only getting about £2,400 a year. It was finally agreed that all the salaries would be improved, costing the College another £10,000 a year in total (£10,00 in 1971 is about £120,000 today).

The improvement was not sufficient to placate Naphtali Wieder. He had been acknowledged to be a fine lecturer and a Talmudic expert and there had been considerable support for him to be made principal after Epstein retired. In the circumstances the Council probably opted for Zimmels as the more malleable candidate. Wieder had taught at the

College since 1948 but now he had been passed over again in favour of Rabinovitch.

He resigned and accepted a lectureship in Hebrew and Jewish Studies at University College, London. Jakobovits tried to get him to stay but he was adamant. He was much missed by the students who admired him even for his sarcasm. Of the efforts of one student he had written, 'This is still below criticism'! He went on to become a Visiting Professor at Bar Ilan University and died in 2001 at the age of 95.

Rabinovitch set the academic bar high and, like Büchler before him, he did not have a very high opinion of the standards of Orthodoxy to be found in the general community. Where among the ultra-Orthodox, for example, a failure to observe *Shabbat*, the strict keeping of the Sabbath, was severely frowned upon, the former President of the United Synagogue, Sir Robert Waley Cohen, was known to drive up from his home in Somerset to bless a congregation on festivals. This serious breach of the commandments had not prevented him regularly being re-elected.

The problem, however, with setting the bar very high is that few of the players clear the pole. One of Rabinovitch's early students who thrived, though, was Jonathan Sacks, the future chief rabbi, who had come from Cambridge, having been encouraged to take up the rabbinate by Rabbi Joseph Soloveitchik, one of the most eminent Talmudists in New York, and by the Lubavitcher Rabbi, Rabbi Menachem Shneerson.

Jonathan Sacks had been President of the Cambridge University Jewish Society and had worked at university in accordance with the relaxed academic atmosphere at the time. He did not consider he had worked very hard, but he got a first class degree in philosophy, which was an unusual distinction. Today, he remembers the very different world he entered at the College:

> Rabinovitch was an intellectual giant and he was extremely demanding of his students. He expected us to have read everything and not just to have absorbed the knowledge but to be critical

about it as well. If a question had to be decided, he objected strongly to the student who looked up the answer in the Shulchan Aruch; you were supposed to work out the answer for yourself.

He represented the American standards of Jewish Orthodox learning, which were really not to be found in Britain. When I got my *semicha* there was a suggestion that I accept a pulpit in America and I went to visit it. I found the level of Talmudic expertise of the congregation outstanding; far more knowledgeable than you'd find in a United Synagogue. It was just a higher level of application.

Nahum Rabinovitch, Principal and towering Talmudist. Copyright: *The Jewish Chronicle*.

I remember, to get my *semicha*, Rabinovitch created a case study and I had to write a responsum which was about as long as a doctoral thesis. It was about an imaginary parcel of food that had been sent to Russia at Pesach time and held up in the Customs. It involved a whole series of very difficult Talmudic problems about if and when you could eat it. My paper was 80,000 words long and it had to be written in Hebrew.

Rabinovitch was a tremendous scholar – still is I'm sure – and I don't think he was ever properly appreciated in this country. He had been chosen by Chief Rabbi Jakobovits and I think he expected that the number of students would be increased by starting a school to provide an additional intake. After all there were very few students when he arrived. There was an attempt to create this but it couldn't be sustained financially. He was certainly highly regarded by London University and he was very popular in the College.[1]

In March 1971 Rabinovitch took up his appointment and set about reinvigorating the institution. The faculty were losing Kahana and Cashdan, both of whom were either past retirement age or approaching it. He would shortly lose Naphtali Wieder. Within a short space of time though the number of additional lecturers rose to sixteen. Rabinovitch cast his net wide and among the newcomers was Zvi Kra, a graduate of New York University, who taught Modern Hebrew, Avraham Shalev from the Hebrew University, and Leon Feldman from Rutgers University in the United States, who arrived to teach Jewish history.

The ability to strengthen the faculty owed much to the sheer professionalism of Rabinovitch. If scholars are prepared to devote their lives to Hebrew education, it is only natural that they should want to carry on their work at institutions with distinguished leadership, and Rabinovitch had a first class international reputation.

Benno Wasserman, who had gained his doctorate at Yale, was another who joined the faculty and, in 1973, with the financial help of the Rothschilds, three visiting fellows were appointed who had been trained at Yeshiva University in New York and Princeton. Two of the lecturers had been appointed to the Board of Studies of London University and Rabinovitch himself served on several university committees, as well as on the Studies Board of the Council for National Academic Awards (CNAA). The criticism of the *Jewish Chronicle* at the end of the Zimmels era was corrected.

Within a few years Rabinovitch had reorganized the syllabus, which now concentrated on Talmud, Bible, Jewish commentaries, philosophy, history, the Hebrew language and Hebrew literature. He wanted the College to be primarily for male students and, by 1975, women were only taking the teaching training courses, rather than the BA in Jewish Studies, where seven out of the twenty-four undergraduates had been women in 1971.

Rabinovitch initially found that running Jews' College involved a tremendous amount of work. There were nine students studying for BA Hons degrees and seven for *semicha*. Eleven were studying to be *hazans* and nine more for postgraduate degrees. Another nine were taking Teaching Training courses and five were taking special courses.

That made fifty students and they were certainly well looked after by the Honorary Officers and supporters of the College, who often undertook more than one role. Committees proliferated, like the inflation which would follow the Yom Kippur War. There were twenty-seven members of the Council, fourteen members of the Education Committee, seven on the Executive Committee, sixteen on the Finance Committee and ten on the Hazanut Committee. Eleven took care of Library affairs, and another eleven were involved in publications. There were sixteen on the House Committee, twenty on the Endowment Committee and seventeen organized functions. Nine took care of Public and Extra-Mural Lectures, six comprised the Medico-Legal Group, seven the Smaller Communities Committee, nine the Chaplaincy Committee and ten the Alumni Association. Seventeen took care of Student Recruitment and there were eleven on the Central Examining Board, while the Institute for the Training of Teachers Executive Committee had fourteen members.

With fifteen staff, and an Honorary Medical Officer, Solicitor, Auditor, Executive Director, Honorary Warden, Matron and Administrative Assistant, that made another twenty-two giving of their time and expertise to help the College. It added up to nearly 250 roles to be filled, mostly by unpaid volunteers.

A few years later, in 1975, another Committee – the Jewish-Christian Relations Group – made a brief appearance, and at one of their five meetings, the Cardinal Archbishop of Westminster gave the address. As the Annual Report stated, 'All the meetings were of a very high standard and greatly appreciated by distinguished audiences.' But the Group only met occasionally afterwards. Of course, the recognition in the Report of so much help was a courtesy, even if those involved did not spend that much time on the tasks during the year. Attend half a dozen meetings, and a listing in the Annual Report was considered well merited.

There was no argument about the quantity of help, but the problems the College faced at the beginning of the decade were one result of the community taking too long to turn its attention away from the Jacobs affair. Dr Zimmels had not been a dynamic leader, the College had kept its public head down for the most part, and its image had become tired. The Chief Rabbi now decided that he needed to give a clear lead to Rabinovitch and condemned the curriculum as having been designed for Theological Schools in general half a century before. He wanted something done to modernise it.

The main objective of the College remained the education of those who would follow careers as Jewish scholars. In 1971 there was an analysis of the BA Honours degrees which the Jews' College students had gained over the previous thirty years. It showed some remarkable achievements. Most notable was the fact that at London University, no less than 39 per cent had gained first class honours; 25 per cent had got 2:1s and 21 per cent 2:2s; 14 per cent had thirds and only one student out of 130 was ungraded. It was normal for less than 10 per cent of students to get first class degrees. Nearly 40 per cent is amazing, and reflects extremely well on both students and teachers. Many of the students went on to higher degrees, and out of the 130, sixteen gained MAs, four M.Phils and twenty PhDs. Again, mind boggling.

Jakobovits also pressed for the scope of the curricula on offer at the College to be increased, in the attempt to make the College more relevant to the general community. The Chief Rabbi's particular field was Jewish Medical Ethics and it was no surprise that a Medical-Legal committee emerged. Its three lectures in 1971 were on Law and Religion, Post-epileptic Automatism, and Authority and Enquiry. All were well attended.

Another initiative was a series of extra-mural lectures organized by Irving Jacobs. These lectures would be held under the auspices of Jews' College but in centres in many parts of the country. In 1972 Jacobs organized fifty lectures in fifteen different centres and managed to arrange that volume of meetings year after year.

Bruno Marmorstein had led the Council during many difficult years since 1962. He was ready to stand down in July 1972, to be replaced by Arnold Lee, who was a major property developer. The strain of the post-Jacobs period had taken its toll on Marmorstein. As he said in his last year as Chairman, the College had been, 'constantly sniped at by the *Jewish Chronicle* ... I believe that they have been leading a campaign to subvert Orthodoxy'.[2] The Chief Rabbi said publicly that he agreed with him. It was true that not all the Directors of the *Jewish Chronicle* were strictly Orthodox, but their approach would have been more concentrated on selling newspapers than on religious viewpoints. That was the business they were in. Strong headlines and powerful journalism were going to attract readers more than bland reporting. It was ever thus.

In newspaper terms, the Jacobs affair was a good story and it ran and ran. Moreover, everybody of any importance in the community had an opinion which they were happy to see publicized. It was also the case that new readers were more likely to come from the left of the community, as the right condemned the paper for not being sufficiently modest in its illustrations, and looked askance at members of its community reading the journal.

The College still had its financial problems and these were, nationally, the same as those which were defeating even the expertise of the Treasury and the Chancellor of the Exchequer. Inflation by 1973 was heading for over 20 per cent a year and for a decade it was seldom under 10 per cent, peaking in 1974 at 24 per cent. Interest rates climbed to 15 per cent and the effect on servicing bank overdrafts was dramatic. In 1969 the deficit in the accounts was £6,000. The total deficits in the next ten years would amount to £400,000, reaching £67,000 in 1976. Bank interest that year was £13,600.

Of course, the College investments diminished in value as well. Most of them returned 3½–5 per cent and with a 15 per cent interest rate, their capital value would inevitably be reduced by about two thirds. Some of the investments didn't even have a maturity date, notably War Loan, which hasn't been paid back in full to the investors to this day.

There would, of course, be generous private contributors who would bail out the College in extremis. The Council even created another special committee to examine the figures yet again. There would also now be far more fund raising events, led by community entrepreneurs like Jarvis Astaire. He raised £12,000 in one evening and another fund raiser produced £8,500. The sale of property would be beneficial as well. Nevertheless, income never balanced expenditure. In 1973, when Leonard Stern, the Honorary Treasurer, finally gave up the unequal struggle after more than ten years in the post, he commented: 'In spite of every possible economy and strenuous efforts to increase the income, our finances give cause for grave concern. It can be clearly seen that the sources of our income are far from adequate to meet our existing needs, let alone our plans for the future.'[3]

Stern was succeeded by a first class accountant, Bernard Garbacz, who was expert enough to be given the unenviable task by the Courts of unravelling the affairs of the Hasmonean Schools at the end of the decade. Garbacz also examined the accounts carefully when he took over and reported: 'On expenditure generally, in the six months I have been in office, I have been able to form the view that expenditure is responsible and non-wasteful, and members of the Staff, whether administrative or academic, are cost conscious in relation to the affairs of the College.'[4]

Garbacz considered every way of alleviating the situation. He even considered renting out parts of Montagu Place. After all, a section of the new Marble Arch Synagogue site had been used for a banqueting house. The old Chief Rabbi, whose baby it had originally been, was not happy and said in Council, 'I am very much against it'. No more was heard of the idea. Revenue from such a source was nipped in the bud, in spite of the fact that income from commercial usage was the original strategy for Woburn House, where the Chief Rabbi had been a member of the faculty before the war.

One of the positive side-effects of the inflation – if unforeseen – coincided with the Chief Rabbi's efforts to increase the number of children educated at Jewish schools. Once they were built, it was necessary to get Jewish parents to send their children to them. This was not easy, as a public school education was still the objective of most middle-class Jewish parents.

The inflation came to the aid of the Chief Rabbi, as so many families found their budgets stretched and their capital reduced. A free Jewish school education became potentially more attractive. Moreover, the academic results achieved by pupils at schools like Hasmonean could be seen to compare very favourably with the public schools over the years. Sending your children to Jewish schools became much more fashionable.

The downside of the inflation, however, was that the cost of building the schools escalated and they cost far more than budgeted. As a result, there had to be economies in the other charitable work of the Chief Rabbi's Jewish Education Development Trust and one of the organizations which suffered was Jews' College, to which a substantial annual donation had to be stopped.

The United Synagogue found its resources severely stretched as well. It provided two tranches of support to the College at the time. One was to subsidise the general expenditure and the other was to support the *Hazanut* department. In 1972 the donation for general purposes was £4,546, but this reduced steadily over the decade to £2,555 in 1979. In 1973 the contribution towards the cost of the *Hazanut* course was £1,043 but by 1977 this was down to £100 and only recovered to £500.

At least there was now a profit from the College's annual function. This raised about £5,000 a year but the deficit was heading for over

£60,000 a year. In 1975 the total income was £38,000 and academic staff salaries and pension contributions alone were over £30,000. Which left the building costs, the rates, bank interest, lighting and heating and any number of other expenses to be covered from less than £8,000. The work of the College continued, though, in spite of all the difficulties, and in the decade seven more students received their *semicha*.

They included a great congregation rabbi, Eddie Jackson, who came from Ireland and would go on to look after the Kenton and Hampstead Garden Suburb Synagogues in London for the next thirty years. Raymond Apple was another, an Australian who was destined to be the rabbi of the Great Synagogue in Sydney and provide spiritual leadership of the highest quality.

One serious problem at the time was to provide the poorer students with bursaries to enable them to continue with their studies. The United Synagogue did provide bursaries for eight students, but inflation was continuously eating into their value. The United Synagogue said it couldn't increase them and was not influenced by the fact that in just four years the College had provided them with seven new ministers, eight teachers and seven *hazanim*. The students could also apply for state grants but these were, primarily, for their education rather than their subsistence.

One former graduate, unhappily, came to an untimely end; in 1973, on the Sinai front in the Yom Kippur War. There the College lost one of its alumni, by the death in action of Mayer Nissim who had originally come from Aden and obtained his BA only six years before. The Council put up a plaque in his memory but its whereabouts today is unknown.

By 1974 Rabinovitch had achieved a first for the College in the approval by the Council for National Academic Awards of a BA Honours degree in Jewish Studies, centred on the College. It was an endorsement of which the College could be proud. The CNAA said:

> Two aspects are considered by the Council: the college and the course. The college must be a suitable place for degree level work and have adequate facilities. The staff must be capable of teaching

at degree level and the pattern of teaching and examination arrangements must be appropriate. Subject to this initial approval of the course by the Council, [the College has] the same freedom as the universities to teach and examine the course and to admit the students.[5]

A number of distinguished non-Jewish scholars had visited the school before the course was approved. The Regius Professor of Hebrew at Cambridge wrote: 'I am satisfied not only that the new plan makes sense as a combination of different branches of Jewish Studies, but also that it will make use of modern scholarship ... as well as traditional Jewish learning.'[6] The professor was probably aware that he was endorsing the views of Samson Raphael Hirsch, but the form of the new courses would not have gained the approval of the principals of many Orthodox yeshivot. Jews' College was still accepting the views of Hirsch, Hertz and Büchler, right back to Nathan Marcus Adler. Indeed Dayan Moshe Swift attacked the course publicly, saying that it was a break in the Torah world because it included both Jewish and Christian scholarship that was critical of the Bible.

The Dayan's views were ignored by both Rabinovitch and the Chief Rabbi. Jakobovits' decision was indicative of his independence of the Beth Din. Ever since Dayan Yechezkel Abramsky had been appointed in 1935, the critics of the Chief Rabbinate had been accusing the incumbent of being in thrall to the Beth Din, but it was never true and Jakobovits was making the point again.

The Principal received his own reward when he was appointed a Visiting Fellow at Clare College, Cambridge. Unfortunately, the academic recognition the College and its staff merited, was unlikely, in Rabinovitch's opinion, to be mirrored in the way its graduates would be treated in the future. As he said as early as 1973: 'At the moment our rabbis are treated like *Shamosim* [beadles] and this can only destroy the type of spiritual leadership we need.'[7]

The varying viewpoints were discussed in public in a newspaper article in which Rabinovitch and the Vice President of the United

Synagogue stated their different views. The US spoke for what they called pastor-rabbis and Rabinovitch for intellectual rabbis who could hold their own with a better educated community. Neither was probably aware that exactly the same arguments had been set out 100 years before and many times in between.

In 1976 in a *Jewish Chronicle* supplement on the College, Chief Rabbi Jakobovits set out his own view on the shortcomings of the College in the past:

> Its sister academies in pre-war Europe and elsewhere to this day, never simply aimed at qualifying candidates for ministerial vacancies; they all pioneered enduring movements such as the Berliner Rabbiner Seminar's Orthodox-Scientific synthesis associated with Hildesheimer and Hoffman or the Breslau School's 'Historical Judaism' inspired by Graetz and Frankel, or Yeshiva University's 'Modern Orthodoxy'.[8]

This was quite true, but it overlooked the fact that there was no shortage of rabbis in Eastern Europe or of rabbinic families in the years leading up to the Holocaust. The community in Britain when Jews' College was started by Nathan Marcus Adler had no such resources or traditions. It had pretty well started from scratch.

One yardstick for judging academics is by how much they get published and where they are asked to speak at conferences. The Annual Reports in Rabinovitch's time now had a special section devoted to publications, as well as a list of the *Learned Papers and Invited Lectures given by Members of the College.* If most of the entries referred to the work of the Principal, it was still impressive. Between 1974 and 1975, for example, Rabinovitch gave lectures in New Jersey, City University and Yeshiva University in New York, John Hopkins in Baltimore and Birkbeck in London.

Rabbi Sidney Leperer made substantial contributions to the *Encyclopaedia of Hassidim,* on the Khmelnitzki Massacres, the Frankists, the first English translation of the Pirkei Avot (Ethics of the Fathers), and the incidents of Blood Libel in Eastern Europe between

1760 and 1914. A few years later, Jonathan Sacks was teaching Philosophy and Talmud at the College and was invited to speak at a conference of Senior Church Leaders at Windsor Castle.

There was also a non-academic life for the students to enjoy. Martin Wise, who was a Freshman at the College in 1976, recorded his impressions of the students in their spare time:

> The Student Union is active in organizing activities, and we have our own games room and a squash court (where you can work off the frustrations of a difficult piece of Gemara) ... Most students get involved with the London communities by teaching in Hebrew classes, taking services, leading Youth Groups etc. ... Everyone stops to relax around the table on Friday night. The atmosphere and singing have to be experienced to be appreciated.[9]

Jakobovits had wanted to see the College expand its activities even further and there were a number of new initiatives at this time. First and foremost was the Sir Israel Brodie and Lady Brodie Residence for Women Students which would provide accommodation in North London on the Finchley Road. This, it was hoped, would be the foundation of the additional educational resource Jakobovits had promised Rabinovitch. The residence would have room for eighteen women students and would be looked after by a warden and his wife. £83,000 had been raised to buy the building and adapt it to its new purpose. £25,000 came from the Harry & Abe Sherman Foundation, £30,000 from the Charles Wolfson Charitable Trust, and £25,000 from Michael Sobell.

It was also recognized this time that there would need to be an endowment fund to look after the maintenance of the residence, and £23,000 had been raised for this purpose. At the end of the day, though, there was only £15,000 left for furnishings and fittings and an indefinite sum was likely to be required to top up the Endowment Fund.

Of course it was a good idea. Of course it was needed; Jakobovits and Rabinovitch were right, but where was the additional money to come from? If the College couldn't eliminate its own deficit, was it wise to take on more heavy commitments? The attraction of new initiatives is the excitement of creation, the likelihood of admiration from society, and even the immortality which comes from the gift being labelled with the name of the donor. By contrast, paying maintenance costs is usually not rewarded with more than an entry in the accounts ledger and a passing reference in the Annual Report. There is seldom any long-term acclamation. The enthusiasm for new concepts is also difficult to keep up indefinitely.

The contrast was with the creation of a Chief Rabbi J.H. Hertz Chair in Rabbinics, which was financed by the entrepreneur, Sir Charles Clore, who endowed it with £75,000. This was in 1973 and, in today's money, it was over £800,000. It was the largest donation the College had ever received.

The Brodie Institute lost money from the beginning and would have lost more without contributions totalling £10,000 from the Chief Rabbi's JEDT. The building was also used for a sixth-form women's school which couldn't be made financially viable either. In 1973 there were twelve residents but only five were students at the College.

Eventually in 1976 the Finchley Road building had to be sold to defray the losses. Not for the first time, the Sephardi Judith, Lady Montefiore College came to the rescue. They bought it and continued to run it as before. A new organisation, the Friends of the Midrasha, took over the financial sponsorship. From the point of view of the Sephardim, the building could be used for the students of their Judith, Lady Montefiore College, and the Haham had managed to obtain the necessary finance from a charity in Switzerland.

Jews' College was relieved of the running costs but all that remained of the initial investment was £15,000. All the rest of the income from the sale had gone to reducing the overdraft. Admittedly few could have foreseen in advance just how much inflation would hit the country. For example, the first £25,000 of the Clore endowment was invested in Treasury 9½ per cent Loan 1999. Now 9½ per cent is an immense return in normal times, but when inflation is running at over 20 per cent, the capital value of the investment drops like a stone. In 1976 the market value of the 1973 £25,000 investment was just under £17,000. It recovered later, but that was the economic climate with which Bernard Garbacz, the Treasurer, had to deal. The lesson was still not learned.

Soon afterwards it was decided to create a Sir Israel Brodie Chair in Biblical Studies to honour the old Chief Rabbi. There was a splendid fund raising dinner where the guest of honour was the Secretary of State for Education, Shirley Williams (now Baroness Williams). The funds for the Chair soon reached £50,000 and Rabbi Irving Jacobs, a former graduate, who had joined the College staff in 1965, became the first incumbent. Unfortunately, by this time, the financial affairs of the College were so desperate that the money, with the old Chief Rabbi's approval, had to be used to reduce the deficit, rather than to increase Dr Jacobs' salary.

In December 1977 the Deputy President of the College, Haham Solomon Gaon, retired from his post as the spiritual leader of the Sephardim. There had been clashes between the lay leaders – the Elders and the Mahamad – and the previous Hahamim on more than one occasion, and this was another example of a family that could be dysfunctional.

There were two potential successors but the Mahamad decided not to appoint either of them due to another dispute. There hasn't, in fact, been a Haham since that time. Gaon soldiered on at the College until 1980 when it was decided to ask Rabbi Abraham Levy to serve as Acting Deputy President.

Levy was an alumnus of the College and has now been one of its most dedicated supporters for over fifty years. The College President was, of course, the Chief Rabbi and the Deputy had been the Haham for many years. As Levy was not the Haham, there was some doubt about the technical breach in the constitution, but he was a very popular figure and he would be confirmed as Deputy President by 1985.

In 1978 the Student Union Society was eighty years old. Over that period there had been a large number of lectures given by eminent speakers and the Society was naturally proud of its longevity. In 1972

Rabbi Shlomo Goren, the Israeli Chief Rabbi, had addressed the society. The current President, Martin Wise, only regretted that he now had only £65 in the kitty to pay for any celebrations.

One advantage he did have was that Marcia Falkender, the Prime Minister's secretary, lived nearby and was well disposed towards the College. With her help, in 1976 the Prime Minister, Harold Wilson, visited the College and in that year alone the Visitors' Book included Lord Justice Scarman, Keith Joseph, who was to be Margaret Thatcher's guru, and Sir Monty Finiston, the head of the British Steel Corporation. Reg Freeson, the Minister for Housing, also came to the College, as well as Sir Derek Ezra, the head of the National Coal Board. Most came to give luncheon lectures to the students at the Union Society meetings. If the College was eminent enough to merit the involvement of the Prime Minister, everybody of importance was likely to follow suit on receipt of an invitation.

In 1977 the CNAA approved a new degree course leading to a Bachelor of Education with Honours. The growth in the number of Jewish schools through the efforts of the Jewish Education Development Trust meant that there was a growing need for good Jewish teachers. The course was, therefore, developed with the Polytechnic of North London, although all the teaching was at the College. The course included a year in Israel, with the help of the Torah Department of the Jewish Agency.

It was a higher standard than a previous initiative with Middlesex University, by which students were able to get a Certificate in Education, even though they had been trained under Jewish academic auspices. The first three to pass the Middlesex exams had been in 1973 and graduates at the College continued to go on to teach at Jewish Schools. In 1973 Clive Fierstone had gone to the North London Jewish Day School and Yossi Houri to the Jews' Free School.

Once again, however, the initiative only made the College's financial position worse. In 1974 it had cost nearly £4,000 to run the course and in spite of £2,600 being donated by the Jewish Agency, the LBJRE and the Jewish Memorial Council, it still lost £1,400. Moreover, only a handful of students enrolled in the early years.

Rabinovitch was anxious to emphasize that the College was not just about training rabbis. In 1977 the Annual Report featured those students who had obtained their BA Hons. degrees and what they were then doing. It was certainly a varied list: Ahron Daum was a postgraduate rabbinical student, Yaacov Grunewald was the rabbi at Pinner Synagogue, Michael Isdaile was the *hazan* at the Heaton Park Synagogue in Manchester, David Kass was a London Student Counsellor, Joseph Munk was a teacher at JFS, Jonathan Sacks was lecturing at the College and Alan Shaw had become an accountant,

Kopul Kahana died in 1978 at the age of 83. He had transformed rabbinic studies during his years at the College, and over half of those who had received *semicha* in its 120-year-old history had earned it on his watch. The best Jewish journalist in his day was Chaim Bermant, and he reflected on Kahana:

> A short figure, with a shortish beard, a peaked yarmulka, and a bemused expression ... and he looked as if he might have alighted from a toadstool. His erudition was vast but he bore it lightly, and no rabbi was ever regarded with greater affection or reverence. He was extremely short-sighted and when he read a book, he looked as if he was wiping his face with it. He gave one a feeling of being helpless, unworldly and lost, which was possibly contrived, for he never missed a thing.[10]

Kahana hadn't just been a lecturer and an authority. In 1966, for example, he had given a responsa on a very difficult subject: was it kosher to eat a product containing gelatine? It might have been more appropriately decided by the Beth Din, but Kahana had no hesitation in giving his own ruling: 'gelatine processed from the outer skins of ritually unclean animals was kosher since the *treifa* elements were completely eliminated by the chemicals used'.[11]

Jeffrey Cohen, College alumnus and then Lecturer in Hebrew at Glasgow University, wrote in 1979 of the effects of Rabinovitch's leadership. He pointed out the move to the right in the curriculum, with three times as many study hours devoted to Talmud as before.

The BA Honours degree had become a far more Talmudically oriented course. Cohen saw the College curriculum becoming narrower, with the *semicha* course likely to take up to eight years. This far exceeded the demands of most yeshivot in Israel. In Cohen's view this could well explain the paucity of Jews' College students who had been awarded their *semicha* since Rabinovitch arrived. In fact, there had only been two.[12] Rabbi Cohen had still been well able to see both sides of the argument. He remembered his tutors with affection:

> Dr. Naphtali Wieder, now of Bar Ilan University, fostered the most exacting standards of academic excellence. He ensured that the ministers of today, if not scholarly themselves, at least held scholarship in the highest esteem. Eli Cashdan, now retired, was a teacher's teacher, whose enthusiasm was infectious and whose lectures were a model of lucidity. No one, having sat at his feet for two or three years, could fail to acquire an effective pedagogic technique.[13]

Rabbi Cohen was the minister of one of the largest synagogues in the country in Stanmore in North London, which he had been instrumental in building up, and which he developed into a model modern community. It was a severe challenge in bureaucratic efficiency, because it had to be run smoothly as well as *halachically*. If, for example, a congregation's membership is in the region of 2,000 and 95 per cent of them are in good health, the rabbi might need to be concerned with fifty or more health problems a week.

Ministers were often lumbered with more demands that they could reasonably fulfil. These included supervision of the synagogue classes, sermons, after-dinner speeches, lectures, attendance at weddings, *brissim*, bar mitzvahs, funerals and tombstone settings. This by no means completed the list and the pressure of work was immense. The value of the College's Talmudic lectures was likely to only be appreciated and assimilated when the minister had the time for study, preparation and revision. It was a long time since the foundation of the

College, when a town like Leeds might only have a handful of Jews with far fewer demands.

The structure of the Jewish educational world was markedly changing, as were general educational opportunities all over the country. By 1963, 70 per cent of the student population were receiving state grants of one kind or another. Higher education was, effectively, free and there were many more universities and university courses. For students working for *semicha*, there was also a far greater international choice, with the foundation of the State of Israel and the proliferation of yeshivot, seminaries and out-reach programmes, all anxious to attract students and would-be immigrants.

Within Britain, Gateshead had grown to be a far larger institution with a renowned faculty. There would be a steady supply of Gateshead-trained rabbis, and the right wing of the community would expand on the back of large families and total commitment. A new problem would, however, emerge when from the 1980s onwards more right-wing graduates of Israeli yeshivot began to be appointed to less Orthodox congregations.

Many of the rabbis would expect a higher standard of observance from their community than had been the normal custom, and there would be social tensions if, for example, the rabbi would not shake hands with a woman or tried to forbid mixed dancing at weddings. The community would become more widely split between the left and right wings and the centre would be the loser. As Jews' College had been created as the institution for training the centre's ministers, critics continued to emerge from both sides of the religious spectrum.

The College had held the fort while these developments had slowly taken place. Its raison d'être in the future could well be different from the objectives at its inception in Victorian times. And there was always the question of whether such an expensive operation could be sustainable for a comparatively small number of students.

There was also the problem of whether the College could continue to attract the high quality of lecturers who had served it in the past. In the nineteenth century when Britain had been the foremost nation in the world, the opportunity to work in the country had its own attractions. When the pogroms drove the Jews from Eastern Europe, Britain's image was enhanced as a safe haven. In the Nazi eras it proved so again, and many of the finest College lecturers, like Kopul Kahana, had found sanctuary in Britain.

The College-connected death toll in 1979 was very sad indeed. Chief Rabbi Israel Brodie died that year and, six months later, Sir Charles Clore also passed away. A third loss was Dr. Zimmels, the former Principal, who was knocked down in a road accident and died of his injuries. His daughter-in-law, Erla, would serve with distinction as the College Librarian for many years. The longest surviving alumnus of the College, Rev. Isaac Livingstone, died in the same year when he was 94. He had been at the College at the turn of the century.

In the future, much would continue to depend on the quality of the religious leadership in Britain and it was fortunate that Immanuel Jakobovits was a very highly regarded Chief Rabbi. The next decade would, however, be very testing.

NOTES

1. Interview with Rabbi, Lord Sacks.
2. *Jewish Chronicle*, 15 June 1973, p.11.
3. JCAR.
4. JCAR.
5. JCAR.
6. JCAR.
7. JCAR.
8. *Jewish Chronicle*, 3 October 1976, p.iv.
9. *Jewish Chronicle*.
10. *Jewish Chronicle*, 24 July 1978, p.18.
11. *Jewish Chronicle*, 5 April 1966, p.19.
12. *Jewish Chronicle*, 9 November 1979, p.25.
13. Ibid.

CHAPTER ELEVEN

Jonathan Sacks, Irving Jacobs and Daniel Sinclair

When Kopul Kahana died in 1978, the Kahana Kagan Foundation was set up in his memory to carry out research into Jewish halachic civil law in which he was an expert. Rabbi Simcha Lieberman had taken over the teaching of Codes but, by comparison with Kahana's day, only four students achieved semicha between 1977 and 1985. Like choosing which football team to play for, a lot depends on the reputation of the manager and the considerable length of the semicha course must also have been a consideration.

The financial position of the College worsened dramatically in the early 1980s. Although the United Synagogue continued to be the major beneficiary in terms of the graduates of Jews' College, in 1981 it only provided 1.1 per cent of the total budget – about £2,000. The total deficit reported in June 1982 was over £140,000 and it was obvious that this situation could not continue. It was, therefore, decided, with great reluctance, to sell the lease of Montagu Place to the Swedish Embassy and to move, temporarily, to the Beth Hamedrash in Finchley Synagogue until a new building could be found.

The Council reported in 1983 that the move had been 'completed in a very satisfactory manner'. This was certainly putting a good face on a disaster. The difference between a building good enough for an embassy and some spare rooms at the synagogue was stark. The 50,000 library books had to be put into a special security warehouse, which obviously made them far less accessible to researchers and readers. Morale naturally suffered.

The Chief Rabbi announced that the College would still widen its range of courses, to offer additional Jewish education to teachers, social workers, synagogue officials and communal civil servants.

Nahum Rabinovitch had done all he could, but gave up the struggle. He announced that he was going to make aliyah to Israel at the end of the year and went on to become the head of a yeshivah on the West Bank. He remains one of the finest Talmudic scholars and a considerable author. He had put a great deal of effort into Jews' College, but he had been unable to become comfortable with the Anglo-Jewish brand of Orthodoxy which was so much less demanding than his own. He also wanted to lead a full-time yeshiva, with students not having to try to marry Torah and academic studies.

Historically, the College had provided rabbis who took a latitudinarian stance; they were, for the most part, tolerant and all-embracing. For its part, the United Synagogue always maintained its central control, which diminished the authority and responsibility of the rabbis, though there could be conspicuous individual exceptions. One, for example, was Dayan Morris Swift who was a Gateshead alumnus and believed a rabbi's task was to discipline his congregation. When he died in 1983 one of his colleagues on the Beth Din wrote: 'His kindness and honesty, rather than his pulpit and platform reprimands, provoked by lack of communal discipline and disloyalty, was a true index of his character'.[1] So it was possible to strike a discordant note if the rabbi had the knowledge and the personality. Rabinovitch even had his disagreements with the Chief Rabbi.

Stanley Kalms had resigned as vice chairman in 1982 but came back as Chairman of the Council in September 1983. Jonathan Sacks became its Principal in March 1984. If any team was going to restore the fortunes of the College, the community could not have hoped for one better.

Stanley Kalms (now Lord Kalms), was a highly successful businessman who had remained fully committed to his Anglo-Jewish roots. When Chief Rabbi Jakobovits had taken office, his main ambition had been to create a network of Jewish day schools. The creation of the Jewish Educational Development Trust was the engine to drive that concept forward, and Stanley Kalms agreed to take the

Irving Jacobs, Principal and one of the finest academics. Copyright: *The Jewish Chronicle*.

wheel. The JEDT became a resounding success with some of the most senior entrepreneurs in the community, like Alan Sugar (now Lord Sugar) of Amstrad, playing major roles in creating new schools. In the coming years Jewish schools would blossom as they had never done before. It was not, therefore, surprising that the Chief Rabbi asked Kalms to see what he could do with Jews' College; he had acted as vice chairman and would now take over the chairmanship from Arnold Lee, a fine lawyer but not as persuasive when fund raising. Kalms had already been able to improve the original offer for Montagu Place.

Jonathan Sacks (now Lord Sacks), was, even as a youngster, a spellbinding speaker. At 25 he was teaching Jewish Philosophy at the College. He was 35 when he took over as Principal, even though he had received his own semicha there only six years before. He was a very fine writer and if there was the disadvantage that he didn't have a very lengthy teaching background, he could communicate with the younger generation better than most.

Kalms remembers:

> Jews' College, under my chairmanship, was saved from closure and re-formed on the basis of a college to train young men for the UK rabbinate. We had in the UK virtually no suitable candidates, which meant overseas recruitment, and even that was not easy. We had therefore a disparate rabbinate with very little communal training, a wide age range, boredom and indifference from communities, and an inadequate response to projecting the Chief Rabbi's philosophy.[2]

In spite of these perceived shortcomings the College graduates since the war had included seven men who would go on to be chief rabbis internationally, the Director of the Taylor-Schechter Geniza Research unit at Cambridge, the Quain Professor of English Language and Literature at University College, London, the Professor of the Department of Jewish Studies at the University of Wisconsin, an adviser to the US Secretary of Defense, the Director of the Jewish Marriage Council, and many head teachers, community rabbis and hazanim.

When Jonathan Sacks took over as Principal, he recalled that there was 'no money and no premises'. Relations with London University were also breaking down. The university was concerned that at the College there was no multiplicity in academic areas, as would be found in most colleges: Jews' College taught only Jewish subjects. At the time, there were eight postgraduate students, fourteen studying for their BAs and eleven for their B.Eds. Three were studying Hazanut and twelve more attended the part-time evening course in Hazanut.

Lord Sacks, student, Principal and President. Copyright: *The Jewish Chronicle*.

In 1984, the Council for National Academic Awards (CNAA) panel of academics assessing Jews' College called a meeting to discuss whether there was any future for the College.[3] Sacks feared that the College would be closed. So he took the bull by the horns and promised the academic panel that within a year there would be a series of courses which would be taught from a non-Jewish standpoint and then from a Jewish one. The CNAA relented.

Satisfying the CNAA was one thing. Getting more students was another. Sacks considered that there were three modern restraints which were working against the College. The first was that there was a much wider choice for prospective students: both Israel and the United States offered many options. Second, many of the other colleges had far more students, which made for wider social contacts. Third, in Israel, they could be studying in the heart of the Jewish world.

To help solve the problems Kalms initiated and funded a scheme which would provide fellowships, worth up to £10,000 a year, for students with secular degrees but a limited Jewish academic background, and yeshiva graduates without academic qualifications. After completing their courses, they would agree to serve a community for five years. It enabled students to either study in Israel or back in Britain. It was a very generous provision, fully in keeping with the benefactors of the College over the years.

One beneficial upshot was that any minister with the necessary qualifications could apply and this was attractive because they could well be earning less than £10,000 a year, tax free, with their congregations. There was only one possible response, and Sacks recalls that the salary of rabbis shot up about 40 per cent as a consequence. If the eventual results were not as good as had been hoped, the probable problem was that the academically well-qualified beneficiaries did not have the pastoral skills, which were necessary, as well as their intellectual ability.

Another solution to the lack of students was the creation of an MA course, which had its foundation in the Young Jewish Leadership Institute, started some years earlier by the Sephardim and the Hebrew University in Jerusalem. Lectures could be attended in the evenings, which attracted existing ministers who wanted to add to their academic CVs. The quality of the courses at Jews' College was already up to first degree standard, so this innovation also received the blessing of the CNAA.

One of Kalms' concerns was the old question of whether the College graduates were sufficiently aware of how to deal with the pastoral duties of a minister. Sacks took the problem on board and came up with a course in Practical Rabbinics. When looking for teachers on the subject, he spread the net further than normal College academic sources. Part of the course was devoted to media training by professional broadcasters from the BBC, there was a professor from the Open University, and Kalms brought in his own senior executives to teach team management. One existing minister they did rely on was Maurice Unterman who taught Homiletics. Unterman was the rabbi of

Lord Kalms, another great benefactor. Copyright: Lord Kalms.

the Marble Arch Synagogue and a fine preacher. His trademark was to walk past the pulpit even when he was going to give a sermon, and then hesitate as if a thought had just struck him. Retracing his steps, he would give the sermon, and the device gave his words an added spontaneity.

What both Kalms and Sacks recognized was that students were learning in an intellectually closed environment. They needed to be taught how to operate in the field. It was, of course, always a feature of their training from the earliest years of the College that they would take services on the High Holydays and help with synagogue Hebrew classes. Their alumni had, however, shown as Chaplains to the Forces during the war that they could cope very well in the field if necessary.

In 1986 Sacks prepared a paper called The Next Three Years and he reviewed the problems of the College. The last few, he felt, had been marked by: 'Crises, uncertainty, student shortages and failures to engage with the needs of the community.' The Hazanut courses had become a disappointment: 'There have been no applicants; there are few vacancies; our own graduates have had difficulty finding employment.' He went on: 'We have not played the roles undertaken variously by the Young Jewish Leadership Institute, Spiro or Yakar.' Even the College prospectus in 1985 had sounded gloomy: 'The vast majority of Jews' College graduates are today in the professions, including teaching, and not in the rabbinate.'

There was no way, however, in which Sacks or any of the other officers of the College were going to sacrifice their principles for the sake of gathering a bit more approval from those who were not on the same wavelength. In 1986, for example, Rabbi David Soetender, a Reform rabbi in his own right and the son of a Reform rabbi, signed on for a course at the College. When his affiliations were reported, he was told he was not acceptable. In such circumstances the Progressives, in their criticism of such decisions, normally compared the current situation with that of past years: Sir Philip Magnus, from Upper Berkeley Street and a senior member of the Council for many years in the past, had been very welcome. The fact that the Progressives had moved far from their religious position in those days was not relevant in their view. The College, on the other hand, would not have viewed with any relish the possibility that young students in the classroom might be listening to the views of a Reform rabbi contradicting the teacher.

The relationship between the College and the community had not changed that much over the years. It was still considered worthy of maximum support, without such support being forthcoming, except from a tiny minority of individuals. The United Synagogue, however, now at last became much more positive in its approach. Fortunately for the financing there was finally a senior officer who was very much in favour of the College; Victor Lucas had been elected President of the United Synagogue in 1984, and although he only served one three-year term, he was instrumental in getting the US to agree to give the College £40,000 a year, in recognition of all the work they put in to producing ministers, teachers and hazanim for the community. It was the first time in its 100-year-old history that the organization had made a really meaningful contribution to the College.

Apart from the fellowships, the first task for Kalms was to find a suitable building for the College. The Council decided that the cost of locating in North London was far more sustainable than the West End. But there was a major problem: to house the library would require many thousands of feet of space. Kalms found a splendid building in Oxhey, near Watford, but Sacks felt strongly that young men, without cars, were not going to find a location that far out of London very attractive.

Kalms eventually found the perfect setting in a former furniture research centre in Albert Road in Finchley. Kalms was the College's lender of last resort for many years. He now financed the reconstruction in cooperation with the United Synagogue, and the new building was opened in November 1984. Chief Rabbi Jakobovits called it: 'The rebirth of what, alas, for many reasons is now probably the oldest institute of higher Jewish learning anywhere in the world.'[4]

There were not just financial problems. When Sacks accepted the role of Principal of Jews' College in 1984, some of the older staff, especially Simcha Lieberman, did not consider him sufficiently expert. It was only six months after Sacks's appointment that the divisive nature of the views of Rabbi Louis Jacobs caused discord again. Jacobs had written a new book called *The Tree of Life* and Sacks reviewed it in the *Jewish Chronicle*.[5] It was a very long and thorough review and, while it criticized the Jacobs's theses, it praised him as a good and pleasant individual.

The content of the review was not appreciated by Rabbi Lieberman. He had been one of Sacks's tutors when he was studying for semicha and, by 1984, he had been at the College for fourteen years. A survivor of the Warsaw Ghetto and the Treblinka concentration camp, Lieberman was highly regarded as a Talmudic scholar. A few years before, the Chief Rabbi had praised his: 'rare talents of qualities, nobility of mind and heart which has won such widespread respect among numerous friends for your scholarship and character'.[6] It is always difficult for a teacher to find one of his pupils promoted over him. There are also often the problems of the generation gap, and to make their personal relations more adversarial, Sacks's approach to the students was less austere than Lieberman's.

Now, according to one of his supporters, Lieberman wrote a 'devastating critique of Jonathan Sacks' review of Louis Jacobs' *A Tree of Life*'.[7] Apparently the critique was written in Hebrew and not widely distributed. It wasn't the first time in the history of the College that there had been internal discord among the academics. Epstein had not welcomed the prospect of Louis Jacobs taking over after his retirement. Now Sacks took over Lieberman's teaching of rabbinics. As Kalms recalled:

> When Jonathan Sacks took over the role of Principal of Jews' College in 1984 after his predecessor, Rabbi Rabinovitch, went to Israel, his appointment was not accepted by Rabbi Lieberman, who had no sympathy with the new ideas and was unwilling to accept Sacks as his 'boss'. Jonathan Sacks had great respect for Lieberman but this was not reciprocated. Leiberman was certainly respected as a Talmudist, but the college needed a wider range of teaching skills. Over a period I had several discussions with Sacks about the difficulty of implementing his plans with Lieberman in total opposition. This was obviously an untenable position. Not, I imagine, unusual in the tangled relationships of academia, the unwillingness to accept some change of direction. There were never any meaningful discussions about better remuneration. At that time it was not remotely possible as the College's financial position remained precarious, although I was the lender of last resort and in fact underwriting our programme.
>
> It was decided between Sacks and myself, with the implicit agreement of Chief Rabbi Jakobovits, that Lieberman would have to go and he was therefore told by Sacks of our decision and offered three months' salary, which was appropriate to the funds available. Lieberman was very active in fighting his corner. He went to the media and unfortunately it became a *Jewish Chronicle*

item with not too much concern about the real facts. Lieberman became the hero and Jews' College the villain, a typical anti-establishment situation adopted in our community.

We proposed that we would let the Beth Din sort out the matter and we would accept their ruling. The interesting thing was that Lieberman absolutely refused to go to the Beth Din. The Chief Rabbi had written to a friend that 'the tensions had been unbearable' before the dismissal, and the letter was leaked. When an academic friend of Lieberman went to see the Chief Rabbi to try to resolve the problem, he later referred to 'the miniature tape recorder I'd accidentally secreted about my person'.[8]

There were few holds barred.

At a meeting at Dayan Ehrentreu's home with the Chief Rabbi, Rabbi Sacks, myself and Professor Geoffrey Alderman, Rabbi Ehrentreu expressed deep disappointment that Lieberman would not accept a Beth Din arbitration. There followed a lot of bitter words and I decided to settle with Lieberman privately. The agreed level of compensation was circa £25,000. [Rabbi Lieberman's salary had been £6,200 a year.] As a layman, the whole issue was distasteful but both sides had reasons for their decisions and the whole incident was, in effect, nothing more than a new team wanting to take over from the old team who had suffered years of frustration.

The hard fact was that there was no role for Lieberman's talents and qualities at Jews' College and they would have certainly been wasted on our candidates. At this stage I was offering a Kalms Fellowship of £10,000 a year for three years, for a training course resulting in a semicha for those who wanted to take up a communal role. Jews' College could never have been a place for advanced teaching. It didn't have that environment or resource. We were not positioned as a Yeshiva. A big storm in a small teacup with all the rabbinical gentlemen put in an invidious position, except Lieberman with his not unreasonable private agenda.⁹

The College authorities refused to defend themselves, as they felt the row reflected badly on the whole community and shouldn't be blown up further. Lieberman was less concerned about this and called in journalists and photographers to his home to provide his account of his dismissal.¹⁰ The Dean of the College, Rabbi Irving Jacobs, went on record regretting Lieberman's departure but this was not held against him in the future, when he was appointed as Dean and given responsibility for secular studies.

Academic disagreements can get very heated and this one was not the way the new team would have wished to mark their first year together. Nevertheless, the Council now set up a new Academic Advisory Panel, headed by Dr Aubrey Newman of Leicester University, a well-known author on aspects of Jewish history, and they devised fresh courses which were also accepted by the Council for National Academic Awards.

The scope of the curriculum took advantage of new educational aids. These included a series of films about business management featuring John Cleese, and a two-year course on counselling. Another innovation was called Traditional Alternatives and set up conferences on major Jewish topics in various parts of the country. The speakers were exceptionally able and authoritative and drawn from all over the world. As many as 1,000 people signed up for one conference with another 1,000 unable to get places. It was a development of Irving Jacobs's lecture programme but on a far larger scale. Sacks was anxious that the College should provide educational opportunities for as much of the Jewish general public as possible. As he put it, his aim was to make the College: 'The Archimedean point from which you could move the Jewish world'.¹¹

Others have memories of those days. Where children have little say in their school education, it is by their own efforts that they gain admission to higher education. The fond memory of that achievement lasts many years and as Rabbi Raymond Apple recalls:

I lived in its dorm, took its teacher's, minister's and rabbinical diplomas, served at various times as president of the students' union, Council member and casual lecturer in education and youth work, and married another College student ... As time went on, most [congregations] questioned the old ministerial model and wanted fully qualified rabbis at all synagogues. In the end the 'reverend' system wound down and almost every synagogue now has a rabbi. The old Minhag Anglia is out of favour. Pastoral skills are still required, but so are shiurim [lectures] and scholarship.[12]

It was in 1985 that Judaism in Britain, totally uncharacteristically, stuck its head above the parapet. It had always been the policy to remain as quiet as a church mouse in a country where it was totally tolerated, but generally looked upon by the public as a somewhat quaint relic of far-off times. That had stood it in good stead from the time of the first Haham, Jacob Sasportas, in 1663. He was only installed after he had signed a document promising not to communicate in any way with the Church of England, for fear of antagonising it. Judaism isn't an evangelising religion anyway.

In 1985, however, the Archbishop of Canterbury decided that the government weren't doing enough to tackle poverty and a pamphlet came out called *Faith in the City*. The Chief Rabbi was asked to sign it as well and found himself in a quandary. He explained publicly that Judaism didn't quite see the problem of poverty as the church did. As far as the Talmud was concerned, 'the best charity is that which helps the poor dispense with charity'. It was not up to the rich to subsidise the poor. It was up to the rich to help the poor get on their feet and stop being poverty stricken. As that was the view of the government, and particularly of the Prime Minister, Margaret Thatcher, Jakobovits found himself in the House of Lords soon after.

At about the same time Jonathan Sacks had been asked to write a paper on the same subject for a think tank. This was published as *Wealth & Poverty – A Jewish Analysis*, and received a lot of publicity in the press as well. As the *Daily Telegraph* wrote in 1985 of his pamphlet, 'It is so good and crisp that it almost makes one want to convert', and, 'Why can't the Chief Rabbi appoint a commission to investigate the problem of the inner cities?'

Fortunately, both Jakobovits and Sacks could handle their suddenly elevated position in the country. Over the years they spoke and wrote without bravado or being patronising. The message was always that this was the way the Jews looked at it. Nobody had to follow suit, but the Jews would stick to their rules and if anybody wanted to copy them, they were very welcome to do so.

From a Judaic point of view, Jonathan Sacks was a product of Jews' College, not Cambridge, where he had gained his degree. The College could take credit for the quality of its teaching and that was what it had been set up to provide. Not that everybody within the community agreed. Stanley Kalms, as Chairman of the Council, would have been pleased that in the same year the CNAA had inspected the College and praised the 'optimism and drive of both staff and students'. They felt the courses were 'on a firmer basis than ever before'.[13] Kalms, however, went on record as saying that middle-of-the-road rabbis were becoming harder to find. He felt the candidates were becoming too right wing.

It was true, but there was a reason for the change. The community had become more middle class and the rabbinical tradition was no longer associated with poor, foreign-speaking immigrants. It was no longer downmarket to be part of the rabbinic tradition. The Chief Rabbi, himself, believed in the traditions of Samson Raphael Hirsch, that it was possible to marry the secular and rabbinic world, but that halachah must always come first.

There was a long-term trend continuing to develop. On the one hand there was increased out-marriage and, on the other, a growth in the Charedi (very Orthodox) part of the community. It was exactly the middle that was being squeezed. The proportion of the community that was Anglo-Jewish was diminishing. The whole country was becoming more secular and while this led to an admirable degree of tolerance, just as it had in the time of Charles II, which benefited Jews as a community, so the two Jewish sides were growing further apart. The ghosts of Sir David Salomons and Sir Robert Waley Cohen were still in opposition to the views of every Jews' College principal from Michael Friedländer and Adolph Büchler onwards.

The wardens of Orthodox synagogues were now expected to keep the Sabbath and their habit of wearing top hats on Shabbat fell into decline. In the United Synagogue and across the country, yarmulkes would be worn by many members in the street and it was becoming cool to be religious. Jews' College had kept the faith during many difficult years, and it had won through to a larger proportion of the community keeping a more observant lifestyle.

There was now a possibility of making Albert Road a centre for a new Orthodox congregation created by a 33-year-old Australian, Rabbi Alan Kimche. It was agreed in 1984 that the Ner Yisrael congregation would worship at the College and as their community was largely composed of young professionals, it would give the College an extra dimension. So successful, however, was the growth of the congregation that they outgrew the facilities at the College and left for larger premises in 1986.

In 1987 there was a need for another major fund raising campaign, this time for £1 million. The aim was to obtain some residential accommodation for the students and to create a Department of Teacher Training with a full-time director. More bursaries and scholarships were needed and the books in the library needed computerised cataloguing. It was also recognized that in order to get more eminent visiting lecturers, it would be necessary to pay higher fees. A quarter of a million pounds was raised by the end of the year.

The fund raisers could also have considered the need to raise money to pay for publications. In 1975 the Chief Rabbi had founded a glossy magazine called *L'Eylah* which contained many good articles of Jewish interest. The only problem was that it was almost bound to lose money; amateur glossy magazines do. Yet in 1985 a decision was made that in future the production would be a joint effort of the Chief Rabbi's office and Jews' College. When every item of expenditure was under the closest scrutiny, the College didn't need the additional burden of a £5,000-plus loss a year on a magazine.

In 1988 the Council for National Academic Awards approved an alternative core area of the syllabus at Jews' College for the study of Jewish Law. This enabled women to study for the degree at the University. The original university course had been directed to Biblical and Mediaeval Studies, but the College had been granted the right to develop their own course on Jewish law, based on the din.

The problem for women was that most of the male students who joined the course had a good deal of previous College training and were, therefore, able to deal with a more advanced curriculum than they could. As a consequence, the new curriculum was pitched at a level which women would be able to tackle, just as intellectually demanding, but starting from a more elementary base. The new course was of particular interest to a former student at the College, Tamra Wright. She had studied Jewish Ethics at the College and had a Doctorate in Philosophy from Essex University. This had been followed by teaching spells at Essex and LSE. She had often been asked to speak at synagogue events and recognized that there were many women who were Talmudically knowledgeable, but who had little outlet for their expertise. She decided the solution was a degree course which would give them a first class CV for teaching. It would take a long time to emerge but she would persevere.

Ten years later, in 1999, Michael Bradfield, the son of the founder of Hospital Plan Insurance Services, wanted to mark his mother Susi's 70th birthday. He decided to found a Susi Bradfield Lectureship at the renamed London School of Jewish Studies (LSJS) to train women in the way Tamra Wright had envisaged so many years before. The support he provided was a very generous £60,000 a year and today there are, annually, over a dozen women taking the free one-year course. As a result the ranks of well-trained women teachers are being regularly augmented.

In 1990 Jonathan Sacks, the Principal of the College, was appointed Chief Rabbi, the third Jews' College graduate in succession to receive that distinction. When he took office in 1991 the Council appointed Irving Jacobs as the new Principal. By this time the reputation of Sacks had burgeoned, ever since he had worked with Chief Rabbi Jakobovits on the question of dealing with the problems of poverty.

In 1990 he was invited to be a Visiting Professor at the University of Essex and to give the BBC's prestigious Reith Lecture. He took as his subject *The Persistence of Faith*. By now a regular contributor to BBC religious programmes and the press, the reputation of the College was enhanced by his association with it, and the number of students was considerably increased as a result. In that year thirteen students were studying rabbinics, seven for their M.Phil and no less than thirty-three for the MA course. There were another sixteeen doing postgraduate studies and a further eighteen studying for their BA Hons. Teacher training had attracted twenty-nine more students. It was a vast improvement on the situation when Sacks had first become Principal only a few years before. Just as his predecessors had been towering academics, so Sacks showed the importance of the Principal possessing a high profile in the academic world to attract an increased student intake. The problem was, of course, that growth meant added expenditure, and the deficit in 1990 was over £50,000. When he wrote his final report, Sacks commented: 'To this day, Anglo-Jewry remains obsessed with buildings and is dismissive of what is needed to train and inspire a [religious] builder. Only if that monumental misplacement of priorities is reversed, will the mainstream of this community have a future.'[14]

He also recognized just how important it was to have an Orthodox entrepreneur backing the College. As he said of his early partnership with Stanley Kalms:

> We knew it would take a superhuman effort to save it [the College] and Mr Kalms gave that effort. He was a dynamo of energy. He was relentlessly demanding and never let us rest on any achievements. His financial assistance was, of course, fundamental, but it was less than half of his contribution. He was concerned about the ability of rabbis to communicate with and relate to their members. Our response was the Practical Rabbinics course.[15]

Stanley Kalms resigned at the same time. He was exceptionally diligent when he took on a responsibility, but he liked to follow an activity for ten years and then turn to other interests. He had taken on the JEDT in 1979 and the College a few years later, and the time had come, he felt, to make a change. He had been devoted to the interests of the College. Sacks remembers that the day before Kalms's company was to make a massive take-over bid, his Chairman spent the afternoon on the work of the JEDT and the evening on the interests of Jews' College. Simon Kaplan, who had taken over from Frank Levine in 1984, also resigned. He had been the College's day-to-day contact with Kalms and put in a great deal of work to ensure that the policies were carried out effectively.

Frank Levine, Ephy Levine's son, had also given a lot of time to other communal bodies as well; for example, he was the President of the Kashrus Commission from 1974 to 1985. Like his father, he had been a pillar of the community and when he died in 1992 at the age of 74, his passing was much regretted.

The faculty would lose one of its foremost lecturers in 1995 with the death of Rabbi Dr Sidney Leperer. He was an alumnus of the College and had been appointed to teach Jewish history in 1974. A first class teacher, he was then in post until he died at the age of 73. When Irving Jacobs resigned, Leperer had held the fort until Daniel Sinclair arrived.

Looking to the future Sacks identified a traditional flaw: the College was still too concentrated on producing ministers for the London and United Synagogue congregations. The reason for this stretched all the way back to the days when candidates for the Council would not be appointed if they didn't have a home in London. The efforts to get the provincial communities involved in the success of the College had been hampered by its image as a London institution, controlled by Londoners and without the interests of the provinces at heart.

The students at the College continued to reflect well on their tutors. In 1992 four of the eight sitting their BA in Jewish Studies got firsts, including a woman, Lisa Nadler. Jacobs was in constant demand to lecture throughout the community, but the strain told on him. He retired through ill-health at the end of 1993 when he was only 55. Sacks, took over again temporarily until a successor could be found.

In the spring of that year it was announced that Rabbi Dr Daniel Sinclair would take up the post in September on a three-year contract. David Pomson, the new Chair of the Council, had met him in Israel in 1994 and discussed the possibility of his taking over as Principal. He would cut a very different figure from predecessors like Friedländer, Büchler and Epstein. He was English, 44, a former pupil at the Jews' Free School and he had earned his semicha in 1991.

Apart from serving as the minister in Edinburgh for three years, he had spent most of his adult life in Israel, where he was an expert in Jewish law and medical ethics. He had law degrees from London, Melbourne and the Hebrew University. When first interviewed by the press in Jerusalem it was noted that he was thin and wiry, and in the non-clerical garb of jeans and trainers. As an Israeli academic this was not unusual, but at the College it was hardly the traditional dress. The College was now looking for a more youthful and modern image than had been the norm.

Sinclair inherited an institution which David Pomson believed had suffered from 'utter neglect'. He wasn't quite right. It's never easy to trace the source of a problem back through many years, but it wasn't neglect that had crippled the College; it was the way it had been taken off-message on two specific occasions. First by Waley Cohen, all the way back in the 1930s, trying to create a centre for Jewish organizations and saddling the College with a rent for Woburn House it couldn't possibly afford. Then by Chief Rabbi Brodie, creating a monument to lost European yeshivas with Montagu Place, a building fit for an embassy, but again with overheads the College could never support. That fascination with buildings, which Sacks had criticized, was the real culprit.

The pious belief that G-d would provide, or at least the community as a whole, had never worked out in practice over more than 100 years. The community still benefited enormously from the graduates of the College but, equally steadfastly, refused to pay for their education. The result, which might well have been foreseen, was that, when benefactors like Montefiore, Samuel, Tuck and Kalms could not be replaced, it was inevitable that the College would founder financially.

Alan Mocatta had, indeed, warned them of this when Montagu Place was first opened. When the inevitable happened, the finger of blame was pointed everywhere but where it belonged.

By 1995 the financial position was such that the Annual Report no longer contained details of the various Balance Sheets, as it had done since 1855. The Treasurer, Bernard Waiman, contented himself with:

> The past year has seen a severe deterioration in the financial condition of the College. When I became Treasurer I was not aware of how dire the situation had become. I have been looking at the expenses of the College but this has not been the major difficulty and although some savings have been made, the problem lies in the lack of income. It is clear that a major fund raising exercise is required to address this position.[16]

Sinclair was anxious to widen the appeal of the College to young people. By the time his period in office was completed, the number of students enrolled on the courses at the College had reached an unprecedented 150, though, of course, most of them were part-time. Only 10 per cent of them were studying for semicha, but Sinclair had also introduced pre-semicha courses for men studying for other degrees, so that they could move on to the rabbinic qualification. He also arranged for Israeli scholars to lecture on their specialities, and there was an annual course of lectures by distinguished overseas academics.

> When I arrived at Jews' College I found a group of mostly young married men, almost all of whom had part-time positions either in education or in the ministry. And that is where they have stayed after graduation.
>
> The introduction of the pre-semicha course has brought in a younger look, some very interesting people who would not have come into a regular rabbinics programme ... a group of highly intelligent people doing all sorts of things from a PhD in physics to degrees in law and international relations ... I imagine some

of them will go into key positions in the rabbinate because of the momentum they will get just by being here and doing the course.[17]

It was also a notable innovation by Sinclair that in 1996 there were three women lecturers who were teaching religious rather than secular subjects: Fiona Blumfield, who had degrees from both Cambridge and London, was covering Bible and Hebrew grammar; Evelyn Stern, with degrees from London and Cornell, was teaching Jewish and Comparative Ethics and Philosophy; and Tamra Wright, with her doctorate from Essex University, was teaching Jewish philosophy. Women had also been admitted to the BA course in Jewish studies.

Jews' College remained one of the very few institutions where, to obtain semicha, it was necessary to have not only the rabbinical knowledge, but also a degree from London University. Most yeshivas had still rejected academic Jewish studies. It was also unusual that semicha students now studied for their university degrees in mixed classes. In 1995 over fifty students at the College got certificates and degrees, including eight who had received semicha. One highlight of Sinclair's time was the College hosting the conference of the International Jewish Law Association in 1996.

There were still a lot of other institutions where semicha could be obtained, in Israel and America. As Rabbi Sinclair recalled:

> A particularly attractive option for an Orthodox person at the time was to engage in an intensive study programme in Hebrew at an Israeli yeshiva or Ulpan for a couple of years after school and then to return to England for a regular university degree ... The Jews' College I encountered in 1997 was no longer the mainstay of the Anglo-Jewish rabbinate ... and it also had a number of competitors in the field of academic Jewish studies.[18]

Sinclair also remembers, with no pleasure, that the main item on the agenda of almost every Council meeting was the dire financial state of the College.

The practical side of Jewish education was not neglected, though the programme was run by a new body, the semi-independent Agency for Jewish Education, which was based at the College.

During Sinclair's years in office eighteen students graduated with a BA, thirty-eight with an MA, twelve received semicha and twelve got Diplomas and Certificates. When he went back to Israel in 1997, the Chairman, not surprisingly, said how sorry everybody was to see him go. The question was now how the College would carry on. David Pomson summed up the situation in his report in 1996:

> When the next history of the College comes to be written ... its chronicler will look upon the period 1995/1996 as one of critical import. Year on year, Chairman and Treasurers alike had warned of the disastrous consequences of that indifference which Anglo-Jewry loves to demonstrate for the welfare of its key institutions. At our most recent graduation ceremony, I described as intolerable the lack of financial support. Cassandra-like, our prophecies of impending doom were condemned to be heard but unbelieved. With liquid assets inadequate for one term's activity, coupled with furore over the proposed auction of some of our treasures, the extent of our difficulties at last achieved recognition ... The question was not so much of rescue, rather of disposal with dignity and discretion. Some more active consciences were allayed with minor handouts; others while claiming to be the closest of friends, not only failed to solicit support on our behalf but singularly failed to make any contribution of a personal nature.[19]

The extent of the difficulties was now finally recognized and the Schaller family very generously decided to buy the Albert Road site for the college. It was a major contribution to keeping the College in existence. The fund raising tapped new potential sources in 1998 when a limited edition of a fragment of a rare torah scroll in the Library was offered to anybody who gave the College £1,000. In the first year sixteen were given out.

That year Daniel Sinclair turned his attention to making, perhaps for all time, the case for the College:

> Anglo-Jewry has always prided itself on its tradition of open-minded Orthodoxy and an ability to tolerate Jews of varying degrees of religious practice within the United Synagogue ... in order to be convincing and effective, however, tolerance must be grounded in Jewish sources and their interpretation over the ages ... vital if we wish to be in position to pass it on to our youth, who require good, solid and convincing arguments for the maintenance of any form of religious life ... the only way in which this type of informed tolerance can be fostered is to train people to study the sources of their Judaism ... seriously and with devotion but in an academic and contextual setting. This, precisely, is the mission of Jews' College.[20]

There were problems too on the academic side. The University of London had decided some years before that any educational body with less than 5,000 students could no longer be part of the university. What it could do instead was link up with one of the existing parts, and the LSJS had, officially, become part of the School of Oriental and African Studies. This was now producing its own difficulties. The SOAS was a hotbed of anti-Israel societies and its Jewish students were subject to much invective. There were numerous complaints from the community, which the School rejected as exaggerated and refused to compromise on its protection of free speech for visiting lecturers.

When Sinclair returned to Israel in 1997 Jonathan Sacks commissioned an in-depth enquiry into the future of the College by the United Jewish Israel Appeal's Strategic Planning Unit. The Jewish boarding school, Carmel College, had just closed and there was concern that the College might follow suit. The enquiry, led by Professor Leslie Wagner, a highly regarded academic, led to the appointment of Professor David-Hillel Ruben as the new Principal.

Ruben was an exceptionally bright American philosophy professor at the London School of Economics and took over from Sacha Stern who had been the Acting Principal on a two-year secondment. It was Ruben's belief that there should be far more part-time courses at the College to attract more students from the ranks of the general public. As he said at the outset: 'The College should be tapping into a huge reservoir of people. Where there are now just two full-time lecturers, the expansion will eventually require at least six academic staff. Its current £500,000 budget would need to increase by 50 per cent.'[21]

Where that kind of money was to come from was not specified. It was also in Ruben's time that, in 1998, the name of the College was changed to the London School of Jewish Studies to reflect its ambition to broaden its attraction to a wider section of the Jewish community.

Another major new initiative was announced in May 1998 when Rabbis Chaim Brovender and Shlomo Riskin of the Ohr Torah Stone Yeshiva in Israel were invited to come to London to set up a branch of their Yeshiva within the College. Brovender had pioneered the right of women to study Talmud at seminary and was a controversial figure. As Lord Sacks recalled:

> The idea was that Rabbi Brovender, who had been a pioneering figure in yeshivah learning for Baalei teshuvah, would create a yeshiva presence in the London School of Jewish Studies, which would balance the academic study programmes as well as being a major study resource for North West London Jewry.
>
> The idea of a link with the institutions Rabbi Riskin had created in Israel, specifically Yeshivat haMivtar, also made a great deal of sense to us. Unfortunately it seems that the chemistry was not quite right. Not that many people were drawn to Rabbi Brovender – just as not that many were drawn to Rabbi Nachum Rabinovitch in the twelve years he spent as head of the College, despite the fact that he was one of the most towering rabbinic scholars to have graced British Jewry. The fault, in other words, was ours, not Rabbi Brovender's ... We learned that you cannot transfer an institution, or even an outstanding Torah personality, from Israel to London and achieve the same results.[22]

As a result, by the summer of 1999, Brovender was back in Israel, though previous lecturers at the College over the years had successfully made the move from outside the country.

It was in 1998 that Eli Cashdan died at the age of 93. He had been a pillar of the College for many years and an inspiration to his students. He had obtained his semicha at the age of 17 and also gained a first class honours degree from the College when he was 22 in 1927, plus an MA in semitics with distinction. There was more to Cashdan than academia, however. He became a barrister and served as a chaplain to the RAF during the war. He was the first Jewish chaplain to be made a Squadron Leader and finished his time in the forces as a Wing Commander. He managed to combine this with assisting Epstein in the translation of the Babylonian Talmud into English, where he tackled the difficult sections on Menahot, the temple offerings, and Hullin, the regulations on animal sacrifices. He went back to Jews' College as a lecturer in 1951 and stayed in post for twenty years.

In 2000 a new Principal, Rabbi Abner Weiss, from America, was appointed. The key question was whether he could improve matters.

NOTES

1. Jewish Chronicle, 7 October 1983, p,22.
2. Lord Kalms in conversation with the author.
3. The panel was chaired by David Jenkins, the future Bishop of Durham. This was the clergyman who had controversial views about the resurrection. Three days after his installation in Durham, York Minster caught fire. The Home Secretary wisely refused to speculate on the possible involvement of the Almighty.
4. JCAR.
5. Jewish Chronicle, 2 November 1984, pp.24–5.
6. Jewish Chronicle, 15 February 1985, p.5.
7. Jewish Chronicle, 5 April 1985, p.20.
8. Jewish Chronicle, 16 July 2004, p.25.
9. Interview with Stanley Kalms.
10. The records about the Lieberman affair are in the Metropolitan Archives, but the file is embargoed until 2051! A fuller assessment of all the details of that disagreement will, therefore, be possible for the future author of the history of the College's first 200 years!
11. Lord Sacks in conversation with the author.
12. Email from Raymond Apple.

13. JCAR.
14. JCAR.
15. Jewish Chronicle, 8 September 1989, p.12.
16. JCAR.
17. Author correspondence with Rabbi Dr Daniel Sinclair.
18. Ibid.
19. JCAR.
20. JCAR.
21. JCAR.
22. Author correspondence with Lord Sacks.

CHAPTER TWELVE

LSJS

David-Hillel Ruben left for a post as head of New York University in London at the end of his contract. The turn of a new century – albeit not a Jewish one – brought a new principal to the College. The South African rabbi, Dr Abner Weiss, was welcomed from California as an expert in pastoral care with a PhD in psychology. He was a charismatic leader, and was soon involved in additional duties, ministering to the Western Marble Arch Synagogue congregation. He was keen to encourage adult education programmes and said that he had raised $1 million in America to revive rabbinic teaching. Not surprisingly, his appointment was hailed as the prelude to a new era.

Weiss also brought with him Rabbi Dror Brama who led the Torah MiTzion programme to create rabbis who would help start *kehillas* – new congregations – where better local organization was needed.

It was, therefore, a disappointment when, after less than two years, Weiss resigned to return to the United States. There was speculation about differing views on Modern Orthodoxy, cross-communal politics and the pressures of trying to keep the College going in the face of almost insuperable financial challenges. In fact, his departure was due to a more prosaic problem, involving a proposed second marriage, which proved impossible to resolve.

The Trustees and the Council agonised over the future. Jews' College had been founded to solve the problem of nascent communities without religious leadership. The position in 2000 was quite different. The major communities were now well established and, if the need was for rabbis, there were alternative *semicha* courses available in Israel and America. The new element in the equation was the very considerable growth in the number of Jewish schools in recent years.

The effect of having so many youngsters taught at Faith Schools was that there was an increasing demand for Jewish teachers. In the past the Jewish schools had depended on non-Jewish teachers for secular subjects and there had always been a serious shortage of Jews in the profession. At this point, however, as the children learned more of the faith, there was a very welcome additional spin-off, as their parents and grandparents sought not to be left behind. So there was a growing demand for adult education courses if they could be organized effectively. There was also a considerable demand for courses for women.

There were practical concerns, where there was a large, potential demand but little supply. In addition, while Talmudic study had been defended by the principals since Louis Loewe, this was now part of the traditional curriculum of Jews' College, rather than the provision of the sole centre for such learning.

There was also a supply of trained rabbis emerging from Gateshead, and while there were occasional clashes between a congregation and the Gateshead minister on the appropriate level of observance of the *mitzvot* in both public and private life, there were now suitably qualified men available. Also the pressing needs of the community had changed since early Victorian times, as the vast majority of Jews were now British-born and had mostly climbed out of poverty.

The flood of Jewish immigrants at the end of the nineteenth century had come from a European world of tight Jewish communities, held together by their strict level of observance, and scrutinized on their behaviour by their fellows. It was a world where their defence against state discrimination was centred on membership of their congregation. If the necessity for this had never existed in democratic Britain, old habits still died hard.

What many needed, 100-plus years later, was proof that Judaism was meaningful in a modern secular society and, for that to be achieved, the first requirement was for far more and better adult education.

The financial leadership of the LSJS now rested with Howard Stanton. The Chief Rabbi had asked him to try to resolve the LSJS problems and he would become Chairman of the Council from 2003–

08. Stanton had been brought up in Stamford Hill and was a very able and determined accountant. A highly successful businessman, he was the Deputy Chairman of the UJIA (United Jewish Israel Appeal) and a committed worker for the community. He would prove to be highly dedicated and successful.

There now came a very unexpected intervention from an unlikely group of six young people. They were without any kind of power base, but they were determined to try to defend the values of the institution. All were passionate about Jewish education. The six were Marc Weinberg, the Executive Director of Bnei Akiva, the Jewish youth movement, Dr Tamra Wright, who was Bradfield Lecturer in Jewish Philosophy at LSJS already, Dr Raphael Zarum, former Education Director of the UJIA, Dr Daniel Rynhold, lecturer in Judaism at LSJS, and businessmen Samuel Rubin and Ian Gamse. Dr Wright, of course, specialized in women's education.

The six had already made a major contribution to the relevance of LSJS within the community. They had started a learning programme before Rosh Hashanah (the New Year) in 2001, knowing that interest in Judaism tended to peak in the period of the High Holy Days. Hundreds of people came to their Ellul lecture programme at the School.

The group of six covered all the bases: Raphael Zarum was a very experienced educator; Tamra Wright had a first class track record in organizing women's programmes as well as academic studies; while Marc Weinberg and Sammy Rubin would be in charge of fund-raising. Sammy Rubin was a successful entrepreneur in the City and he would become a Trustee of the School. Daniel Rynhold would look after the academic programme and Ian Gamse would be responsible for financial matters. Marc Weinberg was well known to Howard Stanton.

The group could point to a number of successful initiatives in adult education in the previous twenty years and, as they said in their written proposal, 'We can create a College which will function as the intellectual, educational and ethical centre of the UK "modern orthodox" community'. Their proposals were accepted and from the outset, the Lishma programme went from strength to strength. Where the initial courses had been in the autumn, soon there were further courses at Passover and Chanukah. Eventually there would be more than 500 signing on for the programmes. Tamra Wright was made Director of Academic Studies from 2003, and Raphael Zarum was appointed Director of Lifelong Learning at the LSJS in 2004. Together they would lead the LSJS forward for the next ten years till the present day.

In 2008 the LSJS launched two new programmes, in association with Kings College, London University and Middlesex University: a Masters in Jewish Studies and a Masters in Jewish Education.

The purpose of Jews' College had been to produce ministers and teachers. The new philosophy of the LSJS was increasingly to spread Jewish learning as widely as possible. This meant that the subjects covered could be much more comprehensive. When the phone is answered today, the caller is informed that they have reached The World Campus for Jewish Education.

So, from an academic perspective, Tamra Wright delivered eight Stanton Lectures in the Philosophy of Religion at the Faculty of Divinity at Cambridge. From a less academically stringent point of view, over 500 students had by 2009 enjoyed a tour of Jewish London. These included The East End Jews and Food Tour, the National Gallery Bible Tour and the Natural History Museum Genesis Tour. These activities were certainly educational, but they were always likely to attract wider audiences than had previously been drawn to Jews' College.

The growth in the number of courses on offer was impressive and by 2012 the Degree Programme and Teacher Training courses covered not only the MA in Jewish Studies and Jewish Education, but also a BA in Applied Professional Studies with the University of Greenwich, a school-centred initial teacher training programme and a graduate teacher programme.

The growth in the college membership has been far greater than it has ever been before. Over 300 students signed up for the first Ellul programme and the annual budget is now over a million pounds. As a result, the Victorian days when hardly any students paid for their education compares with the very substantial income which comes from those on the courses today. This is, however, partly because the community's disposable income is far greater than it used to be.

Initially it wasn't possible to continue with the *semicha* course and this lapsed between 2000 and 2008, at which point the Montefiore College course was reintroduced by the Sephardim. Their senior rabbi at the time, Abraham Levy, had no intention of abandoning their training of rabbis. He reacted to the crisis by announcing in 2006 that the Sephardim would set about restarting their own programme, under the direction of Dayan Saadia Amor. Amor was a Talmudic heavyweight, and a scholar of that eminence would be internationally accepted as a good judge of the qualifications of applicants. Like the Chief Rabbi, the Sephardim considered a *semicha* course essential for the Jewish community in Britain.

Saadia Amor could trace his ancestry back to the Rambam (Moses Maimonides). He had come to Britain in 1956, and fifty years later he became the Rosh Beth Din and head of the Rabbinical Diploma class at the Judith, Lady Montefiore College. Under his tutelage, and in cooperation with the LSJS, many students later achieved *semicha*, being ordained by the Chief Rabbi, Lord Sacks, Abraham Levy and the head of the Jerusalem Beth Din, Dayan Ezra Basri.

The first course was run independently of LSJS at the Sephardi synagogue in Maida Vale, London, but LSJS was able to amalgamate with the Sephardim for the second in 2010. In 2013 no less than nine candidates finished the punishing curriculum and received their *semicha*: Natan Abenaim, Steven Dansky, Yaacov Finn, Meir Lev, Asif Mittelman, Ofir Ronen, David Steinberg, Lee Sunderland and Rafi Zarum. Lucien Gubbay, the Chairman of the Trustees, said that the course was not for the faint-hearted. Unhappily Saadia Amor died in 2015. Today, leading rabbis from Yeshivot Eretz Hemdah in Israel come regularly to London and give shiurim through skype. *Semichas* can be awarded again.

A major change from those early Victorian days was the contribution which came from women lecturers. Where there had been only the occasional woman teaching a secular subject, currently Tamra Wright, Maureen Kendler and Lindsey Taylor-Guthartz are covering Torah topics.

As far as teacher training is concerned, the government's Ofsted inspectors ranked the Jewish Teacher Training partnership, now run by the LSJS, as an 'outstanding provider of Teacher Training in the Jewish community'. It is the only one in the country. From the community's point of view, this is an absolutely crucial area for the future. Teaching a religion in an increasingly secular world is a major challenge. The inspiration a good teacher needs to provide is in competition with a host of other well publicized attractions and role models. If the teacher fails to engage the children, the support that often less knowledgeable parents badly need is not available. Internationally, the effect of Israel and the status of Jewish academics, have all played their part.

Even so, the elephant in the room is always the ongoing costs involved. Charities like LSJS are still the poor relations when it comes to the fund-raising efforts within the community. One hedge fund entrepreneur a few years ago gave his alma mater, Lincoln College, Oxford, £60 million. A prominent Jewish businessman has given the National Theatre £10 million. Both are admirable donations but, just like Jews' College from the outset, that level of support to ensure that the institution could stop worrying about money for a decade or two has never been forthcoming. A very notable exception, however, was a munificent grant of £750,000 in 2010, payable over five years, by the Maurice Wohl Charitable Foundation. The grant was dependent on the LSJS raising the funds on its own behalf, which it did.

At the end of the day, it comes down to personalities. The ability of a teacher to inspire, of a marketing man to produce effective promotional material, of a businessman to spend money wisely and of charismatic leaders. All are normally in short supply and when they retire or disappear from the community, they can leave gaps which may not be filled for years.

So how does one assess the value to the Jewish world of Jews' College over the years? To the non-Jewish world, if anything was known about it at all, it has just been a centre for Jewish study. For non-observant Jews it has been a college teaching a form of the religion which they felt was out of date. It was unimportant to them for most of its later existence because it didn't influence their lives. For ultra-Orthodox Jews it has been traduced as a college whose standards were lower than they believed necessary.

Its relevance has, therefore, been confined to middle-of-the-road Orthodox Jews, but they still represent the majority of the communities in Britain and the British Commonwealth. Even in those circles, there has been continuous disagreement about the kind of graduates it should produce.

What has Jews' College done for them? Well, first of all, it has kept the show on the road. It is all too easy to take this for granted. The fact is that it is perfectly possible for Jewry to disappear; primarily, through assimilation and massacre. There are many countries where you can find Jewish cemeteries but no – or practically no – Jews. In Britain, and the major countries of the British Commonwealth, that hasn't happened. There has always been a small cadre of Jews who have learned and taught traditional Judaism, who have ensured that there were classes to teach the next generation, that there were traditional services in the synagogues and enough effective spiritual leadership to keep the community together.

There have been ministers and rabbis who have comforted the mourners, visited the sick in hospital, inspired their congregations from the pulpit and officiated at bar mitzvahs and marriages, buried the dead and ensured that animals were killed in the most humane way possible according to Jewish law. There have been competent *mohels* to carry out circumcisions, and Dayanim to settle points of Jewish law in the Beth Din. There have been Talmudic experts, often imported from abroad, and the in-depth knowledge of the Torah has remained safe in their hands.

Jews' College trained a lot of these men. Each one played their part in the communities they served. Even if they didn't become ministers, they were better equipped to be educated laymen in their congregations, and they served not only in Britain but in many other parts of the world. In later years, there have been better trained women teachers as well.

You can't put a price on the assistance they provided. There is no monetary value to comforting the bereaved or giving children a spiritual foundation to their personalities. What you can say is that those trained at Jews' College were invaluable in helping individuals to deal with the pressures of life in tens of thousands of cases and, as a consequence, they did a great deal of good.

Compared to these contributions, the financial stresses and strains of running Jews' College over the years has been a very small price to pay, as those with the responsibility realised. It may never have produced the ideal numbers of graduates, which was the aim of those who led the organization. It couldn't do so because there could never be too many of them. Men – and later women teachers – who would make considerable sacrifices to follow their vocation.

There would still always remain Jews in need of comfort, instruction, succour, encouragement and leadership. Jews' College played its part in filling the gap which would always exist, but which would have been far larger without the institution. It would have liked to have done more, but it did a great deal.

Yes, in retrospect, there were errors of judgement, mistaken policies, internal politics and damaging hidden agendas. In the early years fund raising should have been conducted on a more professional level and the Council should have been more concerned about improving the level of Jewish observance in the country, rather than whether the community was aping what they perceived as great English traditions.

There were clashes of personality, as always happens in any organisation, and there was often frustration among the lay leaders that the religious leaders were not prepared to compromise on their spiritual responsibilities. It is difficult for laymen to appreciate just how large is the academic area of study which has been built up within Judaism over the millennia. Or that the study of Rashi, an eleventh-century French Rabbi, was always going to be more important to the principals of the College, than paying the rent.

Judaism is a demanding religion. Throughout the history of Jews' College, almost to the present day, the standards of observance of the majority of the Orthodox community has been in decline. Keeping the sabbath competed unsuccessfully in many homes with watching the family's football team. The attractions of French cuisine undermined the laws of *kashrut*. The desire to be fully accepted by their fellows led to a decline in the wearing of *tsitsit*, yarmulkes and *tephillin* by Jewish boys in schools all over the country. The outside pressures of anti-Semitism also led to an even greater desire not to stand out as different.

Again, Jews' College held the fort until the country changed. Until action was taken to make racism illegal and until the vast majority of the population agreed that it should be. Jews benefited from the condemnation of colour bars, from efforts to obtain equality for women in the workplace, from all the new standards applying to a multicultural society. It gave them confidence to be Jews.

It is also true that they benefited from the public creation of other scapegoats. When there was prejudice against people of a different colour, the Jews became part of the white majority. When crime and terrorism were attributed to other communities, an increasingly secular society became less concerned with the crucifixion. Jews came out from behind their barricades, wearing yarmulkes and standing tall. Jews' College and its graduates had been part of the cement that made the survival possible.

The College always kept up its original Talmudic standards. It was attacked for this because its graduates, through their own example, kept reminding Jewish congregants that they were not abiding by the rules. That they were letting their parents and grandparents down by not following in their religious footsteps. The criticism was not voiced in those terms but, in its ultimate form, it could break up families when the children married out.

For the first time in hundreds of years the community, internally, was starting to become more Orthodox. The credit for this lay, to a great extent, with better education, and that was built on the foundations laid, in large part, over 160 years, by Jews' College.

Finally, it is also insufficiently appreciated just how much the permanent spiritual leaders of Jews' College were prepared to sacrifice for the cause. In any other field of endeavour their standard of living would have been far better. They – and their families – were prepared to make sacrifices of material well-being which their fellow Jews would never have considered. Their commitment was truly a vocation, and their faith in the Almighty was the only spur they needed.

At the end of the day, against all the odds, there is still a majority of Orthodox Jews in Britain. When Chief Rabbi Jakobovits was introduced as a peer in the House of Lords, he recalled that when he was putting on the robes, it was in the Moses Room, and the official helping him remarked that he was the first Chief Rabbi to be made a peer. Jakobovits told the official that he was, in fact, the second; the first was Moses who brought the Ten Commandments to the world, which included the House of Lords.

Jonathan Sacks was also elevated to the Peerage in 2009 and could be said to have become one of the moral voices of the country. After the riots of August 2012 *The Times* ran an Opinion piece on what lessons might be learned from the mayhem. It seemed like a suitable subject for a senior dignitary in the Church of England, but the chosen author was the Chief Rabbi. He still represented less than 0.5 per cent of the population.

When Sacks retired, his successor was the South African, Ephraim Mirvis. He took over as Principal of the College and is just as committed as his predecessors to seeing that it carries on providing the ministers and teachers that the community needed.

The community had largely moved into the middle and upper classes. If it wants to, there are ample funds to sustain the College. The fresh appeal to the general Jewish public is being promoted with energy and professionalism. The key need is to get LSJS higher up on the list of priorities for financial support which the community tackles.

The institution is flourishing today as it has never done before but, as it is said, you can see the future better by standing on the shoulders of the founders. The ghosts of Loewe, Friedländer, Büchler, Epstein and Zimmels can be seen in the continuing dedication to Talmudic education, and Nathan Marcus Adler and Sir Moses Montefiore would be well pleased to see that their creation still serves the community well.

CHAPTER THIRTEEN

And Then There's the Library

The record of civilization is most easily accessible in later years if it is contained in a first class library. The Royal Library of Alexandria, founded in the third century BCE, was a shining example of what could be achieved, and the British Library today continues the great tradition.

From its inception, the founders of Jews' College recognized that a good library would be a fundamental asset if it could be built up over the years. It would be a monumental task though and it recalls the instructions of the sages that: 'You are not allowed to finish the work, neither are you allowed to desist from it.' This applied in full measure to a large number of dedicated members of the College over its 150 years.

It was agreed from the outset that a librarian would be one of the staff. There were initial plans to include the Beth Hamedrash of the Great Synagogue in the College, but this idea was abandoned early on. There was a small Beth Hamedrash library already in existence, but this was not used as the basis for the College library. When it was eventually sold by the United Synagogue in New York in 1999, it realized well in excess of $3 million.

In the early years there were occasional references in the account ledgers to money being spent on buying books, but there was no properly constituted library. New books were requested by lecturers and their purchase authorised by the Council.[1] In 1859 the Jews' and General Literary and Scientific Institution ceased to function and a generous and far-sighted communal worker, Lewis Meyer Rothschild, who originally came from Denmark, bought its library and gave it to the College. It was stipulated that it should be insured for £500

(£43,000 in today's money) and Rothschild – not from the banking family – agreed to pay for this if the College couldn't afford to do so. As a 'thank you' Rothschild was elected to the Council. The press reported that: 'the library consisted of 4,000 volumes, about 2,000 of which are works of fiction, was purchased for £200'. A lot of the books were not included in the gift as they: 'were not considered appropriate for a college for the study of divinity'.[2]

The collection was housed in bookcases which had previously been owned by Lord Macauley and it was resolved that the Beadle should be paid £5 a year for his services as the library attendant. It was a start, but as one press critic pointed out: 'except for a few sets of the Talmud, some Hebrew Bibles, and the various commentaries and Midrashim, it contained scarcely anything useful to Jewish students'.

Happily, the nucleus was supplemented in 1861 by Walter Josephs, who offered the College on trust the Hebrew library he had been left by his late father, who had been one of the founders of the College. It was finally presented to the College as a gift in 1882 and is designated the Michael Josephs Collection.

In later years there were occasional gifts mentioned in the records, such as those by B. Meyers, E.M. Merton and Louis Werner. Rothschild came to the aid of the College again in 1873, when he gave it the collection of Dr Immanuel Deutsch, who had been an assistant at the British Museum employed to work on their books in the oriental book section on the Talmud. His collection included: 'a fine copy of the best edition of the Talmud and many standard works on Semitic languages, and other volumes'.[3]

It was agreed that the Principal, Dr Friedländer, an author in his own right, would now be asked to catalogue the library collection properly. This was to be a recurring theme over the years as the library expanded. It's all very well having a fine library, but if you can't find the books you're looking for, it drastically reduces its usefulness to the proposed reader. A good solicitor is said to be one who knows where to look things up and the same applies to researchers.

In 1875 the College received part of the library of the late J. Henry Moses, who had been the first Treasurer of the College. His collection included a Babylonian Talmud and copies of the *Mishnah*, Maimonides, *Shulchan Aruch* and Bible commentaries. Rothschild gave another donation to the library at the same time. It was also in 1875 that a subcommittee was formed to rectify what Friedländer had called 'the dilapidated state of the books in the Library'. He wanted it to: 'report on the state and condition of the College Library with a view to its being placed in a proper state to render it fit and useful for the College purposes'.[4]

Unfortunately there are no records remaining of the work of the Library Committee until 1897 when its functions were stated. In the meantime the Council decided on what books to buy and which gifts to accept. For example, in 1881, the Council minutes record that Dr Friedländer's request for a multi-volume edition of the *Arba'ah Turim* (the basis for the *Shulchan Aruch*) and the purchase of a *Talmud Yerushalmi* was also approved.

In 1877 the library of Alexander Henry Keyser of Amsterdam was bought and presented to the College by Charles Samuel, now the Treasurer of the College. These biblical and rabbinical works were augmented in the same year by secular books presented by Rev. (later Sir) Philip Magnus. In 1878 the College was given the library of Abraham Benisch, a biblical scholar who was for many years Editor of the *Jewish Chronicle*.

When the College moved to Tavistock Square in 1881 part of the ground floor was used for the library. The books were still not properly classified and the Council in 1883 resolved that: 'Dr. Friedländer be asked, with the help of the Students, to prepare a properly classified catalogue of the Library by January 1st 1884'.[5]

Before this could be completed, however, the death occurred in 1883 of Rev. Aaron Levy Green, who had been the minister of the Great Synagogue in London and Honorary Secretary of the College since it was created. His widow wrote to the President of the College, Rabbi Hermann Adler, and said that her husband's wish had been: 'that his Hebrew and Theological library should be of public utility to the community'.[6] It was that kind of generosity which played such a large part in the building of the collection over the forthcoming years. The

Green Library was offered on trust to the College and gratefully received. By the end of 1883 the books were ready to be transferred and: 'kept as a distinct and separate library, to be opened to the public'.[7] A £500 endowment fund was created for its maintenance and, while the books were integrated into the general collection during the First World War, they are still labelled 'The A.L. Green Library' and can still be consulted to this day.

This magnificent library consisted of about 6,000 books, including incunabula (books printed before 1501) and early prints. It contained all the theological works which were needed by students for the ministry. It also had a unique collection of pamphlets on Anglo-Jewish history and a collection of sermons in English and German.

All of this would also need cataloguing and for the first time in the history of the college an official librarian was appointed. Dr Friedländer formally took on the additional title, dividing the library into twenty-seven separate sections.

In 1884 there came books from the library of J. Jacobs in Hull and, in 1890, more from the libraries of H.A. Franklin and F.D. Mocatta and, in 1895, that of Lionel Cohen. It was in that year that the College formally: 'accepted the trusteeship of the Rev. A.L. Green Library'. From its funds in 1896 came the first books for the 'music class'.

There were other libraries in existence within the community and in 1895 the Council decided to try to arrange for them to be amalgamated. The largest were those of Aria College in Portsea and the Judith Lady Montefiore Sephardi College in Ramsgate. While it did not prove possible to come to an agreement with the Sephardim for a complete fusion, there were beneficial results for the College. The Sephardim agreed to give them £1,000 a year, which they did for the next fifteen years, and to lend them books: 'for the use of Jews' College, such of the contents of their Library as might not be required for the use of the Synagogue or College at Ramsgate'.[8] Unforeseen circumstances were, however, to lead to the Ramsgate Library being lent on trust to Jews' College. The books would no longer be needed in Ramsgate when the Elders of the Sephardim closed the college.

It was then agreed, in June 1897, to lend to Jews' College the Montefiore Library of Printed Books and most of the manuscripts which also contained items from the library of Dr Leopold Zunz. This collection was to form one of the main pillars of the library.

As a result of the agreement, a special committee was formed with Asher Myers, the editor of the *Jewish Chronicle,* in the chair, to deal with the transfer. This developed into the library subcommittee. Asher Myers' house was a centre of Jewish intellectual life in London at the time. He had a passion for books and his own manuscripts display beautiful calligraphy with his signature embossed on the bindings.

Dr Hartwig Hirschfield, who had been the Lecturer in Biblical Exegesis (critical explanation) and Oriental Languages at the Montefiore College was made redundant when the Sephardim closed Ramsgate. He accepted the same position at Jews' College and agreed to be the Sub-Librarian as well. One of his advantages, of course, was that he knew the Montefiore Library.

By 1901 the cataloguing of the printed books had been completed and by 1904 the *Descriptive Catalogue of the Hebrew MS of the Montefiore Library* was in print. Coincidentally, Louis Loewe, the original headmaster of Jews' College, had collected many of the manuscripts; twenty-seven from the Zunz library and 412 manuscripts from the collection of Solomon Joachim Halberstam.

Small gifts were also welcome; Claude Montefiore gave an Encyclopaedia Britannica in 1898 and then a magnificent collection of 10,000 volumes which had belonged to Rev. Albert Löwy. The books were to be part of the library, but each would have its own stamp. Other donations came from Dennis Samuel, Simon Waley and S. Hoffnung, from the library of his late father.

Within a couple of years Hirschfield was able to report that the catalogues of the Green and College Libraries had been completed. At the prize day in 1901 Solomon Schechter, who had had so much to do with moving the Cairo Genizah to England, was able to say that the College now possessed: 'one of the finest collections of philological books and Judaica'. As far as possible all the Judaica and Hebraica were deposited in the Masters' Common Room.

In 1902, when the College moved to Queens Square, it took some time to get all the books there as well. There were now 25,000 of them. It was a pity that the architect was given all kinds of advice about the needs of the College, but the needs of the library were not mentioned. As a consequence the Building Committee decided later that a large room at the rear of the ground floor should be used for the Rev. A.L. Green Library and Dr Friedländer's dining room should house another part.

With the growth of the library, the daily work of a librarian could obviously not now be undertaken by the teaching staff. One of the senior students would, in future, be the library prefect. Rules for lending were now reformulated, including the prohibition on staff taking books away from the College precincts. The full list of Regulations was printed in the Annual Report of the College for the first time in 1903.

It was in 1902 that the Chair of the Library Committee, Asher Myers, died. The Council coped with the additional responsibilities until Marcus Adler, the old Chief Rabbi's son and a noted bibliophile, was appointed in his stead in 1904.

More books were donated by the family of the late Alfred Cohen, and by Albert Jessel and John Stranders, while a fine *Sefer Torah* was presented to it in 1905 by Madame Halfon.

Maintaining such a vast collection was now going to be very difficult. The librarian complained of the woeful condition of the Montefiore library, some of whose books had to be stored in the basement and had gone rotten: 'It made me ill to handle and examine them'. A Visiting Committee was appointed and they came up with recommendations to consolidate the constituent libraries which now had about 23,000 volumes. The Committee wanted all the books on one floor and adequate shelving to be bought. The Council considered the proposals in 1908 after Dr Friedländer had resigned as Librarian and Dr Hirschfield had taken over.

It was at the same time that the United Synagogue appointed a Special Committee to look into the affairs of Jews' College and in 1910 to emphasise: 'the desirability of the reorganisation of the College

Library'. The Committees came up with its plans, but very little actually happened. It was agreed that a card catalogue of the books should be made, but at this point the Library Committee disappears from the records until 1927. The Council and the Education Committee replaced it, with the latter taking it under its wing. The cataloguing was completed in 1914 and Dr Hirschfield was duly thanked.

By the outbreak of the First World War the library was now composed of four parts; the original nucleus, the A.L. Green Library, the Montefiore Library and the Löwy Library. There were also some small benefactions and the books the College had bought itself. It could now lay claim to being the most valuable Jewish Library in Europe with about 35,000 books. As Elkan Adler, the President of the Jewish Historical Society of England said in his Presidential address: 'There is probably not a Rabbinical seminary in the world that has gathered together so valuable and comprehensive a collection.'[9]

There was no opportunity to expand the library during the war but at the end of hostilities the library benefited from a £1,000 grant from the Jewish War Memorial. There were also occasional donations, like those of the *Jewish Chronicle* and Arthur Franklin. They may have been for only around £100 but the equivalent in today's money would buy £4,000 worth of books.

In 1920 Dr Hirschfield was given some help, in the person of S.M. Lehrman (later Rabbi Dr). The library tried to make up for lost time and a good collection of books was bought from the library of Rev. Gerald Friedlander. Israel Brodie, later the Chief Rabbi, also gave a number of rabbinic works. These were augmented in 1926 when a large number of books belonging to the late Dr Israel Abrahams were placed at the library's disposal.

Keeping the collection in apple-pie order was still a major problem. In 1927 the Chair of the Council stated, 'that there remained an enormous amount of work to be done, chief among which was the reorganisation of the Library'.[10] Another special committee was set up under the chairmanship of Elkan Adler (1861–1946), another member of the Chief Rabbi Nathan Marcus Adler's family. This led to £250 being donated to buy more books and new rules for the conduct of the library being formulated. Adler was an avid book collector and his journeys to the Orient enabled him to buy ancient manuscript sheets and fragments. His 1921 catalogue of his collection had 4,200 entries, with some material dating back to the seventh century. He would be Chairman of the Jews' College Library Committee for twenty years.

In addition, in 1928, Rabbi Dr Isidore Epstein became a lecturer at the College and it was agreed that he would also take on the role of Librarian. So Dr Epstein was played in by Dr Hirschfield, who retired in good order in 1929 after thirty years at the College. Dr Epstein supervised the translation of the Babylonian Talmud and became well known internationally for his book, *Judaism*.

With Elkan Adler's encouragement, the Library Committee became very effective. The Chief Rabbi often attended the meetings as well. Discussions ranged over book purchases, subscriptions, the security of the books and lending procedures. Many of the books had great value, and their safety, if they were lent outside the building, was a prime concern.

The College was now going to move to Woburn House. It was decided, 'that the Montefiore Library and the Green Library were to be kept in distinct and separate portions of the Library in the new building ... and all valuable books would be kept in the Librarian's room'.[11] They also made up their minds that they needed an assistant librarian. Rev. Louis Rubin-Zacks, a graduate of the College, became the part-time assistant librarian and the library settled down, sharing its premises with the new Jewish Museum. There was still too few staff to manage all the intricacies of a major library and so it became an Outlier Library of the National Central Library, which made it easier to lend books to provincial libraries and those readers who would have found it difficult to come to Woburn House.

There now arrived some splendid new collections of books from the Chief Rabbi and the Rev. Solomon Levy, who had been the first to receive *semicha* at the College. There was also a major donation by Stuart Green of the collection of his late father, A.A. Green, who was also a past student and a member of the Council for many years. Books from the collection of Dayan Bernard Spiers in 1933, the Wigoder family and Rev. Joseph Polack were other welcome additions.

The problem was, of course, that what was needed was: 'a detailed list of all the books in the Library, shelf by shelf, and when this was done, to use this list for the purpose of a new card index for the Library, and as the basis for future checking'.[12] Good intentions, but even after a search for volunteer help from outside the College, and the agreement of Rabbi H. Klein to supervise the work of preparing the list, the enormous task was still abandoned after a few months. Rubin-Zacks was appointed full-time as assistant librarian to see what could be done on a more permanent basis. The problem, though, remained the necessary continuity of effort and the employment of sufficient staff

In 1935 the Chief Rabbi became Chair of the Library Committee and Jacob Weinberg (later Rabbi), became a temporary assistant after Rubin-Sacks accepted a ministerial position. In his time it was agreed to accept on deposit books from the de Sola and Corcos Libraries, offered by the Jewish Museum and Central Library. These remained in the care of the library until they were moved to the Mocatta Library at University College, London in 1962.

At least the librarian was able to report to the Council in 1935 that: 'The Library is now accessible to readers every day of the week and the number of volumes which have been borrowed by readers during the past twelve months has vastly exceeded that in any previous year. Many books have been added during the past year by purchase as well as by donation.'[13]

Before the war the College bought German-Jewish books from the library of the late Rabbi Dr Adolf Savendi and hundreds of volumes from the library of the late Dr George Wigoder.

When the war broke out it was initially decided to only move the most precious books out of London, but the Blitz put the whole library too much at risk. Several hundreds boxes of books were evacuated and loans and trust owners were told that the College could no longer be responsible if there was any enemy action. The joint meetings of the Education, Executive and Finance Committees discussed library matters in the reduced state of the College. It was during the war that the A.L. Green library was handed over to the College in perpetuity.

When the war ended Dr Epstein was fully occupied with the academic reconstruction of the College and so Rabbi Dr Hersch Zimmels agreed to be the librarian as part of his duties. The Library Committee was reconstituted in 1946 under the chairmanship of Wilfred Samuel, and this was the year when Elkan Adler died after forty years on the Council. In 1947 Dr Zimmels produced a report reviewing the damage done to the books during the war because of inadequate storage, and made proposals for the future working of the library.

Recommendations were made for the safeguarding of the books, the prevention of more losses, more speedy and economical cataloguing, the replacement of damaged and missing books and the employment of someone to 'invigilate readers'. Zimmels also wanted to recruit a qualified librarian but the old system of unqualified assistant librarians was reintroduced. Rev. Michael Elton filled the post and was the first full-time librarian not to have served as a College lecturer as well.

The library had been badly damaged and depleted during the war years, but in 1948 a friend of the College gave £1,000 to buy the valuable collection of the last Principal, Dr Büchler. It included important sets of periodicals and books which had not been in the library before, and it was now possible to create a separate reference section. When the death occurred of Rev. Hermann Mayerowitsch, the *hazan* at the Great Synagogue, his widow gave his collection of all the classic works of *hazanut* to the library.

In 1948 there was a historic library event when a woman was employed for the first time. Ruth Lehmann was a prospective student in Librarianship and was taken on to help incorporate the Büchler Library in the collection. In the next few years she catalogued thousands of new acquisitions.

This was a period when the number of students was increasing, so the library was needed more than ever. The cataloguing continued and the backlog decreased. The Wigoder Library was finally catalogued after being at the College since 1936 and 'transferred to the safety of the Principal's Room'. Gifts from individuals and organizations, as widespread as the University of Uppsala and the Library of Congress, continued to arrive and it was pleasing to see the librarian represent the College on the Executive Committee of the Jewish Book Week. Within the College, the Moral Leadership Courses now included visits to the library on their educational programmes.

Michael Elton was a very good librarian and was awarded the Special Diploma in Hebrew Palaeography (the study of writings from the past) and Epigraphy (inscriptions on statues and coins) at the School of Oriental and African Studies. Seven years later Ruth Lehman was similarly rewarded.

The Holocaust destroyed Jewish libraries all over Europe but remnants survived. In 1949 the Library Committee reported that, '64 cases of Hebraica were being held by Dr. Oskar Rabinowicz on behalf of the Committee on Restoration of Continental Jewish Museums, Libraries and Archives, of which Jews' College had first refusal'.[14] Over the next few years the library received thousands of books from this source; all the reserve shelving was used up and a lot of the books had to be stored in the boxes they came in. Hundreds of volumes of classical rabbinical literature, never before seen at the library, flooded in and these were augmented by donations from the same Continental ruins. The return of the books of the Jewish Central Library, on deposit since 1935, to the office of the Jewish Memorial Council helped to absorb the many new books. A Purchasing Committee was also established to spend with care the small sum available for book purchasing.

The library was gaining national recognition. In 1950 it received 'Approved' status from the Library Association, so that librarian students could carry out their 'approved' service there. It was also a notable event when the Library Association's Special Libraries Meeting was held at Jews' College. There followed an invitation to host the Standing Conference of Theological and Philosophical Libraries in London, which was an opportunity to put on view the treasures of the library. Ruth Lehmann became Chair of the Standing Conference in 1958.

Wilfred Samuel had had to resign due to ill-health in 1951 and Oskar Rabinowicz took his place. More crates arrived that year from the library of Herbert Adler, though there was nowhere to display their contents.

In 1952 the British Museum helped the College to obtain a valuable benefaction of manuscripts and documents which had belonged to Solomon Bennet, an eighteenth–nineteenth-century scholar, well known in his time for attacking the publications of Chief Rabbi Solomon Herschell. Professor Selig Brodetsky, former President of the Board of Deputies and President of the Hebrew University in Jerusalem, gave the College a handsome collection of Hebraica, and Louis Rabinowitz of New York an equally kind gift of American Judaica. Where there was a dearth of modern Hebraica, this was much alleviated by a gift of Israeli Hebraica in memory of Chief Rabbi Hertz.

Michael Elton was lost to South Africa in 1954. Ruth Lehmann was shortly elected an Associate of the Library Association, thus becoming the first Chartered Librarian ever at Jews College. She also became the first woman to be put in charge of the library in 1955. In 1964 she was awarded the Fellowship of the Library Association. She served as librarian for over twenty years.

In 1954 the library was divided up into its separate parts. There was a reference section and a folklore section. One for Talmud translations, Gaonica, Festschriften (books of essays honouring religious leaders during their lifetime), periodicals, Anglo-Judaism, Zionism, Hebrew Law, Religious Codes, *Mussar* (moral instruction), General Philosophy and Art.

In 1955 the College helped in founding the Congress of European Jewish Libraries and the Jewish Book Week Exhibition. Sonia Lefcovitch arrived as assistant librarian that year and worked well on the team for the next twelve years.

The problems of space and resources continued to concern the library. There was never enough shelving, but gifts continued to be received. This was extremely generous of the donors but only exacerbated the problem of how to display them. There was a gift from the collection of the late Rev. Dr Thomas Walker and: a most valuable collection of Jewish and sacred music, including some manuscripts from Rev. M. Cohen in Leeds. The first consignment of Hebraica from the Jewish Agency also arrived and was followed in future years by more publications.

In 1956 Dr Rabinowicz resigned as Chair of the Library Committee and was replaced by Judge Israel Finestein. That year saw the completion of the: 'first stocktaking ever undertaken of the printed books of the Montefiore Loan Library at Jews' College'. They also finished: 'the microfilming of a large number of manuscripts of the Montefiore and Jews' College Collections, on behalf of the Israeli Ministry of Education, Institute of Manuscripts'.[15] It was typical that of the 280 books added to the collection, 190 were gifts.

Meanwhile Ruth Lehmann had been appointed to represent Jews' College on the provisional committee of the Standing Conference of Theological and Philosophical Libraries of Great Britain. The library was even asked to take part in the exhibition organised by the Tercentenary Council at the Victoria and Albert Museum.

The remaining 1,000 manuscripts of the Montefiore Collection at Ramsgate arrived in 1957, as well as the library of the defunct Aria College. The library's card catalogue was microfilmed for the new Association of Libraries of Judaica and Hebraica in Europe, and Rabbi Aron Blumenthal's considerable rabbinical library was deposited on permanent loan.

It was in the same year that the 60,000 printed books moved to Jews' College's magnificent new home in Montagu Place. Nothing had been forgotten in discussions with the architects; lighting, heating, shelving and equipment were all they should be. The collection had been augmented by the gift of 10,000 books on Hebraic and Judaic subjects salvaged from the ruins in Europe by the Archive Trust. The whole removal was completed by the beginning of the academic session of 1957–58 and it resulted in a lot of publicity in the Jewish press and on the BBC.

In 1958, with the establishment of the Jews' College Institute for the Training of Teachers, a new department of secular books was formed and grew quickly. Further books came from the late Dr M.

Bauer, Dr Jacob Ehlrich, Rev. Solomon Einhorn, Dr J. Irger and Dayan Bernard Spiers. The library was flourishing and in its centenary year in 1960 an exhibition of the library's treasures was opened by the Chief Rabbi. Six hundred visitors came, both Jewish and non-Jewish, and £15,000 was raised for the library's upkeep. In 1962 an extensive exhibition of the sources of the *Shulchan Aruch* was organised.

The gifts continued to come in at regular intervals. In 1970: 'generous benefactors this year were the Hebrew University, the Institute of Jewish Affairs, Yad Ben Zvi and the World Jewish Congress. An addition of particular interest which was presented to the Library was the Manuscript Catalogue of the Blumenthal Rabbinics Library.'

That year £1,000 was spent on buying books and this doubled to over £2,000 by the end of the decade, when over 1,000 books were either purchased or donated in 1978. Even with that level of investment, however, it proved difficult to keep the library collection up-to-date. The area that caused the Library Committee most concern was the books of Responsa produced by eminent Talmudic scholars around the world. The decisions they contained were of great importance in keeping the *din* au courant. The medical world was also changing and Chief Rabbi Jakobovits, himself, was tackling the questions which emerged as a result on everything from abortion to organ donation.

Ruth Lehmann retired in 1973 and a Dutch lady, Erla Broekema, took over. When she left to have a baby, Leonard Sokolic and Avrom Shuchatowitz replaced her but it was decided to recruit a new librarian in 1980. The successful candidate was Esra Kahn who was not a professional librarian but had catalogued an important collection of Judaica which had been bought by Jack Lunzer, a noted bibliophile. Lunzer was so impressed by the catalogue that he persuaded Kahn to apply for the post, and then bought 3,500 books from a London dealer in Judaica and Hebraica for the College; it was particularly strong in Responsa literature, Novellae on Talmud, Chassidism and Jewish history. As the only eminent bibliophile on the Library Committee, Lunzer's opinion carried much weight and he offered to pay Kahn's salary. Kahn was appointed and Lunzer kept his word until there was a disagreement some time later.

The new librarian found the cataloguing of the College library very unsatisfactory: 'The collection was in total disarray. If you found a book, it was a miracle. The collection was very out-of-date. Dr Joseph Kaminetzky, the Director of the Torah Mesorah in America came to visit us and pronounced it an antiquarian library.'[16]

Kahn took up his office just in time to see all the librarians of major Jewish collections meet in Cambridge to set up a Hebraica Libraries Group. Stefan Reif, a Jews' College alumnus, was the first convener. Over the coming years the group met to consider the problems inherent in maintaining the libraries, which often gave cause for concern. For example, in 1988 there was a serious problem with the Mocatta Library at University College, London, where there simply were not sufficient staff to deal with the necessary stocktaking. Today, the major collections in Britain, apart from Jews' College, are to be found at the British Museum and the Bodleian in Oxford, but a lot of ancient and very valuable material has been sold over the years by other British libraries to institutions throughout the world.

When Montagu Place had to be given up in 1982, the library books were moved to a repository in Islington while the College was temporarily housed in Finchley. Running a library under those conditions was almost impossible. The best that could be achieved was a reference library in Finchley and a weekly visit to Islington to collect and return books. Furthermore, there was insufficient money available to buy the necessary new books, though the 1983 budget was £7,500 and there were very substantial donations from well-wishers. Such donations, however, were not, necessarily, books that were needed for current purposes. As Esra Khan reported in that year: 'However fine and valuable ours was, it definitely needed urgent action to update its stock. They [the CNAA] specifically pointed to deficiencies in modern textbooks for the students of the College.'[17] When Jonathan Sacks became Principal, he did insist on £10,000 being put into the annual budgets for the library and that continued during his years in office.

There was also the problem that those responsible for creating the library space in Albert Road didn't consult Esra Kahn, as had been promised. One result was that thousands of pounds were spent on huge heaters in the ceiling to warm the area. The problem then was that the hot air played on the books and they became 'cinder dry'. The heaters, therefore, couldn't be used and the money for them was wasted.

The work involved in controlling a library of 60,000 books is immense. In 1983 there were 2,219 newly accessed books and pamphlets to be catalogued and an additional 2,300 to be re-catalogued. This wasn't an unusual year. Furthermore the library was a major resource for researchers, who would welcome advice from Kahn on what literature was available. Typically, Dr Yaakov Gelb came from Petach Tikva to study the history of the Rumanian Jews, Professor Yehuda Ratzaby arrived from Bar Ilan to study Saadyana, Gamil Ahmad el Refaey from Cairo spent a long time on Haskalah literature, and Dr Jadelson came from Tennessee State University to study Israel Zangwill.

The library was eventually moved to Albert Road where it remains today as part of the London School of Jewish Studies. A notable addition was the Jewish Memorial Council Library of 3,000 volumes. It was decided at the outset not to allow the general public in to browse, as there had been pilferage in the past, which is a constant concern for libraries. The move was completed with great difficulty by Kahn, who served from 1980–2003. With his friendly disposition and his thirst for bibliographic curiosities, 'Esra Kahn turned the library into a welcoming place for study and research'.[18] So it was, but the Albert Road setting was a poor imitation of Montagu Place. In 1985 the CNAA regretted: 'a failure to integrate the library into the academic life of the College'.[19]

Unfortunately, the solution to the problem of how to integrate 60,000 books without sufficient financial or staff resources was not a part of the criticism the CNAA was ready to address. By 1985 there was no money to bind pamphlets or to deal with the suggestions of the CNAA. Kahn soldiered on and Erla Zimmels née Broekema, the daughter-in-law of the former principal, joined him and is still involved today.

There was, of course, a great deal of interest in the contents and sheer size of the library. Esra Kahn reported in 1989: 'This past year I have again given a dozen talks to schools and adult groups, mainly on the subject of the Library and its rare books, the History of Hebrew Printing and the Passover Haggadah.'[20] There were certainly some very unusual items; for example, the library possessed a piece of an eighth-century *Sefer Torah* and a book printed in China on rice paper by missionaries, which contained passages of the Bible. Kahn was never too busy to help; in 1992 he was the guest lecturer: 'to a packed house of the newly founded Jewish Genealogical Society of Great Britain and, as a result of the talk, a marked increase in researchers in Jewish genealogy has been noted'.[21]

The lawyer, Charles Corman, was the Chair of the Library Committee from 1985–90 and was followed by Charles Landau. In his valedictory report, Corman pointed out that there were now about 500 new books of Jewish interest produced every year, in English and Hebrew alone. Twice as many as had been published in the past five centuries. While the library was not trying to stock all the new Holocaust literature, it was concerned that the very expensive books of Responsa were still outside its buying capacity. To correct the situation, a sale of surplus books was inaugurated and a Book for Tomorrow scheme was introduced. If sufficient books were donated, the donor would have a special book plate placed in them bearing his name.

In 1986, in his review of the College, Jonathan Sacks identified his concerns about the library: 'The book and periodical purchasing appears to be sporadic and without direction. Important new books are missed; trivia are acquired.'[22] In the library's defence, one problem was that the additions to the library were often gifts from individuals and there was no way of knowing what the contents of their collections were. Furthermore, authors were donating the results of their efforts and the same applied. The librarian was well aware of the absence of many important books but had difficulty in finding the money for them.

Meanwhile the revitalised MA programme was attracting students in the evenings and so the library hours were extended to forty-five a week, including evenings and alternate Sunday mornings. Kahn was still hard at work trying to fully catalogue the collection. He checked and allocated 30,000 books in 1992 but still regretted four years later that 5,000 Hebrew cataloguing sheets were only to be found in handwritten form and badly needed typing.

It wasn't just a question of lending books though. Kahn continued to address the visiting groups, and occasionally travelled abroad to find cheaper sources of the volumes he needed. He also organized exhibitions, like the 1996 display of the works of Rabbi Jacob Emden (1697–1776), a major figure on the Continent.

It was a great pity that the College had to relieve its financial problems by selling 339 of its rare books in 2002, and still there were no funds to buy any more volumes. In addition, the Montefiore Collection was removed by the Montefiore Endowment. The three Jews' College book sales produced over £600,000. The library still gets books from members of the community, however. A collection of 3,000 books on anti-Semitism was one of the most recent donations. The most significant acquisition, though, was the computer programme, Otzar Hachochmah, where the update to the latest edition had 37,500 titles accessible in its programme.

Esra Kahn retired in 2003 to be replaced by Erla Zimmels. With the prolonged discussions about the future of the College, the interests of the library had to be put on the back burner and there were no funds available to buy new books for many years. It was still a massive resource, however, and Erla Zimmels was brilliant at finding the older publications which researchers needed. Many a time, the author can confirm, the most obscure pamphlets would be unearthed after they had lain undisturbed for many, many years.

With so many of the rare books sold, the international reputation of the library inevitably suffered but, in 2010, the library still had no less than 100,000 titles, which is immensely impressive. It has recently been given Dr Epstein's library, yet another example of the affection the library holds throughout the community. The housing of the collection, however, left a great deal to be desired.

In 2015, therefore, a fund raising campaign finally made it possible to house the library appropriately. The new shelving set the books off properly and the library now reflects the international importance of the collection. It still faces the problem which has beset every aspect of the College: how to maintain it. Where is the money to be found to buy new books and to buy the books for which there were no funds over the last ten years.

This is a task which everyone knows must be addressed. There is a need to compile a list of volumes still missing, so that a wealthy benefactor can sign the necessary cheque. This is a task for the future.

NOTES

1. Much of this chapter is based on Ruth Lehmann, *Jews' College Library, A History* (London: Jews College, 1967).
2. JCAR.
3. JCAR.
4. JCAR.
5. JCAR.
6. JCAR.
7. JCAR.
8. JCAR.
9. *The Transactions of the Jewish Historical Society of England*, vol.viii, p.8.
10. JCAR.
11. JCAR.
12. JCAR.
13. JCAR.
14. JCAR.
15. JCAR.
16. JCAR.
17. JCAR.
18. Erla Zimmels, 'The Jews' College Library: 1860–1910', in *Jewish Year Book 2010*, ed. Elkan D. Levy and Derek Taylor (London and Portland, OR: Vallentine Mitchell, 2010), p.20.
19. JCAR.
20. JCAR.
21. JCAR.
22. JCAR.

APPENDIX A

Jews' College Officers

Founders

Chief Rabbi Nathan Marcus Adler
Sir Moses Montefiore

Presidents

1855–1890	Chief Rabbi Nathan Marcus Adler
1891–1911	Chief Rabbi Hermann Adler
1913–1946	Chief Rabbi Joseph Herman Hertz
1948–1965	Chief Rabbi Israel Brodie
1967–1991	Chief Rabbi Immanuel Jakobovits
1991–2013	Chief Rabbi Lord Sacks
2013 –	Chief Rabbi Ephraim Mirvis

Deputy Presidents

1912–1919	Haham Moses Gaster
1950–1994	Haham Solomon Gaon
1994–2014	Rabbi Abraham Levy
2014–	Rabbi Joseph Dwek

Chairmen

1879–1887	Sir Barrow Ellis
1888–1908	Chief Rabbi Hermann Adler
1908–1919	Joshua Levy

1919–1924   Samuel Emanuel
1925–1945   Saemy Japhet
1945–1961   Sir Alan Mocatta
1962–1972   Bruno Marmorstein
1972–1983   Arnold Lee
1983–1989   Lord Stanley Kalms
1989–1996   David Pomson
1998–2002   Clive Marks
2003–2008   Howard Stanton
2008 –   Professor Anthony Warrens

Principals

1855–1858   Dr Louis Loewe
1858–1863   Rev. Barnett Abrahams
1865–1907   Dr. Michael Friedländer
1907–1939   Rabbi Adolph Büchler
1939–1945   Chief Rabbi Joseph Herman Hertz
1945–1961   Rabbi Dr. Isidore Epstein
1964–1968   Rabbi Dr. Hirsch Zimmels
1971–1983   Rabbi Nahum Rabinovitch
1984–1990   Chief Rabbi, Lord Sacks
1990–1993   Rabbi Dr. Irving Jacobs.
1994–1997   Rabbi Daniel Sinclair
2000–2002   Rabbi Abner Weiss
2003   Rabbi Lord Sacks

APPENDIX B

Jews' College Rabbis

1896 Rabbi Solomon Levy, MA, New Synagogue.
1898 Dayan Asher Feldman, BA, Hon. Sec of Jews' College for thirty-two years; Beth Din.
Dayan Moses Hyamson, BA, Stoke Newington Synagogue; Beth Din for thirty-five years; Chief Rabbi pro. tem 1911–13.
Rabbi Abraham Wolf, MA, Manchester Reform Synagogue; Professor of Logic at University College, London.
1899 Rabbi Benjamin Michelson, BA, Newport Synagogue, Brisbane, Australia; Welfare Minister, United Synagogue; South Hackney Synagogue.
1900 Rabbi Michael Adler, BA, Central Synagogue, London.
1901 Rabbi Maurice Simon, BA, author of scholarly books.
1908 Rabbi Barnet Cohen, BA, Sheffield Synagogue
1909 Dayan Harris Lazarus, MA, Brondesbury Synagogue; Chief Rabbi pro tem 1948–1965.
1913 Dayan Louis Mendelsohn, MA, Nottingham, Bristol, Dublin and West Ham District Synagogues; Beth Din.
1920 Rabbi W. Hirsch, BA, Middlesborough, Shanghai and Pretoria Synagogues.
1923 Chief Rabbi Sir Israel Brodie, KBE, BA, B.Litt (Oxon), Melbourne Synagogue; Senior Chaplain to the Forces; Chief Rabbi.
1923 Dayan Mark Gollop, BA, Southend, Bayswater and Hampstead Synagogues; Beth Din; Senior Chaplain to the Forces.
Rabbi Samuel Gross, B, Dalston Synaogue.

1926	Rabbi Solomon Mestel, MA, Richmond, Nottingham, Melbourne (Australia) and West Ham Synagogues.
1933	Professor Israel Abrahams, MA, Chief Rabbi, South Africa.
	Rabbi Dr Simon. Lehrman, MA, Manchester, Liverpool and New London Synagogues.
	Rabbi Pinchas Shebson, Grimsby, Southend and Westcliffe Synagogues.
	Rabbi Jack Danglow, OBE, CMG, VD, MA, Minister in St Kilda Australia and Victoria, Australia.
1937	Rabbi Dr Isaak Emil Lichtigfeld, Frankfurt Medal of Honour, Chair of Conference of German Rabbis; Frankfurt Synagogue; Hesse Synagogue.
1943	Rabbi J. Vilenski, BA, Manchester Synagogue.
1948	Rabbi Dr Isaac Cohen, BA, PhD, Chief Rabbi of Ireland.
	Rabbi Dr Alexander Carlebach, PhD, North Hendon Adath; Binyan Zion Synagogue, Jerusalem; Chief Rabbi of Northern Ireland.
	Rabbi Isaac Chait, MA, United Sheffield Hebrew Congregation; Palmers Green and Southgate Synagogue.
	Rabbi Dr Solomon Gaon, BA, PhD; Haham of the Spanish and Portuguese Congregations.
	Rabbi S. Rapoport, BA, Higher Crumpsall Manchester Synagogue.
	Rabbi Solomon Warshaw, BA, Brighton, Bayswater, Cardiff, Glasgow, Stanmore, Pinner, Leeds and Yeshurun Synagogue, Edgware.
1949	Dayan Dr Myer Lew, BA, PhD, Stoke Newington and Hampstead Garden Suburb Synagogues; Beth Din.
	Rabbi Stanley Woolf, BA, Princes Road Synagogue, Liverpool.
	Rabbi Dr Jacob Posen, BA, PhD, Upton Park and Nottingham Synagogues.
	Rabbi Dr Arnost Zvi Ehrman, Nairobi, Kenya, Bristol, Streatham District and Watford District Synagogues.
	Rabbi Raphael Wittler, BA
	Rabbi Max Warschawski, Strasbourg Synagogue.

1950	Rabbi Dr Abraham Melinek, BA, PhD Stoke Newington and Willesden Synagogues.
	Rabbi Dr Eugene Newman, MA, PhD, Golders Green Synagogue for twenty-three years.
1951.	Rabbi Dr Izaak Rapaport, OBE, M.Phil. PhD, Leicester and Melbourne, Australia Synagogues.
1952	Rabbi Morris Nemeth, BA, Hampstead, Streatham and District, Greenbank Drive, Liverpool and New West End Synagogues.
	Rabbi Dr Joseph Rabinowitz, BA, PhD, Bradford, Higher Broughton and Dalston Synagogues.
	Rabbi Dr I.H. Levine, BA, PhD, Capetown and Bulawayo Synagogues.
	Rabbi I. Waller, BA, West Ham District Synagogue.
1953	Rabbi Isaac Zwebner, MA, Bulawayo Synagogue, Zimbabwe.
1954	Rabbi Myer Berman, MBE, BA, Wembley Synagogue for forty years.
	Rabbi Lipa Baum, BA, Pollokshields, Glasgow, Luton, Regents Park, Belsize Park and Woodside Park Synagogues.
	Rabbi J. Weinberger, St Albans Synagogue.
1955	Rabbi Dr Harry Rabinowicz, BA, PhD, St Albans, Ilford, Dollis Hill, Cricklewood and Willesden Synagogues.
	Rabbi Isaac Newman, BA, CF, Barnet and District Synagogue.
1956	Rabbi Shalom Coleman, BA, Perth, Australia Synagogue
	Rabbi Sidney B. Leperer, BA, PhD, Walthamstow and Leyton, North Finchley, Woodside Park and Hove Synagogues.
1957	Rabbi Joseph Shaw, BA, Sutton, Palmers Green and Southgate Synagogues.
1958	Rabbi Isaac Fabricant, BA, Brighton and Hove Hebrew Congregations.
	Rabbi Chaim Cooper, BA, Kingsbury Synagogue, East London Synagogue and Hull Synagogue for forty years
	Rabbi Abraham Chaitowitz, BA, Stanmore Synagogue for thirty-one years.
	Rabbi Dr Solomon Goldman, MA, PhD, St Johns Wood Synagogue.

Rabbi Sidney Katz, BA, B.Sc., Great Synagogue, Pretoria, for thirty-eight years.

1959 Rabbi Raphael Cymberg, MA, Cockfosters and New Southgate Synagogue.

1960 Rabbi Ephraim Gastwirth, BA, South Hampstead, Sunderland and Blackpool Synagogues.
Dayan Hans Grunewald, Munich Synagogue.
Dayan Simon Herman, BA, Federation of Synagogues; Whitefields Synagogue, Manchester.

1961 Rabbi Maurice Rose, MA, Sutton Synagogue.
Rabbi Dr Norman Solomon, MA, Hampstead Synagogue
Rabbi Simeon Lowy, MA, The Philippines and Harrogate Synagogue.

1962 Rabbi Ronald Lubofsky, BA, Cockfosters and New Southgate; Great Synagogue, Sydney; St Kilda, Melbourne, Australia.
Rabbi Sidney Silberg, MA, Ealing, Newcastle, Bournemouth and Hendon Synagogues.
Rabbi Bent Melchior, Chief Rabbi of Denmark.
Rabbi Emil Nemeth, BA, Highgate Synagogue
Rabbi Cyril Shine, BA, Central Synagogue, London.

1964 Rabbi Philip Ginsbury, MA, Streatham, Brixton and South London Synagogues.

1968 Chief Rabbi Cyril Harris, BA, Kenton, Edgware and St Johns Wood Synagogues; Chief Rabbi of South Africa.
Rabbi Abraham Levy, BA, Senior Sephardi Rabbi, Bevis Marks and Lauderdale Road Synagogues.
Rabbi Philip Somen, MA, Brixton Synagogue and Commercial Road Great Synagogue.

1969 Rabbi Philip Greenberg, BA, Giffnock and Newlands Synagogue., Glasgow.

1970 Rabbi Raymond Apple, BA, LLB, Senior Rabbi of the Great Synagogue, Sydney, Australia and AB Beth Din.
Rabbi Toviah Rapalowicz, Edinburgh, Adelaide and Sydney, Australia Synagogues.

	Rabbi Dr Bernard Susser, BA, LLB, M.Phil, PhD, Yellville, Johannesburg, Belsize Park, Notting Hill, Plymouth, Sunderland and Brighton and Hove Synagogues.
1971	Rabbi Michael Goldman, BA, Newbury Park Synagogue.
	Rabbi Eddie Jackson, BA, Kenton and Hampstead Garden Suburb Synagogues.
1977	Rabbi Yaacov Grunewald, Pinner Synagogue for thirty-four years.
	Rabbi Lord Jonathan Sacks, MA, PhD, Dunstan Road and Western Marble Arch Synagogues; Chief Rabbi.
1982	Rabbi Geoffrey Hyman, BA, Woodside Park, Sutton, Belmont and Ilford Synagogues.
1985	Rabbi Joel Portnoy, Hales Synagogue, Manchester.
1986	Rabbi Meir Salasnik, Bushey Synagogue.
	Rabbi Dr Julian Shindler. MA, PhD, Senior appointments in the Chief Rabbi's Office.
1988	Rabbi Ian Goodhardt, Reading Synagogue.
1994	Rabbi Yaacov Yehuda.
1996	Rabbi Victor Seedman
1993	Rabbi Stanley Coten, Kingston and Surbiton, Ruislip and District Synagogues.
	Rabbi Leonard Brook, St Annes Synagogue.
1995	Rabbi Ronen Broder, West Ham and Upton Park Synagogues.
	Rabbi Yisroel Elia, Lauderdale Road Synagogue
	Rabbi Adam Hill, Leicester Synagogue, Central Synagogue, Birmingham, Potters Bar Synagogue.
	Rabbi Dovid Muster, teacher at Hasmonean High School.
	Rabbi Shmuel Nassim, made Aliyah.
	Rabbi Moshe Perez, Nottingham Synagogue.
	Rabbi Chananya Silverman, Enfield and Winchmore Hill Synagogue.
	Rabbi Leonard Tann, Singers Hill Synagogue, Birmingham.
	Rabbi Rallis Wiesenthal, Chicago, USA.

1997	Rabbi Michael Davis, Waltham Forest Hebrew Congregation.
	Rabbi Jason Kleiman, Beth Hamedresh Hagodol Synagogue
	Rabbi Shmuel Neumann, Hendon Synagogue.
1999	Rabbi Alexander Chapper, Ilford Federation Synagogue.
	Rabbi Shalom Gittelman.
	Rabbi Danny Kerbel, Hackney, Yeshurun, Gatley and Stockport Synagogues.
2001	Rabbi Barry Lerer, Watford Synagogue
	Rabbi Stephen Sacks, osteopath.
	Rabbi Zvi Solomons, Reading Synagogue.
2013	Rabbi Natan Abenaim, Institute Européan Emmanuel Levinson, Paris.
	Rabbi Steven Dansky, Mill Hill Synagogue
	Rabbi Yaacov Finn, Shenley Synagogue
	Rabbi Meir Lev, Sutton Synagogue
	Rabbi Asaf Mittelman, Rav of Yeshiva in Israel.
	Rabbi Ofir Ronen, Wolfson Hillel Jewish Primary School
	Rabbi Samuel Rubin, Trustee LSJS
	Rabbi David Steinhoff, Head of Kashrut for Sephardi Kashrut Authority
	Rabbi Lee Sunderland, Romford Synagogue
	Rabbi Raphael Zarum, Dean of LSJS

APPENDIX C

Jewish Chaplains to the Forces in the Second World War

Name	Synagogue	Date at Jews' College
*H.I. Alexander	Hendon	1934
Saul Amias	Edgware	
*Arthur Barnett	Western Served in First and Second World War	1905–07
*A. Berman		1934
*M. Berman	Wembley	1932
Emanuel Berry	Llandudno Died 1944	
*C.M. Bloch	Portsmouth	1932.
*Harry Bornstein	Hampstead Garden Suburb Died 1943	1937
*Israel Brodie	Jews College Served in First and Second World War	1923
Solomon Brown	Leeds	
*Eli Cashdan	Hendon	
*Bernard Casper	Manchester	1934
*Isaac Chait	Sheffield	1924
*Bernard Cherrick	New, Stamford Hill	
*Dr A. Cohen	Birmingham	
*Barnett Cohen	Sheffield	1908
*P. Cohen		1931

*I.K. Cosgrove		
Salis Daiches	Edinburgh	
Moishe Davis		
*Emmanuel Drukker	Newcastle	1912
I. Dvorkin	Reading	
L.I. Edgar	Liberal	
*Michael Elton	JC Librarian	1937
*B. Epstein		1938
*I. Fabricant	Brighton	1930
J. Gill (Lifschitz)		
Morris Ginsberg	Richmond	
*S. Goldman	Nottingham.	1935.
*Mark Gollop	Dayan, Beth Din	1923
B. Greenberg		
E.T. Hamburger		
L.L. Hardman	Hendon	
C.L. Heilpern	Bournemouth	
D. Hirsch	Hull	
*W. Hirsch	Jews' College Staff	1920
*Bernard Hooker	Liberal Synagogue	
*Solly Hooker	Harrow	
*Simeon Isaacs	S.E. London. Central Synagogue	1931
*Jacob Israelstam	Bradford; Warden JC Hostel	1931
Maurice Jaffe	Jerusalem	
*B. Joseph	Hackney	1931
*Simon Lehrman	Liverpool	1933
*Israel Levinson	Served in First and Second World War	1906
*Isaac Levy	Bayswater; Hampstead	1931
*Maurice Lew	West End Great Synagogue; India Command	1931

B. Lucki
J. Margulies
*Benjamin Michaelson   Brisbane   1899
Alan Miller
*Wolf Morein   N. London   1924
                    Died 1941
Abraham da S. Pimentel   Manchester
A. Plasrow   Southend
*H. Rabinowitch   1931
*I. Rapaport   1940
Samuel Rodrigues-Pereira   Ramsgate
I.T. Rosen   Manchester
*Louis Sanker   Bristol   1932
J. Schachter   Belfast
*A. Shapiro
Stanley Solomons   Birmingham
*Arthur Super   Leeds   1931
*Bernard Unterman   Leicester
*Maurice Unterman   Cardiff
Ephraim Urbach
*M. Wagner.
*J. Weintrobe   Swansea   1930
Wilfred Wolfson   Plymouth
*Benjamin Wykansky   Brondesbury

*Jews' College graduates and staff.

APPENDIX D

The Rabbinical Diploma

Rules and Regulations and Subjects of Examination

(1) Candidates for the Diploma of Rabbi shall be required to have passed the Third or Final Hebrew and Theological Examination of the College and the Degree Examination of some recognized University, or some Equivalent Examination.

The Council shall be empowered, in exceptional cases, to dispense with the qualification of the University Degree. The Third and Final Hebrew and Theological Examination of the College shall be obligatory for all Candidates.

(2) Every candidate must, at least three calendar months before the Examination, inform the Principal of his proposed candidature, and must obtain from him within that period a Certificate, confirmed by the President, that in respect of his religious and moral life, he is a fit and proper person to be entered for the Examination.

(3) The Examination shall be held during the month of December in each year, and the first Examination for the Diploma shall be held in the year 1903.

(4) The Scheme and Subjects of Examination shall be as follows:-
I. TALMUD
Candidates must be able, after a preparation lasting not more than two hours, to expound a sugya [topic], in any one of the following Masechtoth [tractates]:-

Shabbat, Pesach, Yom Kippur, Marriage, Divorce and Kashrut with the Commentaries of Rashi and Tosafoth.

II. SHULCHAN ARUCH

Candidates must pass (a) a viva voce [oral exam] and (b) a written Examination:

(a) Viva Voce:
Answers to questions about the Shulchan Aruch, divorce, marriage and witnesses.

(b) In writing:
Not less than ten searching questions about responsa in the above to be answered in writing. The Candidate to be permitted the use of the Shulchan Aruch open during this part of the Examination.

III. During the twelve months preceding the Examination, opportunities shall be given to Candidates to become conversant with the practical portions of the slaughter of animals, giving get [a divorce], with the answers to how to confirm that an animal has been correctly slaughtered.

IV. The Examination shall not last longer than three days.

(5) To Conduct the Examination, the following (or such of them as shall be able and willing to act) shall be constituted as the Board of Examiners:-

The President (the Chief Rabbi); the Haham; the Principal; the Theological Tutor; and a Member of the Beth Din to be nominated by the Council, and to hold office for the ensuing Examination.

The President shall be the Chairman of the Examiners, with an additional casting vote in the event of an equality of votes.

(6) As soon as possible after the Examination, and within one calendar month, the Principal shall draw up a Report for the Council upon each Candidate separately; each such Report shall state the recommendation of the Examiners, and in the case of a successful student that he has been recommended to the President of the College (the Chief Rabbi) as competent for xxxxx, the Diploma of Rabbi.

In the case of an unsuccessful Candidate, the Report shall clearly state in what subject or subjects he has failed to satisfy the Examiners. A Candidate who has failed to pass on one occasion shall be allowed to enter for any subsequent Examination, provided that he comply with the Regulations set forth above.

(7) The Diploma with the Seal of Jews' College attached shall be presented to the successful Candidate or Candidates at the Public Distribution of Prizes next following the Examination.
(8) The Diploma shall be in Hebrew and English:
    I. The Hebrew, written in accordance with the customary form and phraseology.
    II. The English printed in the following terms:-

JEWS' COLLEGE, LONDON.

XXXXXX

DIPLOMA OF RABBI

As a result of an Examination conducted within the College, by the BOARD OF EXAMINERS for the Hatorah Haaroah, consisting of:-

....

THE PRESIDENT (THE REVD THE CHIEF RABBI)

....

THE HAHAM

....

THE PRINCIPAL OF THE COLLEGE

....

THE THEOLOGICAL TUTOR

....

MEMBER OF THE BETH DIN

....

This DIPLOMA testified that the Hatarath Horaah has been conferred upon

....

with all the rights, privileges, and status appertaining thereto.

Signed
[Seal of Jews' College]
President of Jews' College

Date

APPENDIX E

Jews' College Publications

Jews' College always tried to provide an educational resource for the wider Jewish community in Britain. One way in which this was achieved was through the publication of learned papers by members of the staff. The College started to underwrite this initiative in 1908.

Adolph Büchler, The Political and the Social Leaders of the Jewish Community of Sepphoris in the Second and Third Centuries

Samuel Daiches, The Jews in Babylonia in the Time of Ezra and Nehemiah According to the Babylonian Inscriptions

H. Hirschfield, Jefreth b. Ali's Arabic Commentary on Nahum, with an Introduction, Abridged Translation and Notes

Adolph Büchler, The Economic Conditions in Judaea after the Destruction of the Second Temple

Samuel Daiches, Babylonian Oil Magic in the Talmud and in the Later Jewish Literature

H. Hirschfield, Qirqisani Studies

A. Marmorstein, The Doctrine of Merits in Old Rabbinicial Literature

Adolph Büchler, Type of Jewish Palestinian Piety from 70 BCE to 70 CE

H. Hirschfield, Literary History of Hebrew Grammarians and Lexicographers, Accompanied by Unpublished Texts

A. Marmorstein, The Old Rabbinic Doctrine of God. 1. The Names and Attributes of God

Adolph Büchler, Studies in Sin and Atonement in the Rabbinic Literature of the First Century

Samuel Daiches, Studies in Psalms. The Meaning of Ben Odom, Odom and Kindred Terms. Part 1

Isidore Epstein, The Responsa of Rabbi Simon B. Zemah Duran as a Source of the History of the Jews in North Africa

A. Marmorstein, The Old Rabbinic Doctrine of God: II Essays in Anthropomorphism

A. Cohen, Jewish Homiletics

New Series

Israel Brodie and J. Rabbinowitz (eds), Studies in Jewish History (The Adolf Büchler Memorial Volume) (London: Oxford University Press, 1958).

J.H. Zimmels, Ashkenazim and Sephardim (London: Oxford University Press, 1958).

H.J. Zimmels, J. Rabbinowitz and Israel Finestein (eds), Essays Presented to Chief Rabbi Israel Brodie on the Occasion of his 70th Birthday, 2 vols (London: Narod and Soncino Presses, 1965).

Also published

Isidore Harris, History of Jews' College (London: Luzac & Co., 1906)

Albert Montefiore Hyamson, Jews' College, London, 1855–1955 (London: Jews' College, 1955).

H. Hirschfeld, Descriptive Catalogue of the Hebrew MSS of the Montefiore Library (at Jews' College Library) (Together with a Catalogue of the Hebrew Manuscripts in the Jews' College Library, compiled by A. Neubauer) (Reprint 1969).

Ruth Lehmann, Jews' College Library, A History (London: Jews College, 1967).

Jeffrey Cohen, Moments of Insight. Biblical and Contemporary Jewish Themes (London and Portland, OR: Vallentine Mitchell, 1989).

Bibliography

Apple, Raymond, 'Kovno and Oxford: Israel Brodie and his Rabbinical Career', www.oztorah.com/2008/o2/kovno-oxford-Israel-Brodie-his-rabbinical-career

Black, Gerry, JFS: The History of the Jews' Free School, London, Since 1732 (London: Tymsder Publishing, 1998).

Gollancz, Hermann, Personalia (Oxford: Oxford University Press, 1928).

Harris, Isidore, History of Jews College (London: Luzac & Co., 1906).

Henriques, Robert, Sir Robert Waley-Cohen, 1877–1952 (London: Secker & Warburg, 1966).

Hyamson, Albert, Jews College, London, 1855–1955 (London: Jews College, 1955).

Jacobs, Rabbi Louis, We have Reason to Believe (London: Vallentine Mitchell, 1965).

Lehmann, Ruth, Jews' College Library, A History (London: Jews College, 1967).

Picciotto, James, Sketches of Anglo-Jewiish History (London: Soncino Press, 1956).

Sacks, Jonathan, Will We Have Jewish Grandchildren?: Jewish Continuity and How to Achieve it (London and Portland, OR: Vallentine Mitchell, 1994).

Taylor, Derek, British Chief Rabbis (London and Portland, OR: Vallentine Mitchell, 2007).

Taylor, Derek, Chief Rabbi Hertz, The Wars of the Lord (London and Portland, OR: Vallentine Mitchell, 2014).

Zimmels, Erla, 'The Jews' College Library: 1860–1910', in Jewish Year Book 2010, ed. Elkan D. Levy and Derek Taylor (London and Portland, OR: Vallentine Mitchell, 2010).

Index

Abelson, Joshua, 73.
Abrahams, Barnett, 38, 42, 89.
Abrahams, Dr Israel, 46, 48, 53, 76, 89, 92, 277.
Abramsky, Dayan Yeheskel, 180, 197, 225.
Academy, 132-138, 141, 142, 157.
Aden, 211, 224.
Adler, Alfred, 107.
Adler, Celestine (Lehfeld), 38.
Adler, Elkan, 46, 277, 278, 280.
Adler family, 9, 14.
Adler, Henrietta, (Worms), 20.
Adler, Herbert, 282.
Adler, Chief Rabbi Hermann, 40, 42-4, 54, 59, 60, 74, 84, 85, 90, 91, 95, 97-100, 103, 108, 112, 115, 117, 118, 137, 273.
Adler, Marcus, 276.
Adler, Michael, 74, 123, 124.
Adler, Mordecai, 14.
Adler, Chief Rabbi Nathan Marcus, 7-11, 14, 15, 20, 21, 24, 25-30, 32, 33, 36, 42, 46, 49, 50, 53, 56, 63, 68, 69, 97, 100, 112, 137, 184, 225, 226, 270, 277.
Adolph Tuck Hall, 153, 168.
Agency for Jewish Education, 256.
Albert Road, 243, 249, 256, 285, 286.
Alderman, Professor Geoffrey, 245.
Alderney Road Cemetery, 21.
Alexander, Joshua, 18, 46.
Aliens Bill, 99.
Allenby, General, 125.
Alexandria, Royal Library of, 271.
Alliance Building Society, 9.
Alter, Rabbi Yehudah Aryeh Leib, 87.
America, 57, 63, 93, 99, 121, 126, 131, 181, 183, 193, 199, 207, 217, 218, 239, 255, 257, 259, 261, 285.
American Association for Jewish Studies, 183.
Amor, Dayan Saadia, 265.
Amsterdam, 1, 6, 107, 273.
Amstrad, 237.
Anderson, Hans Christian, 57.
Anti-Semitism, 269, 288.
Antoine, Mr. 89.
Apple, Marian, 177.
Apple, Rabbi Raymond, 176, 200, 224, 246.
Aramaic, 3.
Archive Trust, 283.
Aria College, 60, 115, 147, 274, 283.
Aria, Lewis, 60.
Aristotle, 75.

Arnold, Dr, 17, 86.
Arons, Mrs, 177.
Artillery Ground, 39.
Ashkenazi, Rabbi Zvi, 107.
Ashkenazim, 9, 19, 49, 54, 76.
Association for the Diffusion of Religious Knowledge, 43.
Association of Jewish Scientists, 215.
Association of Libraries of Judaica and Hebraica in Europe, 283.
Assyrian Studies, 97.
Astaire, Jarvis, 223.
Australia, 73, 176, 195, 196, 202, 211, 234, 249.
Austria, 18, 120, 121.

Babylonian Talmud, 180, 259, 273, 278.
Balfour Declaration, 20, 126, 170.
Bar Ilan University, 204, 215, 232, 286.
Barned, Israel, 30.
Barnstein, Rabbi Henry, 70, 71, 83.
Barnett, Arthur, 165.
Barnett, Henrietta, 166.
Barnett, Dr Lionel, 89.
Basri, Dayan Ezra, 265.
Baum, Dr M., 284.
BBC, 240, 251, 283.
Bearsted, Lord, 145, 190.
Beckman, Barnett, 117.
Bedford, Duke of, 76.
Behrend, Dr. Henry, 56.
Belgium, 96.
Belsen, 166.
Benifold, J. S., 38-40, 44.
Benisch, Abraham, 273.
Benjamin Levi Educational Trust, 141.
Bennett, Solomon, 282.
Benoliel, Joshua, 19.
Berlin, 43, 64, 120.
Berman, Myer, 27.
Bermant, Chaim, 201, 231.
Berry, Emanuel, 166.
Beth Din, 85, 90, 97, 98, 118, 137, 147, 198, 201, 225, 231, 245.
Beth Hamedresh, 2, 5, 6, 17, 18, 22, 30.
Billig, Levy, 116.
Bing, Rabbi Abraham, 6, 7.
Birkbeck College, 226.
Bischoffsheim, Henry Louis, 91.
Blitz, 167-169, 279.
Blumenthal, Rabbi Aaron, 283.

Blumenthal Rabbinics Library, 284.
Blumfield, Fiona, 255.
Bnei Akiva, 263.
Board of Deputies, 13, 18, 19, 126, 130, 139, 155, 206, 282.
Board of Shechita, 98, 126, 141.
Bodleian Library, 56, 94, 95, 192, 285.
Book of Common Prayer, 56.
'Book of Jewish Thoughts', 123, 170.
Bornstein, Harry, 166.
Bosnia, 180.
Bradfield, Michael, 250.
Bradfield, Susi, 250.
Brama, Rabbi Dror, 261.
Breslau, 152, 202.
British Academy, 37.
British Library, 271.
British Museum, 89, 272, 282, 285.
Brodetsky, Professor Selig, 282.
Brodie, Fanny, 185.
Brodie, Chief Rabbi Israel, 146, 147, 159, 163, 165, 170, 179, 181, 183-186, 191, 195-202, 206, 234, 253, 277, 284.
Broekema, Erla, 284.
Brovender, Rabbi Chaim, 258, 259.
Brown University, 204.
Büchler, Adolph, 83-105, 108, 109, 112-116, 118, 120, 122, 125, 126, 142, 146, 148, 151, 154-159, 163-165, 170, 173, 183, 192, 215, 225, 249, 253, 270, 280.
Burma, 166.

Cairo, 286.
Cairo Genizah, 275.
Cambridge, Duke of, 8.
Cambridge University, 17, 44, 63, 64, 89, 92, 113, 114, 116, 129, 130, 135, 154, 161-163, 179, 180, 204, 209, 216, 238, 248, 255, 264.
   Clare, 225.
   Jewish Society, 216.
   Wolfson College, 161.
Canada, 190, 215.
Carmel College, 188, 257.
Cashdan, Eli, 178, 188, 189, 204, 211-213, 218, 232, 259.
Casper, Chief Rabbi Bernard, 165.
Central Committee for Jewish Education, 148.
Central Jewish Committee for Problems of Evacuation, 168.
Chaikin, Rabbi Avigdor, 89, 90.
Chaplains to the Forces, Great War, 123, 124, 126.
Chaplains to the Forces, Second World War, 165, 212, 241, 299-301.
Chapman, John, 39, 44, 58, 59, 90, 96.
Charedim, 248.
Charles II. 1, 248.
Charles Wolfson Charitable Trust, 227.
Chaitovitz, Abraham, 27.
Cheder, 160.
Cheltenham, 162.
Chicksands Road Board School, 70.
Chief Rabbi's Religious Emergency Council, 170.
China, 287.
Chofetz, Chaim, 87, 189.
Christian Theological College, 94.
Church of England, 3, 17, 54, 56, 100, 108, 125, 148, 247, 270.
City & Guilds Institute, 66.
City of London School, 47.
City University, New York, 226.
Cleese, John, 246.
Clifton College, 121.
Clore, Sir Charles, 228, 234.
Cohen, Abraham, 163, 176.
Cohen, Alfred, 276.
Cohen, Arthur, 58.
Cohen, Barent, 84.
Cohen, Barnett, 165.
Cohen, Dr, 161.
Cohen, Francis, 89, 123.
Cohen, Rabbi Harris, 48, 89.
Cohen, Herman, 46, 60.
Cohen, Isaac, 14.
Cohen, Rabbi Jeffrey, 186, 205, 231, 232.
Cohen, Lionel, 274.
Cohen, M., 283.
Cohen, Moses, 73.
Cohen, Sir Robert Waley, 129-133, 136, 137, 139, 140, 142, 155, 157, 165, 170, 197, 215, 249, 253.
Cohen, Dayan Susman, 48.
Concord Hotel, 166.
Concordia Estates, 155.
Condor, Major Claude, 56.
Conference on Jewish Material Claims against Germany, 205, 213.
Congregationalists, 74.
Conservat, 91.
Conservative Hebrew Union College, 116.
Conservative Judaism, 64, 207.
Continental Jewish Museums, Libraries & Archives, Committee of Restoration, 281.
Cooper, Chaim, 27.
Corman, Charles, 287.
Council for National Academic Awards, (CNAA), 219, 224, 230, 239, 240, 246, 248, 250, 285, 286.
Cousinhood, 129.

Daiches, Dr Samuel, 96, 97, 110, 119, 124, 158, 159, 171, 202.
Daum, Ahron, 231.
Davies, David, 77.
Davies, Ven. C. Witton, 213.
Dazevedo, Haham Moses, 3.
Denmark, 6, 196, 271.
Deutsch, Dr Immanuel, 272.
Dickens, Charles, 57.
Disraeli, Benjamin, 66.

Index

District Rabbis, 148.
Doyle, Mary, 20.
Dropsie College, 112.
Duschinsky, Charles, 171.

East End, 57.
Education Act 1870, 34.
Egypt, 114, 162.
Ehlrich, Dr Jacob, 284.
Ehrentreu, Dayan Chanoch, 245.
Eicholz, Alfred, 89.
Einhorn, Solomon, 284.
Eleazer, Magnus Prize, 70.
Ellis, Sir Barrow, 53, 58, 63, 67.
Ellul Lectures, 263, 264.
Elton, Michael, 166, 280-282.
Emanuel, Samuel, 126, 139.
Emden, Rabbi Jacob, 288.
Epstein, Gertrude, 177.
Epstein, Dr Isidore, 138, 146, 147, 168, 169, 172-177, 179, 180, 182, 185, 187-189, 192, 195-199, 207, 212, 215, 244, 253, 259, 270, 278, 280, 288.
Essex University, 250, 251, 255.
Esther, Book of, 54.
Euclid, 45.
European Jewish Liberals, Congress of, 282.
Evans, Outsize, 206.
Ezra, Sir Derek, 230.

'Faith in the City', 247.
Falkender, Lady Marcia, 230.
Federation of Synagogues, 15, 49, 111, 142, 205, 213.
Feldman, Dayan Rabbi Asher, 73, 74, 85, 96, 110, 114, 170.
Feldman, Leon, 218.
Feuchtwanger, Rabbi, 206.
Fierstone, Clive, 230.
Filer, Abraham, 116.
Finchley, 285.
Finestein, Judge Israel, 283.
Finiston, Sir Monty, 230.
Finsbury Square, 20, 22, 41, 47, 57, 184.
France, 211, 268.
Frankfurt, 146.
Frankel, 226.
Franklin, Arthur, 115, 277.
Franklin, David, 185.
Franklin, H.A., 274.
Franklin, Jacob, 18.
Freedman, D.J., 73.
Friedländer, Bertha, 43, 95, 145.
Friedlander, Gerald, 73, 277.
Friedländer, Michael, 35, 40, 43, 45, 48, 50, 53-82, 84, 90, 95-98, 107, 112, 203, 249, 253, 270, 272-274, 276.
Friends of the Midrasha, 228.

Gallipoli, 114.
Gamse, Ian, 263.

Gaon, Haham Solomon, 180, 190, 191, 208-210, 228, 229.
Garbacz, Bernard, 222, 229.
Gaster, Haham Moses, 56, 68-72.
Gateshead, 142.
Gateshead Seminary, 72.
Geffen, John, 123.
Geffen, Lionel, 89.
Gelb, Dr Yaakov, 286.
German Jewish Aid Committee, 96.
German Reparations, 191.
Germany, 122, 159, 160, 211.
Gestetner, David, 77.
Gibbon, 75.
Gibraltar, 188.
Gillis, Bernard, 206.
Ginsberg, Professor, 170.
Glasgow, 231.
Goldbloom, Rev. J. K., 175.
Goldsmid, Isaac Lyon, 18.
Golomb, Moshe, 177.
Gollancz, Rabbi Professor Sir Hermann, 36, 37, 47, 63, 74, 83, 124.
Gollancz, Sir Israel, 36, 37, 56, 83, 84.
Gollop, Dayan Mark, 118, 165, 170.
Goodman, Tobias, 6.
Goren, Chief Rabbi Shlomo, 230.
Gower Street, 47.
Graetz, 75, 226.
Grand Rabbin, 152.
Great Universal Stores, 161.
Greece, 75, 97.
Green, Aaron Levy, 6, 18, 22, 53, 55, 58, 273.
Green Rev. Aaron, 32, 46, 48, 85, 119.
Green, Jack, 206.
Green, Stuart, 278.
Greenberg, Rabbi William, 70, 71, 83.
Greenspan, Rabbi Nashman Shlomo, 87, 88.
Greenwich University, 264.
Grossnass, Dayan Arieh Leib, 211.
Grosvenor House Hotel, 185.
Grunewald, Rabbi Hans, 196.
Grunewald, Yaacov, 27, 231.
Grunfeld, Dayan Isidor, 160, 198, 201.
Grunfeld, Judith, 160.
Gubbay, Lucien, 265.

Hailsham, Lord, 206.
Halachah, 3.
Halberstadt, 2.
Halberstam, Solomon, 275.
Halevi, Judah, 192.
Halfon, Madame, 276.
Hamburg, 54.
Hampshire, 60, 116.
Hanover, 7-10, 14.
Harris, Chief Rabbi Cyril, 187, 196, 209, 212.
Harris, H.L., 43.
Harris, Isidore, 38, 43, 47, 48, 134.
Harris, Lebus, 125.
Harris, Pincus, 169.

Hart, Rabbi Aaron, 2, 107.
Hartog, Professor Alphonse, 40, 44.
Hartog, Numa, 44.
Hasmonean Schools, 222, 223.
Hasmonean School for Girls, 205.
Hass, Simon, 175.
Hast, Marcus, 61.
Hebraica Libraries Group, 285.
Hebrew, 175, 179, 208. 218, 255.
Hebrew Cultural Movement, 175.
Hebrew Union College, 118.
Hebrew University College, Cincinnati, 134.
Hebrew University, 116, 218, 240, 282, 284.
Henrietta Barnett School, 166.
Henry, Henry Abraham, 6.
Henry, Michael, 39.
Herschell, Chief Rabbi Solomon, 3, 4,5,7,15, 282.
Hertz Chumash, 170.
Hertz, Chief Rabbi Joseph Herman, 64, 73, 117, 118, 120, 121, 130-140, 142, 144, 146, 147, 155, 160, 162, 164, 165, 170, 173, 176, 179, 196, 225, 278, 279, 282.
Hertz, Rose, 145.
Hertzl, Theodore, 69, 121.
Herzog, Rabbi Isaac, 134.
Hillel House, 191.
Hirsch, Rabbi Samson Raphael, 9, 225, 248.
Hirsch, Samuel, 110, 192.
Hirshfield, Dr Hartwig, 74, 159, 192, 275-278.
Hoffnung, S., 275.
Holland, 6, 284.
Holloway Prison, 61.
Holocaust, 169, 171, 179, 183, 226, 281, 287.
Hölzel, Herman, 6.
Hospital Plan Insurance Services, 250.
Houri, Yossi, 230.
House of Lords, 270.
    Moses Room, 270.
Hull, 274.
Hungary, 61, 94, 117, 146, 173.
Hurwitz, Hyman, 48.
Hyamson, Dayan Moses, 85, 90, 91, 93, 94, 112, 118, 176.
Hyman, Rabbi Aharon, 87.

Imperial Continental Gas Association, 8, 122.
India, 53, 63.
India Command, 166.
Indian Council, 54.
Institute of Jewish Affairs, 284.
Inter-University Jewish Federation, 177, 199, 207.
International Congress of Historical Studies, 112.
International Jewish Law Association, 255.
Ionides, Hon. Nellie, 192.
Ireland, 134, 224.
Irger, Dr. S., 284.
Isaac, Simeon, 166.

Isaiah, 45.
Isdaele, Michael, 231.
Isle of Dogs, 19.
Isle of Man, 171.
Israel, 166, 175, 176, 179, 180, 183, 209, 211, 230, 236, 239, 244, 253-255, 258, 266.
Israel, Minna, 91.
Israeli Ministry of Education, 283.
Israelstam, Jacob, 116.
Isserles, Moses, 206.

Jackson, Rabbi Eddie, 224.
Jacobs, Rabbi, Dr Irving, 181-183, 210, 212, 221, 229, 235, 237, 246, 250, 252.
Jacobs, Joseph, 56, 274.
Jacobs, Lawrence, 195.
Jacobs, Rabbi Louis, 65, 178, 188, 192, 195-204, 209, 220, 221, 243, 244.
Jadelson, Dr, 286.
Jaffe, Maurice, 166.
Jakobovits, Chief Rabbi Immanuel, 199, 202-204, 206, 208, 209, 212, 215, 218, 220, 221, 223, 225-7, 229, 234, 236-8, 243-245, 247, 248, 250, 270, 284.
James II., 1.
Japhet, Saemy, 91, 115, 142, 145, 155, 167.
Jerusalem, 69, 116, 124, 282.
Jessel, Albert, 108, 111, 112, 276.
Jessel, Sir George, 19, 102, 108.
Jewish Agency, 230, 283.
Jewish Book Week, 281, 282.
Jewish Central Library, 281.
Jewish Education Development Trust, 223, 228, 230, 236, 237, 252.
Jewish Geneological Society of Great Britain, 287.
Jewish Historical Society of England, 162, 277.
Jewish Marriage Council, 238.
Jewish Memorial Council 169, 205, 213, 230, 281, 286.
Jewish Museum, 155, 156, 278, 279.
Jewish Preachers Conference, 146.
Jewish Publication Society of America, 112.
Jewish Quarterly Review, 92.
Jewish Religious Education Board, 81, 115.
Jewish Theological Seminary, New York, 64, 85, 91, 125, 152, 176, 207, 208.
Jewish War Memorial Fund, 129, 131, 133, 135, 277.
Jews' College:
    110th anniversary dinner, 206.
    A.L. Green Library, 274, 276-278, 280.
    Academic Advisory Panel, 246.
    Adult Education Courses, 261.
    Alumni Association, 219.
    Book purchasing committee, 281.
    Büchler Library, 280.
    Building Committee, 276.
    Centenary Building & Endowment Fund, 183, 185, 190.

Index

Central Examining Board, 219.
Centre for Medical Ethics, 183.
Chaplaincy Committee, 219.
Corcos Library, 279.
Corporal punishment, 33, 86.
de Sola Library, 279.
Diplomas, Probationary, Associate & Fellow, 61.
East End Jews & Food Tour, 264.
Economy Committee, 157.
Education Committee, 219, 277.
Endowment Fund, 205, 219, 227.
Executive Committee, 219.
Finance Committee, 219.
Friedländer, Memorial Lecture, 107, 151.
Goldbloom Lectureship in Jewish Philosophy, 208.
Hazanut, 89, 110, 174, 175, 190, 211, 212, 219, 233, 238, 242, 243, 280.
Heenan, Cardinal, 206.
J.H. Hertz Chair in Rabbinics, 228.
Higher Biblical Criticism, 200, 209.
Homiletics, 110, 119, 162, 163, 176, 207, 240.
Hostel, 153.
House Committee, 219.
Institute of Jewish Education, 187.
Institution of Teacher Training, 191, 219.
Israel Independence Day, 203.
Israeli Hebraica, 282.
Jewish-Christian Group, 213, 220.
Jewish Pedagogy, 135.
Journal, 46, 62.
Jubilee Dinner, 91, 93, 124.
Jubilee Lunch 192.
Jubilee Volume, 12.
Kalms Fellowship, 245.
Ladies Auxiliary Committee, 145, 153.
Library, 64, 101, 156, 192, 219, 235, 243, 249, 256, 271-289.
Lishma programme, 263.
Literary & Debating Society, 11, 56, 63, 89, 211, 227, 271.
Lord Mayor's Commemoration Scholarship Association, 34.
Löwy Library, 277.
Marianne Samuel Scholarship, 66.
Medico-Legal group, 219.
Moral Leadership course, 281.
National Coordinating Council of the Friends of Jews College, 203.
National Gallery Bible Tour, 264.
Natural History Museum Genesis Tour, 264.
Newsletter, 203.
Office for Small Communities, 207.
Officers, 291, 292.
Postgraduate Department, 204.
Practical Rabbinics, 240, 251.
Pre-semicha course, 254.
Preparatory Class, 108, 110, 113.

Publications, 307, 308.
Purim party, 203.
Rabbi graduates, 293-298.
Rabbinical Diploma Course, 174, 180, 189.
Rabbinic Examining Board, 147.
Rabbinical Diploma, 303-306.
Rabbinical Studies Programme, 167.
Residence for Women Students, 227, 228.
Responsa, 287.
Scholarships, 77, 122.
Sir Israel Brodie Chair in Biblical Studies, 182, 227.
Smaller Communities Committee, 219.
Student Library, 105.
Student Recruitment, 219.
Student Union, 229.
Susi Bradfield Lectureship, 250.
Teacher Examination Committee, 160.
Teacher graduates, 80.
Teachers' Institute, 177, 211, 283.
Teacher Training, 244, 249, 266.
Visiting Committee, 276.
Wigoder Library, 280.
Women courses, 261.
Women students, 250.
Jews' Free School, 4, 6, 16, 18, 28, 49, 50, 66, 230, 231, 240, 253.
Johannesburg, 93, 117, 126.
John Hopkins University, 226.
Joseph, Delissa, 46, 76, 145.
Joseph, Sir Keith, 230.
Joseph, Morris, 47, 64.
Josephs, Walter, 272.
Joynson-Hicks, William, 143, 145.
Judisch-Theologisches Seminary 152.
Judith, Lady Montefiore College, 180.

Kagan, Rabbi Yisrael Meir, 189.
Kahan, Eliezer, 116.
Kahana, Ada, 178.
Kahana Kagan Foundation, 235.
Kahana, Rabbi Kopul, 173, 175, 178-182, 187, 189, 190, 204, 212, 213, 218, 231, 234, 235.
Kahn, Augustus, 89, 171.
Kahn, Esra, 284-289.
Kahn, Lord, 206, 236-238.
Kaiser, 121.
Kalir, 56.
Kalms, Lord, 240, 241, 243, 244, 248, 251-253.
Kalisch, Arye Jehuda, 6.
Kaminetzky, Dr Joseph, 285.
Kaplan, Simon, 252.
Karaites, 192.
Kashrus Commission, 252.
Kass, David, 231.
Kendler, Maureen, 265.
Kennicott, Bishop, 3.
Kenya, 117.

Keyser, Alexander Henry, 273.
Khmelwitzki Massacre, 226.
Kikuyu, 117.
Kilner, George Washington, 61, 158, 159, 169.
Kimche, Rabbi Alan, 249.
Kindertransport, 171.
Kings College London, 141, 264.
Kitto, Miss J., 205.
Klein, Rabbi H., 279.
Knox, Father Kenneth, 189.
Kra, Zvi, 218.

L'Eylah, 249.
Land-Rabbiner, 7, 8.
Landau, Charles, 287.
Landynski, Rabbi Nachman, 144.
Lange, Michael, 89.
Laski, Nathan, 139.
Laski, Neville, 139.
Lawrence, Zachariah, 73.
Lebus, Mrs. Harris, 125.
Lee, Arnold, 221, 237.
Lee, Sir Sidney, 56.
Lefcovitch, Sonia, 282.
Lehrman, Rabbi Dr S.M., 277.
Lehrman, Simon, 165.
Lehmann, Ruth, 280-284.
Leicester University, 246.
Leipzig University, 43.
Leperer, Sidney, 226, 252.
Levin, Walter, 73.
Levine, Ephraim, 162, 170, 207, 252.
Levine, Mrs. Ephraim, 184.
Levine, Frank, 252.
Levinson, Israel, 165.
Levy, Rabbi Abraham, 188, 189, 196, 209, 229, 265.
Levy, Elkan, 199, 207.
Levy, Harold and Hannah, 177.
Levy, Isaac, 199.
Levy, Joshua, 53, 119.
Levy, Lawrence, 18.
Levy, Moss, 6.
Levy, Rabbi Solomon, 73, 84, 147, 278.
Lew, Maurice, 16, 205, 210.
Library Association, 281, 282.
Library of Congress, 281.
Lieberman, Rabbi Simcha, 235, 243-246.
Lindo, Nathaneel, 19.
Lipkind, Goodman, 73.
Lipson, Eric, 162.
Lipson, Solomon, 125.
Lithuania, 6, 93, 142, 146, 173, 179.
Liverpool, 98.
Livingstone, Isaac, 165, 234.
Loewe, James, 32.
Loewe, Dr Louis, 32, 35, 38, 42, 69, 72, 159, 262, 270, 275.
London Ambulance Service, 91.
London Board of Jewish Religious Education, 191, 230.

London County Council, 114.
London School of Economics, 250, 257.
London School of Jewish Studies, (LSJS), 250, 257, 258, 261-270.
London Society for Promoting Christianity among the Jews, 3.
London Underground, 91.
London University, 17, 38.
  Students Representative Council, 211.
Löwy, Rev. Albert, 275.
Lubavitch, 216.
Lucas, Sampson, 18.
Lucas, Victor, 242.
Lunzer, Jack, 284.
Luzzatto, Moses Chayyim, 175.
Luzzatto, Samuel David, 5.
Lyon, Chief Rabbi Hart, 2, 3.
Lyons, Mrs, 46.

Macauley, Lord, 272.
Maconochie, George, 40, 45.
Magnus, Sir Philip, 65, 66, 119, 132, 134, 242, 273.
Maimonides, Moses, 44, 75, 206, 215, 265.
Manchester, 61, 74, 139, 197.
Mandela, Nelson, 212.
Mann, Jacob, 116, 134.
Marks, David Woolf, 15.
Marks & Spencer, 163.
Marmorstein, Rabbi Arthur, 146, 173, 175, 192, 203.
Marmorstein, Bruno, 189, 203, 212, 213, 221.
Masorti, 199.
Maurice Wohl Charitable Foundation, 266.
Mayerowitsch, Hermann, 280.
Medici, 5.
Meir, Rabbi, 142.
Melchior, Chief Rabbi, Bent, 196.
Memorial Foundation for Jewish Culture, 213.
Mendes, Abraham, 48.
Mendelsohn, Louis, 118.
'Mentor', 114, 119.
Merton, E.M., 272.
Mestel, Solomon, 116, 142.
Metternich, Klemens von, 17.
Meyers, B., 272.
Michael Josephs Collection, 272.
Michaelson, Benjamin, 73, 74, 165.
Middlesex University, 230, 264.
Midrash, 56.
Miller, Sergeant, 39.
Minhag Anglia, 54, 56, 247.
Minister of Town & Country Planning, 184.
Mirvis, Chief Rabbi Ephraim, 270.
Mocatta, Sir Alan, 161, 184, 185, 195.
Mocatta, F.D., 274.
Mocatta, E. L., 84.
Mocatta Library, 279, 254, 285.
Mohel, 10, 92.

Montagu, Ewen, 199, 200.
Montagu Place, 184, 185, 187, 204, 213, 222, 235, 237, 253, .254, 283, 285, 286.
Montague, Hyman, 45.
Montague, Samuel 49, 88.
Montefiore, Claude, 56, 68, 74, 77, 105, 131, 132, 134, 275.
Montefiore endowment, 76, 288.
Montefiore, Lady Judith, 32, 228, 265, 274, 283, 288.
  School, 77.
Montefiore Library, 74, 159, 275, 277, 276, 278, 283.
Montefiore, Sir Moses, 8, 9, 13, 15, 18, 21, 22, 29, 32, 49, 53, 69, 112, 114, 122, 253, 270.
Morein, Wolf, 166.
Moses, 270.
Moses, J. Henry, 272.
Mosque, Central, 213.
Moss, Abraham, 171.
Munk, Rabbi Eli, 198.
Munk, Joseph, 231.
Myers, Asher, 275, 276.
Myers, Barnett, 36.

Nadler, Lisa, 252.
National Central Library, 278.
National Theatre, 266.
Nemeth, Rabbi Morris, 213.
Ner Yisrael, 249.
Neubauer, Dr Adolf, 56, 95. 192.
Neumegen, Leopold, 48.
New College, 61.
New Testament, 85, 108.
New York, 117, 146, 176, 216, 219, 226, 271, 282.
New York University, 218.
Newman, Dr Aubrey, 246.
Nietto, Haham David, 5.
Nissim, Mayer, 224.
North Africa, 180, 181, 211.
North London Jewish Day School, 230.

Odessa Rabbinical School, 125.
OFSTED, 266.
Open University, 240.
Oppenheim, Rabbi David, 192.
Order of Merit, 170.
Organisation of Observant Traditional Jews of Great Britain, 134.
Otzar Hachochman, 288.
Oven, Joshua van, 3.
Oxford University, 17, 60, 74, 94, 113, 135, 154, 161, 209, 285.
  Balliol College, 74.
  Lincoln College, 266.
  Mansfield College, 73.
  Wolfson College, 161.
Oxhey, 243.

Padua, 5.
Paris, 5.
Pass, Elias de, 2.
Passover, 123, 170.
Pastoral Tour, 135, 138.
Peckar, Rev, 110.
Perse School, Cambridge, 191.
Petach Tikva, 286.
Phillips, Sir Benjamin, 39.
Picciotto, Moses, 53.
Pincasovitch, Rev. 174.
Pinchbeck, Dr Ivy, 169.
Plitnick, Rabbi Zalman, 206.
Polack, Joseph, 60, 279.
Polack's House, Clifton College, 116.
Poland, 173, 178, 179, 202.
Polytechnic of North London, 230.
Pomson, David, 253, 256.
Portman Square, 46.
Portsea, 60.
Portsmouth Prison, 44, 61,
Poulson, Mr, 177.
Prague, 43.
Presbyterian College, 76.
Princeton University, 219.
Provincial Bank of Ireland, 9.

Queens Square House, 76, 86, 88, 89, 155-157, 276.

Rabinow, Rabbi Shmuel Joseph, 180.
Rabinovitch, Rabbi Nahum, 190, 215-234, 236, 244, 258.
Rabinowicz, Dr. Oskar, 281-283.
Rabinowitz, Joseph, 116.
Rabinowitz, Louis, 282.
Ramsgate, 61, 68-73, 76, 83, 114, 159, 180, 181, 274, 283.
  Library, 274.
Rapaport, Rabbi, 43.
Raphall, Morris Jacob, 6.
Rashi, 268.
Ratnajiri, 63.
Ratzaby, Professor Yehuda, 286.
Refaey, Gamiel Ahmed al, 286.
Reform, 63, 91, 113, 130, 131-4, 137, 146, 200, 242.
Reif, Dr Stefan, 285.
Reith Lectures, 251.
Riskin, Rabbi Shlomo, 258.
Robert Montefiore School, 114.
Roberts, Mr, 39.
Roco, Rev., 110.
Roman Catholic Relief Act 1829, 4.
Rome, 97.
Rosen, Rabbi Kopul, 189.
Ross, Rabbi Dr Jacob Joshua, 204, 209, 210.
Roth, Cecil, 192.
Rothschild, Amschel, 8.
Rothschild family, 4, 30, 66, 68, 77, 141, 169, 218.

Rothschild, Mrs James de, 205.
Rothschild, Lewis Mayor, 64, 271-273.
Rothschild, Lionel de, 8, 137, 138.
Rothschild, Lord, 91, 120.
Rothschild, Baroness Meyer de, 53.
Rothschild, Sir Nathaniel de, 49.
Ruben, Professor David-Hillel, 257, 258, 261.
Rubin-Zacks, Louis, 278, 279.
Rubin, Samuel, 263.
Rugby School, 17.
Rumania, 286.
Russia, 120.
Rutgers University, 218.
Rynhold, Dr Daniel, 263.

Sabbath Schools, 81.
Sacharov, Rabbi Abraham, 142, 146.
Sacks, Chief Rabbi, Lord, 1, 117, 216, 227, 231, 235, 236, 238-244, 246-248, 250-253, 257, 258, 261, 265, 270, 285, 287.
Sacramental Test Act 1828, 4.
Salaman, Redcliffe, 114.
Salomons, Sir David, 21, 34, 249.
Samuda, Joseph d'Aguilar, 19.
Samuel Brothers, 49.
Samuel, Charles, 49, 50, 53, 58, 64, 66, 67, 71, 76, 77, 88, 112, 253, 273.
Samuel, Dennis, 275.
Samuel, Frank, 77.
Samuel, Harold, 190.
Samuel, Isaac, 89.
Samuel, Marcus, 129.
Samuel, Samuel, 141.
Samuel, Wilfred, 280, 282.
Sanhedrin, 97.
Sandelson, David, 171.
Sanker, Louis, 166.
Sasportas, Haham Jacob, 1, 180, 247.
Sassoon, Albert, 44.
Sassoon, Arthur, 91.
Sassoon, David, 44.
Sassoon, Edward, 93.
Sassoon, Flora, 141.
Sassoon, Sassoon, 45, 46.
Saul, Bendet and Victor, 48.
Savendi, Dr Adolph, 279.
Scandinavia, 211.
Scarman, Lord Justice, 230.
Schaller family, 256.
Shechita, 175.
Schechter, Solomon, 48, 56, 63, 91, 125, 275.
Schiff, Dr, 91.
Schiff, Chief Rabbi David Tevele, 54.
Schiff, Jacob, 91.
Schiff, Otto, 96, 115.
Schiller-Szenessy, Rabbi Solomon, 65, 67.
Schneerson, Rabbi Menachem, 216.
Schonfeld, Rabbi Dr Solomon, 160, 170.
School of Oriental and African Studies, 257, 281.
Schwab, Abraham, 5.

Sebag-Montefiore, Robert, 114, 115.
Secessionists, 56, 64.
Semicha, 5, 70, 83, 84, 89, 96, 119, 120, 125, 147, 154, 167, 171, 174-6, 179, 180, 190, 196, 203, 209, 211, 219, 224, 231-3, 235, 255, 265.
Semitics, 125.
Sephardi Elders, 70, 71, 76, 229, 274.
Sephardim, 1, 6, 9, 19, 43, 44, 61, 68-71, 74, 84, 111, 141, 159, 161, 180, 190, 195, 196.
  Elders, 74, 97, 121, 122, 180, 188, 209, 213, 228, 229, 240, 265, 274.
  Mahamad, 229.
Settle Road Board School, 70.
Sfas Emes, 87.
Shaare Tikvah School, 1.
Shah of Persia, 37.
Shalev, Avraham, 218.
Shatnes, 104.
Shaw, Alan, 231.
Shechita, 178, 206.
Shell Petroleum, 129, 131, 190.
Sherman Foundation, Harry & Abe, 227.
Shine, Rabbi Cyril, 179.
Shochet, 10.
Shuchatowitz, Avrom, 284.
Shulchan Aruch, 6, 16, 32, 42.
Shutske, Max, 116.
Sieff, Israel, 163.
Silverman, Alfred, 201.
Simon, Morris, 74.
Sinclair, Rabbi Daniel, 235, 252-7.
Singer, Rabbi Simeon, 11, 40, 47, 63, 68, 70, 72, 84-7, 146, 203.
Snowman, Dr Jacob, 92, 191.
Sobell, Michael, 227.
Society for the Protection of Women and Children, 85.
Soetender, Rabbi David, 242.
Sokolic, Leonard, 284.
Sola, David Aaron de, 6.
Sola, Sam de, 32, 34, 38.
Solomon, James, 66, 95, 96.
Solomon, Henry, 36, 44, 48, 55, 66.
Soloveitchik, Rabbi Joseph, 216.
Soncino, 193.
South Africa, 73, 130, 141, 147, 158, 165, 196, 204, 211, 212.
South African Board of Deputies, 185, 213.
South African Zionists, 120.
Spain, 1.
Spiers, Dayan Bernard, 279, 284.
Spiro, 242.
Stanton, Howard, 261, 262.
Stephany, Myer. 177, 207.
Stern, Sir Edward, 91, 141.
Stern, Evelyn, 255.
Stern, Leonard, 222.
Stern, Sacha, 257.
Stranders, John, 276.

Index

Suez Canal, 66.
Sunderland, 96.
Sugar, Lord Alan, 237.
Super, Arthur, 166.
Swedish Embassy, 235.
Swift, Dayan Moshe, 225, 236.
Swift, Harris, 199.
Sydney, 126.
Synagogue Guild for Social Services, 161.
Synagogues:
    Bayswater, 37, 47, 60, 89, 176.
    Becontree, 163.
    Bevis Marks, 6, 34.
    Birmingham, 6, 88.
    Birmingham Reform, 212.
    Blackpool, 116.
    Borough, 89.
    Bradford, 116.
    Brighton, 6, 73, 116.
    Bristol, 6, 166.
    Bulawayo, 27.
    Cardiff, 73.
    Central, 73, 152, 168, 175, 176, 179.
    Cricklewood, 184.
    Dalston, 73, 116.
    Dollis Hill, 184.
    Durban, 147.
    Edinburgh, 253.
    Finchley, 235.
    Frankfurt, 28.
    Garnethill, 162.
    Gateshead, 142, 144.
    Golders Green, 117.
    Golders Green Beth Hamedresh, 198.
    Great, London, 3, 4, 6, 8, 9, 34, 48, 61, 85, 147, 273, 280.
    Great, Jerusalem, 166.
    Great, Sydney, 176, 224.
    Hambro, 4, 6, 36, 43, 48.
    Hampstead, 64, 176.
    Hampstead Garden Suburb, 165, 224.
    Harrogate, 116.
    Heaton Park, 231.
    Hull, 27.
    Jamaica, 34.
    Johannesburg, 137.
    Kenton, 224.
    Lauderdale Road, 265.
    Liberal, 118, 131, 132, 165.
    Leeds, 74, 166, 184.
    Liverpool, 6, 9, 165.
    Liverpool Old, 47.
    Louisiana, 44.
    Manchester, 6, 21, 73, 88, 163, 184.
    Manchester Central, 198.
    Manchester Reform, 21.
    Marble Arch, 166, 185, 233, 241.
    Melbourne, 27, 116, 146, 181.
    Merthyr, 48.
    Middlesborough, 146.
    Munich, 28, 196.
    Munks, 198.
    Nairobi, 27, 116.
    New, 9, 48, 73.
    New West End, 47, 87, 89, 123, 162, 198, 207.
    Newcastle, 142.
    North London, 47.
    North West London, 73.
    Nottingham, 116.
    Newport, 73.
    Orach Chaim, 176.
    Perth, 73.
    Pinner, 27, 231.
    Port Elizabeth, 73.
    Richmond, 116.
    St. Johns Wood, 190, 199.
    St. Johns Wood Masorti, 199.
    Seal Street, Liverpool, 6.
    Shanghai, 27.
    Sheffield, 84, 162, 165.
    Singers Hill, 212.
    Southend Reform, 166.
    Stanmore, 27, 186, 232.
    Stoke Newington, 48.
    Strasbourg, 28.
    Sunderland, 142, 144.
    Sutton, 181.
    Sydney, 89.
    Toronto, 215.
    Torquay and Paignton, 116.
    Upper Berkeley Street, 64, 66, 74, 118, 129, 130, 134, 242.
    Wandsworth and Balham, 116.
    Wanstead and Woodford, 184.
    Wembley, 27.
    West End, Great, 166.
    West Ham, 116.
    Western, 6, 73, 165.
    Western Marble Arch, 261.
Synagogue ministers, 78-80.

Talmud Association School, 43.
Talmud Torah, 2, 4.
Tann, Leonard, 211, 212.
Tavistock House, 57, 65, 75.
Tavistock Square, 48, 273.
Taylor-Guthartz, Lindsay, 265.
Taylor-Schechter, Geniza, 238.
Teff, Solomon, 206.
Temple, 64.
Tennessee State University, 286.
Thatcher, Margaret, 247.
The Times, 270.
Theodores, Professor Tobias, 37.
Theological and Philosophical Libraries, 281, 283.
Torah MiTzion, 261.
Torah Mesorah, 285.
Toronto University, 215.
Transvaal University, 130.
Treblinka, 243.

Trocadero, 91.
Tschernowitz, Rabbi Dr Chaim, 124.
Tsedakah, 11.
Tuck, Sir Adolph, 71, 88, 91, 100, 108, 111, 122, 124, 125, 145, 253.
Tuck, family, 155.
Tuck, Raphael, 88.

Union of Israel Synagogues, 166.
Union of Orthodox Jewish Congregations of America, 176.
Union Society, 11, 177, 189, 191.
Unitarians, 74.
United Jewish Israel Appeal, 257, 263.
United Synagogue, 15, 18, 48, 54, 59, 64, 77, 92, 98, 100-102, 108-10, 115, 117, 120-3, 125, 129, 130, 132, 133, 136, 137, 140, 141, 144, 149, 152, 153, 155, 161, 167, 169, 170, 174, 186, 198-201, 207, 213, 217, 223, 224, 226, 235, 236, 242, 243, 249, 252, 257, 271, 276.
University of Capetown, 204.
University College, London, 17, 18, 34, 47, 70, 116, 125, 126, 141, 152, 159, 208, 215, 279, 285.
University College School, 47.
University of Leipzig, 94.
University of London, 53, 60, 61, 85, 88, 163, 174, 183, 191, 204, 208, 211, 218-20, 238, 255, 257.
  Academic Procession, 174.
University of Wisconsin, 235.
University of Witwatersrand, 204.
Unterman, Rabbi Maurice, 166, 240.
Uppsala University, 281.

Victoria, Queen, 121.
Victoria and Albert Museum, 283.
Vienna, 96, 146, 202.
Vilna Gaon, 206.
Volozhiner, Rabbi Hayyim, 6.
Von Lammel School & Orphan Asylum, 116.

Wagner, Professor Leslie, 257.
Waiman, Bernard, 254.
Waley, Simon, 275.
Walker, Dr Thomas, 282.
War Bonds, 122.
War Office, 123.
War Memorial Council, 136, 138-41, 147, 155, 156.
Warsaw Ghetto, 243.
Wasserman, Benno, 218.
Wasserman, Jacob, 161.
Wassersug, David, 61, 73.
Weinberg, Rabbi Jacob, 279.
Weinberg, Marc, 263.
Weissenberg, Dr E., 208.
Weiss, Rabbi Abner, 259, 261.
Weiss, Rabbi Isaac, 70.
Weitzman, David, 206.
Weiwow, Louis, 116.
Werner, Louis, 272.
Wieder, Naphtali, 178, 182, 188, 203, 206, 207, 212, 213, 215, 218, 232.
Wigoder, family, 279.
Wigoder, Dr George, 279.
Willesden Cemetery, 87, 201.
Williams, Dr, 187.
Williams, Dame Shirley, 229.
Wilson, Harold, 230.
Wilson, Colonel, 39.
Windsor Castle, 227.
Wise, Martin, 227, 230.
Woburn House, 151, 152, 155-7, 159, 167, 223, 253, 278.
Wolf, Abraham, 73.
Wolfson, Sir Isaac, 161, 199.
World Jewish Congress, 284.
Wright, Tamra, 243, 255, 263-5.
Würzburg, 6.

Yad Ben Zvi, 284.
Yadin, General Yigal, 192.
Yale University, 218.
Yakar, 242.
Yeshiva, 2, 3, 10.
  Breslau, 94, 226.
  Budapest, 94.
  Collegio Rabbinico Italiano, 152.
  Ecole Rabbinique de France, 5.
  Eretz Hamdan 265.
  Etz Chaim, 87, 142, 147, 175.
  Gateshead, 144, 186, 213, 233, 236, 261.
  Hildesheim, 173, 226.
  Istituto Rabbinico Lombardo-Veneto, 5.
  Manchester, 187, 198.
  Metz, 5.
  Nederlandisch Israel Ietisch Seminarium, 6.
  Ohr Torah Stone, 258.
  Saadath Vachurim, 6.
  Vienna, 95.
  Yeshivat Hamivtar, 258.
Yeshiva University, 219, 226.
Yiddish, 54, 117, 120.
Yom Kippur War, 224.
Young Jewish Leadership Institute, 240, 242.

Zarum, Rabbi Rafi, 263, 264.
Zimmels, Erla, 234, 286, 288.
Zimmels, Dr Hirsch, 177, 178, 189, 195- 202, 206, 207, 209, 210, 212, 215, 219, 220, 234, 270, 280.
Zionism, 69, 120, 121, 196.
Zionist Federation, 175.
Zimbabwe, 190.
Zunz, Dr. Leopold, 275.